## ADVANCE PRAISE

"In a world obsessed with scale and certainty, *Unconvention* is a refreshingly honest look at how underdogs win by staying small, staying human, and staying true. Sri reminds us that what looks naive—like care, proximity, and purpose—might actually be strategic brilliance."

↪ **JOSHUA BERRY,** Award-winning author of *Dare to Be Naive*

"Sri Kaza's *Unconvention* wonderfully reframes what many see as small business limitations as their greatest competitive advantages. Through practical frameworks and compelling examples, Kaza shows how authenticity, focus, and genuine connection create business models that not only outcompete corporate giants, but bring deeper fulfillment to owners, employees, and customers alike."

↪ **ASHISH KOTHARI,** Author of *Hardwired for Happiness* & CEO of Happiness Squad

"As an entrepreneur, what I loved most about *Unconvention* is how clearly it affirms what so many small business owners feel but rarely hear: that being small can actually be your greatest strength. Through stories that are real, relatable, and rich with insight, Sri Kaza brings strategy to life and shows how connection, clarity, and purpose are what truly drive success."

↪ **LESLIE RAE,** Cofounder of The SmartBusiness Academy

"Having built businesses that serve accountants and their small firms, I've seen firsthand how the principles in *Unconvention* create lasting competitive advantage. Sri Kaza articulates with remarkable clarity how small businesses can succeed, not despite their size but because of it. His Underdog Principles provide a strategic framework that transforms how entrepreneurs approach everything from pricing to customer acquisition to talent management."

↪ **IAN VACIN,** Cofounder of Karbon, a practice management solution for accounting firms

"Sri has a gift for entertaining storytelling combined with real-life experience in the business of going up against the big guys. A great read for any aspiring entrepreneur or small business leader seeking practical advice for success."

↳ **JEFFREY PIERSON,** Former head of the Small Business Investment Company, US SBA

# UNCONVENTION

# UN CONVENTION

## A SMALL BUSINESS STRATEGY GUIDE

### SRI KAZA

IDEAPRESS PUBLISHING

WASHINGTON, DC

IDEAPRESS
PUBLISHING

**Copyright © 2025 by Sri Kaza**

All rights reserved. No part of this book may be reproduced, stored, or transmitted by any means—whether auditory, graphic, mechanical, or electronic—without written permission of both publisher and author, except in the case of brief excerpts used in critical articles and reviews. Unauthorized reproduction of any part of this work is illegal and is punishable by law.

Ideapress Publishing | www.ideapresspublishing.com

All trademarks are the property of their respective companies.

Cover Design: Jason Anscomb
Interior Design: Jessica Angerstein

Cataloging-in-Publication Data is on file with the Library of Congress.

Hardcover ISBN: 978-1-64687-205-3

---

**Special Sales**

Ideapress books are available at a special discount for bulk purchases for sales promotions and premiums, or for use in corporate training programs. Special editions, including personalized covers, a custom foreword, corporate imprints, and bonus content, are also available.

1 2 3 4 5 6 7 8 9 10

# CONTENTS

**CHAPTER ONE**
It's Not Business, It's Personal | 1

**CHAPTER TWO**
Vaporware | 31

**CHAPTER THREE**
Delicious and Fulfilling | 61

**CHAPTER FOUR**
Any Color, as Long as It's Black | 83

**CHAPTER FIVE**
Even a Hole in the Ground Has Value | 119

**CHAPTER SIX**
Meet Me Where I Am | 153

**CHAPTER SEVEN**
More Than a Mile in My Shoes | 193

**CHAPTER EIGHT**
Would You Like Fries with That? | 229

**CHAPTER NINE**
No Days Off | 255

**CHAPTER TEN**
Are We Winning Yet? | 277

*CHAPTER ONE*

# IT'S NOT BUSINESS, IT'S PERSONAL

## A Successful Formula

The seeds of this book were planted in early 2017. My friend John Pan reached out to me about some challenges at ForwardLine Financial, the commercial lender he had recently joined. The company specialized in providing financing to small businesses. We had worked together years earlier at a company that helped these same types of businesses claim complex tax credits. That work had shown me firsthand how difficult it was for small businesses to access the same benefits larger companies routinely enjoyed.

"It's the same problem we solved together before," he said. "The team is struggling to scale the company. Would you be open to meeting our CEO, Craig Coleman?"

Craig had founded ForwardLine in 2004, building it into a nationwide small business lender and payment processor. Under his leadership, the company achieved fifteen consecutive years of growth and steady profitability. In 2015, he led a successful sale to a private equity firm, though he remained actively involved in the business. The investors saw untapped potential and envisioned using technology to offer funding to many more small businesses.

"In 2004, our approach to financing was unique in the market," Craig told me. "We worked directly with the owners of Main Street small businesses, taking the time to understand their needs." He explained how the market had evolved since then. "Others have entered the market and copied our products, but we've kept our edge through our understanding of these businesses. Our focus has always been on helping them get the best solution. Championing small business is part of ForwardLine's DNA."

"The market is changing, though." he continued. "Tech-based lenders are making gains, and that's why our new ownership is investing heavily in technology." He explained their plans to streamline the application process, making it easier for business owners and faster for the underwriting team to make an offer. "By April, it will take only two minutes for a business owner to get an answer." Both he and the new investors were convinced that combining their small business expertise with modern technology would unlock massive growth.

The potential was clear—an easier and faster application process should mean more business. I understood their excitement. Having worked with John on scaling up different businesses through technology at Tax Credit Co., I had some experience in this area. I shared a few of my lessons with Craig, gently suggesting that successfully integrating technology with their existing approach might not be as easy as "combine and stir."

The conversation struck a chord with Craig. He invited me to meet with his team, including Larry, his chief marketing officer. During our discussion, Larry explained how their product—a short-term, working capital loan that didn't require collateral—worked. But when he mentioned the interest rates they were charging, I was taken aback.

"Wow, that's a lot more than I'd ever want to pay," I said.

"Issuing these loans carries significant risk," Larry explained. "There is no guarantee that we're going to get our money back. But small businesses don't have access to corporate bonds, and traditional financing is often out of reach. This capital, despite its price tag, gives them opportunities to expand their businesses in ways they wouldn't have been able to do otherwise."

Although I was skeptical about the product, I liked the team and felt like they had a solvable challenge. I stayed in touch with the ForwardLine executives through that summer, occasionally checking in with Larry and John. On one check-in call in the fall of that year, Larry told me that the technology investment wasn't yielding the expected returns.

"On paper, the tech is working perfectly," Larry said. "We're processing more applications and collecting more data than ever, but we're getting fewer businesses across the finish line."

"If the product is the same," I said, "what's changed in your process?"

Larry sighed. "We've automated everything. Applications are online, data processing is lightning-fast, and we're handling more volume with fewer people. But we've lost the personal touch. We used to spend time understanding each business. Now we just process applications, and we're nowhere near the numbers we expected."

This was familiar territory; I'd seen this scenario play out many times. Larry clearly understood the value of those relationships, but he couldn't imagine returning to a system where his team spent thirty minutes on every application call. I explained that while technology could speed up processes and reduce costs, it couldn't replace the vital elements his team captured during those longer conversations.

"You have to hold on to what made you successful in the first place," I said. "It was about understanding your customers and building those personal connections. Your technology captured the data but missed the essence of these connections. Scaling up isn't just about automation. You need a formula that includes the human understanding, not just the algorithms. Your challenge is finding a way to make a ten-minute conversation as meaningful as your old thirty-minute ones."

Larry then revealed the real reason for his call. Craig was moving to the board, and they were bringing in a new CEO, Steve, to focus on securing funding from capital markets. They needed a chief operating officer—someone with experience in scaling businesses.

"We want you to consider the position," Larry said. "The board and Steve would like to meet with you."

I had some productive discussions with Steve and several of the board members and was excited about the challenge, but I needed to understand the business better before making a commitment. I called Larry back a few days later.

"Larry, if these loans are really helping your customers, they would say so, right?" I asked.

"Absolutely," he replied, immediately pulling together a list of clients for me to contact.

Within days, I was speaking with business owners across the country. The first call changed my perspective entirely. A furniture store owner walked me through his seasonal strategy. "I stumbled on this massive inventory of outdoor furniture last winter," he explained. "The supplier needed to clear space. They were practically giving it away at 25 percent of wholesale. I knew I had to move fast. Sure, I had to keep up with loan payments through the cold months, but once summer hit, I made six times my investment. Now, it's part of my business model every single year."

My next call was with a jeweler. "We were at this show when we spotted these amazing pieces," she told me. "They were way beyond our normal budget, but we just knew they'd sell. ForwardLine got us the financing within a day. When those pieces hit our display cases, they flew out the door. We cleared enough to cover the loan costs and then some. Now we travel to Europe annually for shows, select our pieces, bring them home, and our customers keep coming back."

Five more businesses shared similar experiences. Each had spotted an opportunity they couldn't pass up, needed capital quickly, and turned those investments into healthy profits despite the loan costs. These weren't business owners reluctantly accepting expensive money; they were entrepreneurs using it to grow their businesses in ways that actually worked.

My doubts began to fade. While these businesses were successful, traditional banks wouldn't touch them without collateral. Many told me they'd take another loan in a heartbeat if the right opportunity came along. It was becoming increasingly clear to me that without access to this capital, some of these businesses might not have survived, let alone grown.

The position was starting to look different now. I accepted the COO role, confident that with Steve securing our funding and my focus on operations, we could help even more small businesses grow.

## The Business Case

As a team, we came up with an ambitious plan to scale the business. The goal was audacious: triple our revenue in six months and grow tenfold within two years. We even established a company mission: supporting the financial health of America's small businesses.

When we shared this vision at our all-hands meeting to kick off 2018, it was met with smiles and polite applause. While the team appreciated that the new leadership had big goals, nobody seemed to believe they were achievable. With only two salespeople hitting their targets in 2017, the idea of eighty being able to do the same seemed impossible.

I spent time with the sales team, understanding their challenges. They explained how their best deals came from building relationships with business owners, from really getting to know them and their businesses. But these connections weren't possible through email or online applications.

The company relied heavily on direct mail marketing—sending letters offering business financing. While this brought leads to our website and call center, it wasn't building relationships. Each day, hundreds of business owners would respond to these offers, drawn by the promise of quick funding. To understand what was happening, I began listening to recorded calls—forty to fifty each month—hearing business owners describe their needs while my team worked through a standard finance application.

What I found was that every business owner had their own unique situation, but in our haste to process the financing application, we were failing to understand their underlying problem or opportunity. How would they know that our offer was the right solution if we never took the time to understand their needs?

"So many of these business owners that call in don't even know what they're going to do with the money," said David, who would later lead our originations team. I could hear the frustration in his voice.

"A small business owner doesn't pick up the phone without a reason," I replied. "Their intuition tells them there's an opportunity. Our job is to help them figure out what that opportunity is."

When we dug deeper, we discovered that part of the problem stemmed from our drive for efficiency. In making the online application "easier," we'd stripped away questions that seemed unnecessary for the financing decision. Yet those questions had been essential to our consultative selling approach, helping us understand what business owners actually needed. To scale effectively, we needed a new formula. Rather than pushing the fast application processes, we needed to go back to understanding each business's unique situation.

I worked with David to develop a structured approach that balanced collecting the data needed by our technology with understanding the business owners' challenges and acknowledging them. "We can't just go back to our original process," I told him. "It's too long and inconvenient. The analytics team figured out how to make a financing decision with sixteen questions. We need something similar—a simple set of questions that gets to the heart of what a business owner needs."

Instead of only capturing information for the application, we taught our team to explore possibilities with business owners. "When someone calls without a clear plan, remind them that money is expensive. Help them think through what they could achieve with that capital and whether the return will justify the cost," David explained to his team.

Sometimes, this meant suggesting they borrow less than requested. A landscaper might call wanting $50,000 for two new trucks. After reviewing their numbers, we might suggest starting with one truck for $30,000. "Get that truck running at full capacity, then we can discuss financing the second one," we'd advise.

One of the sales guys raised a valid concern: "What if the loan costs more than it's worth to them?"

"Then we tell them that," I said. "If we talk someone into a loan that doesn't make sense, they'll never come back. But if we help them realize it's not the right time, they'll call again when they have a better opportunity."

Years earlier, Craig had rebranded his sales team as funding consultants, focusing on helping owners make their decisions. I reminded the team that their real role was to be a consultant and help to develop business cases. This sparked some pushback. "When I hear that word, all I can picture is someone taking someone's watch and telling them what time it is. I'm not sure we're really consulting on anything," someone on the team shot back.

"Think about it differently," I replied. "Imagine someone rushing to meet a deadline, their hands full, asking you for the time. Yes, they're wearing a watch. But do you mock them, or do you help them solve their real problem? 'It's six o'clock. Your deadline's at eight? Okay, what do you need to accomplish in those two hours?'"

His skepticism faded as the word "consultant" took on a new meaning for him. Instead of simply selling loans, we were problem solvers helping business owners turn their instincts into solid business opportunities.

To refine our approach, I continued listening to customer calls each week. We analyzed what worked and what didn't, developing questions that helped uncover viable business cases. Every business owner had to determine what to invest in, how much to invest, what return to expect, whether the cost made sense, and how they planned to manage those costs. When we helped them answer these questions, the right decisions became obvious.

Our formula worked. The team embraced the idea of understanding each business owner's story, and combined with our improved technology and operations, we hit our six-month target. We'd tripled our business, just as we'd promised. This meant we could bring in more people, teach them the formula, and reach more small businesses that needed our help.

We celebrated by taking the whole company to a Dodgers game—an entire busload of us. Over the next eighteen months, the momentum continued, and we grew the business. Each milestone brought with it its own celebration, sometimes a big company outing, other times a celebration at our offices.

We continued on our upward trajectory, building a team of more than a hundred people at sites in multiple cities and helping almost twenty thousand small businesses with financing. I occasionally visited some of them, seeing firsthand how they'd put our funding to work. By early 2020, we'd built thousands of business cases and developed a clear understanding of how to help small businesses succeed.

By late 2019, we had grown tenfold, exactly what we'd told the team we'd do. This time, the celebration was held at our spacious offices in Woodland Hills, California. We planned an afternoon party with team-building games, food, drinks, and a mariachi band. That day, there was an earthquake, our caterer canceled, and the building's power went out just as the band arrived. Determined to celebrate, team members went down fourteen flights of stairs to help carry the instruments up. All we had was tequila and the mariachi band, but nothing was going to stop the music that day.

Just as we were feeling unstoppable, COVID hit. The lockdowns erased years of progress overnight. Small businesses across the country had to close their doors, which meant they couldn't pay their creditors, including us. With businesses shuttered, we couldn't issue new loans either. We had no choice but to shut down our own operations and furlough most of our employees. Our survival now depended entirely on whether our small business clients could weather this storm.

I found myself in an unusual position. For the first time in my career, I was in the boardroom advocating a proposal that wasn't about maximizing our profitability. "We have every right to protect our own interests," I acknowledged. "But our leadership team believes it's more important to take care of our customers, especially in the long term. Demanding they continue making their loan repayments might help our immediate cash flow, but it's not in anyone's best interest. If we do what's right for our customers now, we all have a better chance of making it through this with a business worth growing."

The board unanimously supported this approach. We adjusted our terms to whatever would keep these businesses alive. Instead of chasing repayments, we focused our energy on helping our clients stay afloat. We reduced payments, relaxed terms, and stayed in close contact with each business. Our thinking was that if we could help these businesses survive the lockdowns, they'd have time to recover and eventually repay their loans. Push too hard now, and we'd recover pennies on the dollar while forcing many of them to close permanently.

## When Big Thinking Failed Small Business

While we worked to keep our small business clients afloat, the government launched its own rescue plan: the Paycheck Protection Program (PPP). Businesses could borrow money to keep employees on their payroll and cover basic expenses during the lockdowns. The government promised to forgive these loans if businesses maintained their staffing levels for eight weeks. The concept made sense: keep people employed, even if their businesses couldn't operate. This would prevent mass resignations and the disruption that would follow when the economy reopened.

We had an early view of the program's development when ForwardLine was invited to participate in Congress's planning discussions. Having worked with thousands of small businesses, I knew their reality. During these sessions, I raised a point that really concerned me: Small businesses don't have the sophisticated record-keeping systems of larger companies. They needed a simpler application process, and the program needed incentives that would encourage lenders to help smaller businesses. But like so many programs designed by big-business leaders for small businesses, my warnings went unheeded. The final design proved just how disconnected these decision-makers were from small business realities.

ForwardLine couldn't tap into PPP ourselves since our private equity ownership made us ineligible, but we saw how we could help our clients access these loans. Direct lending wasn't an option—we'd need capital to fund the loans while waiting for government reimbursement—but we could work as brokers, preparing applications for other lenders.

The program launched just three weeks after the lockdowns began. The government allocated $350 billion for the first round, but the program's design favored large companies from the start. The fee structure told the story. A bank processing a $10 million loan would earn $200,000 for reviewing paperwork that was typically well organized and complete. The same bank processing a $50,000 loan for a small business would earn just $2,500 despite having to chase down scattered documentation and help business owners compile their information. The government thought offering 5 percent on smaller loans would motivate lenders. But who would choose to earn $2,500 for more work when they could earn $200,000 for less?

When applications opened on April 3rd, we had thousands of small businesses ready to apply, many of them our existing customers. We'd gathered their information and prepared their paperwork. But our applications were immediately rejected. The big banks had already filled the pipeline with their largest customers—companies borrowing millions who had their documentation perfectly organized. By April 16th, just two weeks later, the entire $350 billion was gone, mostly to these large borrowers.

Our small business clients faced an impossible situation. They had no revenue coming in but were told to keep paying employees if they wanted loan forgiveness down the line. They needed to produce tax returns, profit and loss statements, and bank reconciliations while trying to keep their businesses alive. Many couldn't pull together the required documentation fast enough, and had no financial institutions motivated to help them through the process. The program that was meant to save small businesses had left them behind.

The program's flaws were obvious from the start—exactly what I'd warned about during the planning discussions. A program meant to save small businesses was built on big-business infrastructure, with incentives that pushed banks toward their largest customers, the ones who, in my opinion, needed the funding the least.

The second round of PPP funding, launched a month later, addressed some of these issues. The government approved more lenders, including companies like ours, that understood small business needs. With additional licenses granted and more organizations able to process loans, small businesses that had been pushed to the back of the line in the first round finally had a better chance at accessing the funds. Forward-Line got its opportunity to broker these loans, allowing us to help the clients we'd originally prepared applications for. But even with these improvements, many small businesses still couldn't get the funding they desperately needed.

As PPP money began flowing through the system and lockdowns lifted, we gradually collected enough on our outstanding loans to resume lending. For any of our small business clients to have made it through this period without declaring bankruptcy was a massive achievement. Survival alone was a victory. By late 2020, we'd reopened our doors, though as a very different company. Most of the executive team, including Larry and Steve, along with many of the people who were a critical part of the company's remarkable growth, had to move on. I stayed on as the new CEO with a skeleton crew, working to rebuild the business to its pre-COVID size and prepare it for sale, which our investors still wanted.

We achieved that goal in 2023, selling ForwardLine to a new buyer. We'd rebuilt our volume and were once again helping numerous small businesses. But something didn't sit right. Yes, we'd accomplished our goal of scaling the business and selling it. But what about our mission to improve the financial health of America's small businesses? Almost 30 percent of our loyal clients from before COVID had closed their doors, and there were more just struggling to survive.

When I shared my unease with a colleague, he brushed it off, quoting a statistic used in conventional thinking: "A third of small businesses fail within their first three years anyway. Just be happy with your success."

I couldn't accept that answer.

## Rethinking Small

The conversation brought back memories of watching *You've Got Mail* years ago with a group of friends, when we still rented videos from Blockbuster. The film follows Kathleen Kelly, played by Meg Ryan, who owns an independent children's bookstore called The Shop Around the Corner on Manhattan's Upper West Side. Her world is shaken when a giant chain bookstore, Fox & Sons Books, announces plans to open nearby.

The story unfolds as a romantic comedy. Through an online chat room, Kathleen connects with Joe Fox (played by Tom Hanks), not knowing he's actually the executive behind the mega-bookstore threatening her business. They fall in love despite being on opposite sides of this retail war. In the end, she loses her bookstore but finds happiness with the very person who put her out of business. Hollywood calls this a happy ending. But I didn't quite see it that way.

As we sat around discussing the movie after it ended, my friends were puzzled by my reaction. "The guy got the girl," one said. "What's the problem?"

"But her bookstore didn't survive," I said. "Her passion, her livelihood, gone. Why did the underdog have to fail?"

"That's just how it works," another friend sighed. "Big businesses always win. Scale always wins."

I never bought that explanation. And now, feeling empty after ForwardLine's sale, that question returned with new urgency: Was it really true? Are small businesses really destined to fail when faced with bigger competitors?

I needed answers. What made some small businesses do better than others? What was the secret to having a good business case? And how could we use this information to help other small businesses succeed?

I had access to more than twenty thousand business cases that we'd documented over the years. Surely there were patterns in the data that could explain it.

I dug into the numbers, looking for correlations. Was their success tied to the size of their loan? Was it their growth rate? Inventory management, perhaps? The raw data showed nothing conclusive, although there were some interesting links. For example, businesses that borrowed between 10 to 15 percent of their annual revenue tended to fare better than those asking for very large or very small amounts. Nothing in the data blew my socks off.

The real answers, I discovered, weren't in the spreadsheets—they were in the stories. Six years of developing business cases at ForwardLine had given me insight into thousands of successful strategies. I went back through our cases, listening to recorded calls and revisiting my conversations with business owners who'd succeeded over time. A pattern began to emerge. While others followed conventional business strategies rooted in pursuing profits, these business owners followed a more personal path. I discovered three principles that set them apart. These principles, when combined with their commitment to their original vision, gave them an edge over their competitors, not just in terms of how successful they were, but in terms of how well they weathered the challenges they faced.

The first of these principles was *positioning*—these small business owners built their businesses around finding and serving customers who understood their vision and truly valued what they offered. When opportunities arose, they stayed true to their vision, even when that meant serving a smaller market. Then there was *proximity*—their closeness to customers gave them unique insight to their needs, allowing these businesses to deliver more complete experiences. That closeness proved invaluable during tough times, with loyal customers rallying to support the businesses they'd come to care about. And finally, there was *purpose*—like the others, they ran their businesses for profit, but their decisions factored in their personal values and needs, balancing purpose with profit.

I call these the *Underdog Principles* because, in a world where big businesses have deeper pockets, bigger teams, and more resources, small businesses start with what looks like a disadvantage. Yet positioning, proximity, and purpose are intrinsic to every small business. Whether the underdog succeeds or not depends on their ability to recognize and actively use these principles.

Think about how many small businesses naturally gravitate toward serving particular customers. A neighborhood coffee shop becomes the morning hub for local creatives. A specialty bike shop draws serious cyclists from three counties away. Yet not every business recognizes this natural focus as a strength they can build upon.

The same goes for customer relationships. Small business owners often know their regulars by name, remember their preferences, and understand their needs in ways that go beyond any corporate data analysis. These personal bonds develop naturally, but the most successful businesses actively nurture them.

Then there's purpose. Some business owners start their venture with a clear mission in mind, while others discover it along the way. For some, it's about creating a life that allows them to spend more quality time with their families. For others, it's about supporting their communities or championing causes they believe in. When I talk with business owners who say they're in it "just to make money," something else invariably emerges. They light up when describing how they solve problems for their customers. They beam with pride when talking about providing good jobs or building something that matters. This sense of purpose influences every decision they make.

As a small business owner, your success isn't measured by market domination or the size of your customer base. Your smaller, focused market—your positioning—gives you the freedom to focus on the customers you genuinely want to reach. You can build your entire business around their specific needs instead of trying to be everything to everyone. This closer connection to your customers—your proximity—allows you to understand and serve them in ways no big business can. Your purpose doesn't need to be world-changing; it might be creating a better life for your family or making a difference in your community or simply doing the work you love in a way that matters. What's important is staying true to what drives you personally.

When you understand and harness your three unique strengths, you can build something that no corporate giant can replicate.

## THE UNDERDOG PRINCIPLES

| POSITIONING: | PROXIMITY: | PURPOSE: |
|---|---|---|
| The ability to serve a focused set of customers who value what makes you unique | The deep understanding of customers that comes from direct, personal interactions | The freedom to build something meaningful beyond just making money |

## How Hollywood Got It Wrong

While researching this book, I learned that *You've Got Mail* was inspired by actual events on Manhattan's Upper West Side back in the nineties, when big-box bookstores like Barnes & Noble were displacing independent bookstores. The movie's portrayal was accurate in many ways. Fox & Sons Books, like its real-world counterparts, offered cafés, a wider selection of books, and discounted prices. Small bookshops, with their higher prices and limited inventory, appeared outmatched. This pattern was supposed to repeat everywhere. Big stores would open, and small stores would close. But something unexpected happened. Like David against Goliath, many independent bookstores continued to thrive against all odds.

Though my work at ForwardLine hadn't brought me into contact with bookstores before, they presented the perfect case study for testing my theory about the three Underdog Principles. While interviewing independent bookstore owners across the country, it became clear that their success wasn't despite being small but *because* of it. Following the same path as successful small businesses everywhere, they found ways to turn their size into an advantage, serving their customers in ways that no big, impersonal chain store ever could. Here's how they did it.

Let's begin with Jonathon Welch, the founder of Talking Leaves in Buffalo, New York.

## Talking Leaves: Independent, Idiosyncratic, and Still Standing

Talking Leaves's story began with a late-night conversation in a Buffalo bar in the fall of 1974. Jonathon Welch, then a middling graduate student in an English PhD program at SUNY Buffalo, and his fellow students had just learned that their favorite off-campus bookstore, which had been operating since 1971, was closing. The owner planned to sell and move to New York City to be closer to her daughters.

"My entry to the bookstore world was accidental, sort of," Jonathon recalled. That night at the bar, inspired by a cooperative bookstore he had belonged to in Madison, Wisconsin, a group of students and community members hatched a plan to save the store themselves. Their solution was ahead of its time—crowdfunding before the term existed. They approached anyone they knew who might have spare cash, offering 5 percent simple annual interest to be repaid over five years. About twenty lenders believed in their vision, and on January 1, 1975, the store on Main Street reopened, with Jonathon as its cofounder.

"I was one of two people hired to work twenty hours a week," Jonathon told me. "Part of my role involved managing the volunteer staff who would later become the first members of our co-op."

"None of us had any bookselling or book industry experience, and no serious retail experience, so we flew by the seat of our pants," he admitted. He took what he thought would be a year's leave from his PhD program to help establish the store and catch up with his studies. That temporary break has now stretched across five decades.

From the beginning, Talking Leaves carved out its own space in Buffalo's literary landscape. "Our mission was to stock the books other stores didn't—the non-commercial, adversarial, marginal books, authors, and subjects from small and independent presses," Jonathon explained. "We featured books from political and social movements and from underrepresented communities—Black, Indigenous, third-world, queer voices that weren't finding shelf space elsewhere."

The store, whose motto is "Independent and Idiosyncratic Since 1971," soon became a gathering place for readers seeking something beyond the mainstream. "We wanted to be a place for safe but active conversation, where people could discover unfamiliar ideas and be challenged by them," Jonathon said. Rather than letting market trends drive their inventory, they let cultural and political discourse shape their shelves.

They've built the store around their readers. "The point became to meet our customers where they are," Jonathon explained. "We provide the books they know about and can order anything they want while constantly exposing them to the unfamiliar, the challenging, and the uncommon. We hope they'll take a chance on something new and different, hoping their curiosity will at least meet, if not match, ours."

This decision to be different became their greatest asset. "We operate on the margins of the retail world," Jonathon explained. "And we've weathered everything from blizzards to recessions to Amazon because what moves and motivates us is culture and politics, not economics."

The store has become part of many readers' lives. Mick Cochrane, a longtime customer, wrote, "Talking Leaves may be the only place on earth I'll ever be a regular, and I confess that I love it. Jon and his wife, Martha—and most of the people who answer the phone in the store—know my voice, and I know theirs. Jon knows which books I want to read before I do, and he sets them aside for me."

They've never invested much in marketing, preferring to let their customers find them organically. "It's largely through word of mouth that we get discovered," Jonathon said. The way they see it is simple: Treat your customers with dignity and respect, and give them space to browse and engage with staff, books, and other customers on their own terms, in at least modest comfort and safety.

It's the everyday interactions between people that are really important. "Retail is human interaction," Jonathon observed. "Amazon's Jeff Bezos used to talk about friction, about how, in his ideal business world, transactions would be frictionless. For us, it's that very friction, those moments between browsing and buying—the conversations, the discoveries, the connection—that makes everything work," he continued.

The book world has changed a lot since 1975, but Talking Leaves still serves the readers it set out to serve. "We know we're not for everyone," Jonathon acknowledged. "That's why we need many independent stores, each with its own character. It gives readers real choices." Now in its fifth decade of bringing lesser-known voices and challenging ideas to curious readers, Jonathon remains modest about their success. "So far, our luck has held," he said with characteristic understatement.

What made Talking Leaves work was a perfect example of positioning—knowing exactly who you serve and why. With this in mind, I headed to Chicago's Lincoln Square, where Suzy Takacs had built her neighborhood bookshop on something equally powerful: proximity—that special kind of connection that transforms customers into friends and a store into the heart of a community.

## The Book Cellar: Uncorking a New Chapter in Bookselling

Wine and books. For Suzy Takacs, these two pleasures had always paired perfectly at the end of a long day. This simple pleasure sparked an idea in 2004 while she was working as a nurse practitioner in the Chicago suburb of Evanston.

"I kept thinking about how much I love ending my day with a good book and a glass of wine," she told me. "These are my two favorite things in life. I figured there must be others who feel the same way."

The neighborhood had no bookstore, and Suzy began imagining a space that would combine her two favorite things. She even came up with a name: The Book Cellar. The timing, however, seemed questionable. Independent bookstores across the country were closing their doors as Borders, the retail giant, strategically positioned new stores near successful shops. But Suzy saw an opportunity to create something unique—a place where wine and literature could come together.

With no business experience but plenty of passion, Suzy got to work. "It wasn't just my favorite books and wines. I took time to curate the inventory and learn from others," she told me.

Finding the right location came with its own challenges—she needed a spot that was safe from the expanding Borders chain, plus she had to secure a liquor license. But luck was on her side when she found an ally in her local alderman, who had a soft spot for small businesses and helped her navigate all the complexities. And so, on June 12, The Book Cellar became the first independent woman-owned bookstore in the USA to feature a wine bar, opening its doors to both literary and wine enthusiasts alike.

Suzy quickly discovered she wasn't alone in her vision of pairing books with wine. "While some customers come just for the wine and others just for the books," she shared, "I wanted to create natural pairings that would bring both worlds together." And she did just that. Wine tastings became a natural complement to author events, with readers sipping carefully chosen vintages while discussing new releases. She even began hosting special evenings where wine authors would share their expertise, creating an atmosphere that was unique to The Book Cellar.

While Suzy held firm to her wine and books vision, she kept her ears open when the community suggested adding espresso to her café menu, like other bookstores were doing. She decided to have her café serve lattes, but in true Book Cellar style, it became another way to bring people together. The café created its own stories, like the one about a young woman, now in her late twenties, who first discovered the store as a child.

"There was this little girl," Suzy told me. "She would sit in the café every weekend with her grandfather. They'd spend hours here together. Even now, all grown up, she's still in touch. She's part of our history."

Like any small business, The Book Cellar has weathered its share of storms: the 2008 financial crisis, the rise of ebooks, Amazon's growing dominance, and Suzy's personal battle with cancer. Each time, her community rallied around the store. During COVID, loyal customers even organized an online campaign to keep the store's doors open.

"The store's purpose has evolved over time," Suzy reflected. "It began as a way to share what I love, but it's become something more meaningful. We're part of people's lives now." That connection with her community has become another of her favorite things, right up there with books and wine.

This deep connection to her community continues to shape her decisions. When the city announced it would be removing parking spaces in 2024, Suzy knew she had to speak up. "The new alderman will work with me because I know my customers. If they're going to spend time here browsing books or visiting other shops on the block, they need somewhere to park." Her customers backed her up, showing just how strong these relationships have grown.

What's kept The Book Cellar going through the years isn't just its unique combination of wine and books. It's the genuine understanding Suzy has of her customers, including recommending the perfect wine to go with their latest read, creating a space where people can come together over morning coffee to discuss the latest bestseller, and appreciating how families have made her store part of their lives across generations. Big retailers might be able to stock books and serve wine, but creating the kind of warm, personal atmosphere that makes The Book Cellar special can't be manufactured or mass-produced; it's something that comes from years of genuine connection with customers.

If Suzy showed me the power of genuine customer connections, my next conversation revealed how personal purpose could transform a bookstore into an agent of change. In Maplewood, New Jersey, I met Jonah Zimiles, whose path to bookselling began unconventionally—in a federal courthouse.

## [words]: Beyond Books and Business

Not every bookstore owner starts with dog-eared novels and dreams of endless reading. For Jonah Zimiles, the journey began when he clerked for Judge Max Rosenn of the Third Circuit Court of Appeals after graduating from NYU Law School. It was there, among case files and legal briefs, that he would discover an unexpected lesson about the power of community service.

"The judge would walk around town during our lunch breaks," Jonah remembers. "Everyone would stop him, and he would listen and talk to them. He had this philosophy—you've got to have your family, you've got to have a good job, and you have to serve your community."

Those words stayed with Jonah through fifteen years of corporate law. "That clerkship helped me land the big job out of law school, which led to other big roles," Jonah explained. But working around the clock at prestigious firms left little room for family or community. When his second child was diagnosed with severe autism, Jonah and his wife, Ellen, who was then a partner at KPMG, faced a turning point. Two high-powered careers weren't compatible with supporting their son's needs.

"Even though I had moved into focusing on nonprofit work, it was just too hard for us to manage." So Jonah stepped away from law to become a stay-at-home father.

During those seven years at home, Jonah volunteered one morning a week at his daughter's school bookstore. Later, when Ellen was preparing to leave KPMG to start her own consulting firm with private equity backing, Jonah helped analyze the business offers she was receiving. She noted his talent for distilling complex proposals into clear one-page summaries. "I don't know why you went to law school," she remarked. "You should have gone to business school. You're really good at this kind of stuff."

That comment sparked something in him. Their son's situation had stabilized enough that Jonah could consider returning to work, though returning to a traditional law career no longer appealed to him. He enrolled at Columbia Business School, initially planning to play a consulting-type role for autism organizations. There, Dean Glenn Hubbard spoke to students about "inspiring the entrepreneur in each of us," encouraging even those headed for corporate careers to think entrepreneurially. The message resonated with Jonah and Ellen, who had been discussing the critical need for helping people with severe autism transition from school to employment.

Then came the 2008 financial crisis. As Jonah graduated, Maplewood, their New Jersey town, was reeling from Wall Street's collapse. Ellen, whose career had actually thrived during the crisis, spotted their local bookstore, a small space on a side street, up for sale. She suggested they take it over, seeing an opportunity to give back to their struggling community while creating something meaningful.

"I wasn't sold on owning the bookshop at first," Jonah admitted. "I hadn't studied retail at business school, and unlike most people who dream of opening a bookstore, I wasn't driven by an extraordinary passion for books." But as he considered the opportunity, Judge Rosenn's words about community service came back to him. "I needed something where family could come first but where I could also create a meaningful impact in my community and focus on a cause I personally care about: helping people with severe autism transition into the workforce. That's when I saw how the bookstore could be a vehicle for something bigger. I told Ellen I'd do it on one condition: We needed the biggest storefront in town. If we were going to serve the community and make a real impact, we couldn't do it in a cramped space."

They soon found an ideal location with a welcoming storefront that could become the inclusive space Jonah envisioned. "We named it [words] and opened our doors in January 2009. While we set it up as a for-profit business, making money was never our primary goal. We were building a social enterprise to serve our community," he told me.

As [words] was taking shape, a neighbor who worked in marketing shared with Jonah what would become guiding wisdom: "Remember, you're not selling books; you're selling the bookstore experience." Those words shaped how Jonah built the business.

Unable to match the profit margins of Barnes & Noble or Amazon's vast reach, Jonah knew that [words] couldn't compete through conventional marketing. Instead, they found their edge through community engagement. They bring the community together through various events throughout the year, including sponsoring Maplewoodstock, a free two-day music and arts festival that draws thousands. While [words] isn't always at the forefront of these events, the bookstore has become woven into the fabric of community life in a way advertising dollars simply can't buy.

One of their most successful initiatives is their annual Where's Waldo hunt. "We didn't want to leave kids out of our community mission, we want to get them reading too," Jonah told me. "The publisher funds this initiative where we partner with twenty local businesses to hide Waldo figures in their shops. Over a thousand kids participate, going from store to store with their albums. The other businesses love it because we're driving foot traffic to them, and we love it because it brings families into our store and helps us promote children's books. It ends with a huge party where we give out prizes to the kids."

As [words] grew, it became the perfect vehicle for what Jonah and Ellen had envisioned all along—helping people with severe autism transition into the workforce. Through partnerships with schools and autism organizations, [words] provides transitional employment opportunities for school leavers with severe autism. These individuals work alongside job coaches for a few hours each week, gaining skills they can use in future employment. "They have passion and want to work, but they need help bridging the gap to employment. We give them the support they need to get a real job," Jonah explained.

From its inception, [words] saw double-digit sales growth for twelve consecutive years, even as the broader industry contracted. They were even named one of five finalists out of twenty-five-hundred independent bookstores for *Publishers Weekly*'s Bookstore of the Year.

That sales growth streak came to an end when the pandemic hit. "You know, COVID did a real number on us, and it wasn't just the sales," Jonah lamented. "We lost the in-person interaction. We lost longtime employees who moved away or couldn't put their health at risk. We lost the ability to serve the community in the way we envisioned."

"But our customers didn't accept that, and they became our lifeline. They organized online fundraisers, kept ordering books, and helped us weather the storm. Their support showed us that [words] had become more than just a bookstore to them, it was part of their community."

"When we started rebuilding our team after COVID, we turned to a technique that had worked well in our autism program called 'job crafting'—finding what someone is good at and passionate about, and then building their role around those strengths," Jonah explained. "When I interview anyone, I don't say, 'I need someone to do X.' Instead, I say, 'I have a whole bunch of things that need doing, and you have skills and passions we could use.' If you're an artist, maybe you'll do our displays. If you're a frustrated teacher, perhaps you'll train new employees."

This approach creates opportunities for meaningful work for everyone who joins the [words] team, whether they're building skills for future employment or finding their long-term home at the store. "I really believe that this forms a huge part of how we build deeper connections with our customers."

Walk into [words] today and you'll find their sales staff—passionate readers themselves—not just recommending books, but sharing what other people in the neighborhood are reading, discussing community events, and facilitating conversations about everything from literature to local issues.

Jonah remains committed to his original vision. While [words] welcomes anyone looking to buy a good book, at its core are the customers who share its deeper purpose—people who want to be part of something meaningful, who want to engage with their neighbors, and who believe in the power of a business to make a difference in its community. For the thousands of families whose lives have been touched by [words], no competitor, however large, can match what this bookstore means to them.

## Being Small Is a Superpower

These independent bookstores tell a story that disproves the Hollywood theory of inevitable small business failure: Small businesses *don't* have to lose to bigger competitors.

Fifteen years in corporate America showed me the inner workings of big business, with its relentless drive toward scale and efficiency. My decade at companies like Tax Credit Co. and ForwardLine opened my eyes to a different world, working alongside thousands of small businesses as they developed their strategies. These businesses succeeded not by following conventional wisdom but by breaking free from it. Their power lay in embracing what made them different and leveraging their unique strengths. While big businesses push for efficiency and standardization, small businesses create experiences that only they can deliver. This is why I wrote this book—to show small business owners that success comes from embracing what makes them different.

In the chapters ahead, I'll take you behind the scenes of both worlds. You'll see how big businesses tackle strategic decisions, from defining their market position and setting their prices to building customer loyalty and making the most of their resources. Then you'll discover how successful small businesses approach these same decisions differently, and more effectively. You'll learn, like I did, that success isn't about copying big-business methods but about harnessing your unique strengths to build exactly the business you want the way you want it.

*CHAPTER TWO*

# VAPORWARE

## One Step Ahead

In my final year of university, with a chemical engineering degree nearly in hand, I found myself at a crossroads. I had a few job offers in my field, but I was drawn to the world of consulting. Recruiters from big-name firms would come to our campus and talk about the exciting work they did: helping companies to grow, become more efficient, and tackle complex challenges. They would invite us to join their firms as consultants, promising a career filled with variety and the chance to make a real difference.

The idea of diving into different business situations, learning on the fly, solving problems, and then moving on to the next challenge appealed to me. Although the recruiters' presentations were often vague, with a lot of hand-waving and buzzwords, I knew I wanted a career that would keep me on my toes and constantly engaged, even if I didn't fully grasp what consulting actually entailed.

I had no idea why these recruiters believed I could be a consultant. I had no business background whatsoever. But being twenty-one, I didn't know what I didn't know. If they said I could do it, who was I to question them? Although my knowledge of running a business was limited to what I'd seen in movies, I imagined myself walking into boardrooms, sharing my wisdom with executives, and helping them steer their companies to success.

After going through interviews with several large consulting firms, I finally landed a job at Pricewaterhouse (now known as PwC) in San Francisco. It was during my first few days there that I discovered the truth: A consultant was just a fancy title for a coder. The firm wasn't looking for business consultants. They had actually been looking for programmers.

As a chemical engineering student, I spent most of my time learning about math and problem-solving. But there was one unexpected skill I picked up along the way: coding in FORTRAN, a programming language from the 1950s that's about as old and procedural as they come. I never thought this seemingly irrelevant knowledge would come in handy, but as it turned out, my limited programming experience was exactly what Pricewaterhouse was looking for.

I joined the firm in the late 1990s, right in the midst of the Y2K panic. For those who don't remember, Y2K was the fear that when the clock struck midnight on January 1, 2000, the world would descend into chaos. People believed planes would fall from the sky, computers would crash, and, for some inexplicable reason, everyone would lose their left shoe (but never the right one). It was a strange time, to say the least.

Amidst this madness, many Fortune 500 companies were scrambling to switch from their outdated enterprise resource planning (ERP) software to systems, applications, and products in data processing, known as SAP, a system that didn't contain the dreaded Y2K bug. Pricewaterhouse already had small internal consulting groups that focused on corporate software installations. With the Y2K deadline looming, these teams were busier than ever. And that's precisely where I found myself, learning to code in yet another ancient language called Advanced Business Application Programing, ABAP, which was used by SAP.

Pricewaterhouse was eager to bring on as many potential programmers as they could find, sending us out to client sites to work on their SAP installations. Our job was to write the small bits of code needed to ensure that the software they had purchased would continue to function when the clocks ticked over into the new millennium. As one of these newly recruited programmers, I knew nothing about business and only slightly more about coding.

As it turns out, I had just a little bit more knowledge than the average person working for my clients. I'd sit with the clients, tinkering with settings and writing code in the background to get things working smoothly. It wasn't that I had any deep insight into their business or what they were doing. My role was simply to help people who weren't comfortable with software get it installed and running. I figured that's probably what consulting was all about—being the bridge between the technology and the end users.

It was a wild time, with everyone racing against the clock to ensure a smooth transition into the new millennium. And there I was, a freshly minted chemical engineer, suddenly finding myself at the center of this bizarre technological drama.

## Slideware

While I was busy fighting the Y2K bug, the dot-com era was in full swing. It seemed like everyone was becoming an overnight millionaire, and like many others, I got caught up in the excitement. In hindsight, I should've paid more attention to Alan Greenspan, the Federal Reserve Board chairman at the time. He warned us about "irrational exuberance," suggesting that the stock market might be overvalued. But when you're young and dreaming of success, caution often takes a backseat. For a brief moment in my twenties, I was worth over a million dollars on paper. As we all know, that bubble eventually burst, but I learned some valuable lessons before reality delivered a harsh wake-up call to a young man who thought he had it made.

The allure of a cool startup promising big things was hard to resist, so I said goodbye to Pricewaterhouse and took a chance on something new. I then found myself a job as a coder at a Silicon Valley tech company called Blue Martini Software. At the time, everyone wanted to get into e-commerce, but building a website wasn't as simple as it is today. We didn't have user-friendly tools like Shopify or Magento that let you create an online store with just a few clicks. Building an e-commerce website required complex custom software, and that's where Blue Martini came in.

Blue Martini's software was the cutting edge of e-commerce website building, but it came at a steep price—a million dollars for a license, plus another 30 percent in annual fees just to keep it running. Plus, it was all written in Java, the programming language everyone was calling the future. The only problem was that I didn't know anything about Java. But when opportunity knocks, you answer the door and figure things out as you go. I may have been a chemical engineer turned accidental Y2K consultant, but I was ready to take on the challenge of mastering Java and helping businesses build their online storefronts. I had no idea what I was getting myself into, but I was excited to find out.

When I joined Blue Martini, I quickly realized that the company was still in the process of developing its groundbreaking e-commerce software. We had a product, or at least parts of one, and some demos to show potential clients. But there were certain features and functionalities that existed only in our imaginations.

Back then, online video demos weren't really a thing. We didn't have the luxury of creating slick YouTube videos to showcase our software. Instead, we relied on good old-fashioned Microsoft PowerPoint slides. In the tech world, this was called "slideware," essentially, software that exists only in the form of slides.

Looking back, it's kind of mind-boggling to think that companies were willing to shell out a cool million based on little more than a PowerPoint presentation and some persuasive salesmanship. But that was the reality of the early days of e-commerce. Everyone was scrambling to get a piece of the pie, and if you could paint a compelling-enough picture of what your software could do, you had a shot at making it big. This was just part of the thrill of working in a startup: You sell the dream, and then you hustle like crazy to make it a reality.

Our clients were a diverse bunch. Some were entrepreneurial types who had snatched up specific domain names, like games.com, guitars.com, or bbqs.com, with grand plans to launch their own e-commerce empires. Others were established businesses looking to expand their reach by taking their products online. From time to time, I'd be called upon to join the company's sales team at client meetings, lending an extra layer of technical credibility to their pitches.

In those early meetings, I'd sit back and listen as the potential client enthusiastically described their business, the products they wanted to sell online, and their vision for their website. Inevitably, they'd turn to us and ask the million-dollar question: Could we make it happen? I couldn't help but notice that our sales guys always responded with an unwavering "yes!" Eventually, I found myself chiming in with my own confident affirmation. I may have been a Java novice, but I could envision the possibilities of our software, and that was good enough for me. In my mind, there was no doubt—of course we could do it. After all, it was just a matter of writing the code.

I quickly realized that getting a client's buy-in had less to do with the actual capabilities of our technology and more to do with how confidently we could say yes. If we could make them believe, based on our sales pitch, that their product would be built to their exact specifications and expectations, then we were already halfway there. The rest came down to human connection, the trust we established through our enthusiasm and assuredness, which ultimately gave them the confidence they needed to take the leap with us.

## Selling Java

One day, one of our sales guys approached me and asked me to accompany him to an important meeting. Starbucks was interested in buying our software to sell their whole-bean coffees online. As we prepared our pitch, we came up with a brilliant idea. We'd install the software on my laptop, add some enticing images of different coffee beans with varying prices, and demonstrate to the Starbucks team just how effortlessly we could help them sell their coffee online.

Not once did it cross my mind to question whether people would actually buy coffee online. Instead, I found myself caught up in the excitement, thinking, *Okay, let's see if we can make this work. I'll show you a demo of how this software functions, even though we can't quite replicate the experience of sipping on a freshly brewed cup of java. But hey, I can still try to win you over with some enticing images of coffee beans!* Looking back, I can't help but chuckle at my own naivety and enthusiasm.

When we finally pitched to Starbucks, we found ourselves in front of their supply chain people, who couldn't have cared less about selling coffee online. Their main interest was whether our software could be used to track and move coffee beans and other inventory between their stores. Without missing a beat, our sales guy enthusiastically said, "Yes!" He exuded confidence. When asked for my input, I just followed his lead and was equally confident. I explained that we already had buttons for buying and selling, so all we needed to do was change the labels to "ordering" and "inventory transfer."

Looking back, I can't believe how oblivious I was to the absurdity of the situation. Here I was, a twentysomething-year-old kid, telling Starbucks that we could take software designed for online shopping and modify it to streamline their supply chain processes. But in that moment, I managed to sound like I knew exactly what I was talking about. The sales guy seemed impressed, and that was all that mattered.

After that meeting, I started gaining a reputation for being good at sales, even though I was pretty much just winging it.

## On an Island

Just shy of a year into my time at Blue Martini, Bill Evans, the company's head of Asia, approached me with an intriguing proposition. He asked if I'd be interested in transferring to Japan, stepping out of my role as a programmer, and taking on the challenge of being a salesperson for all of Asia. The business wanted to expand its software into the Asian market, and for some reason, Bill seemed to think I was the right person for the job.

Bill had already set up a partnership with a little company called NetYear to handle the installations, so my primary focus would be on partnership development and sales.

There was, however, one small caveat: At the time, our software was only designed to work with the English language. The entire English alphabet, consisting of just twenty-six characters, could comfortably fit into one byte. In contrast, languages used in Asia have a much larger set of characters—over fifty thousand, in fact—that our current system couldn't accommodate without using two bytes. But according to Bill, this wasn't a problem. Our engineers were already planning to update our software to support these languages and had estimated that it would take about six months to make it happen. This meant, once again, I would be selling something that didn't yet exist.

Despite this challenge, the opportunity sounded too cool to pass up, so I said yes. A few weeks later, armed with a newly purchased Japanese dictionary and phrasebook, I packed up my belongings and boarded a flight to Tokyo, ready to embark on my new adventure.

One of my first potential clients was Takara Standard, a company that manufactures a brand of customized bathrooms and kitchens called System Kitchen. In Japan, I discovered, people don't piece together their bathrooms or kitchens by buying individual components. Instead, they order the entire room as a single, prefabricated unit. The floor, walls, cabinets, appliances, and plumbing fixtures arrive as one package, precision-engineered to fit the exact dimensions of their space. The shower, toilet, sink, and even the light fixtures are all part of this unified system, perfectly coordinated and custom-designed to specification. *Who buys an entire room as a single product?* I asked myself. Apparently, everyone in Japan.

Traditionally, Takara's customers would pore over catalogs, chatting with sales reps to get everything just right. But Takara wanted to bring this whole process online. That's where we came in. Our job was to create an online configurator that would let customers design their dream kitchen or bathroom with a few clicks.

Little did I know that I was about to learn that everything in Japan revolved around relationships, and complex ones at that.

Back in Silicon Valley, I was used to attending meetings at clients' offices to pitch our product. It was a straightforward process: walk in, dazzle them with your presentation, and walk out with a deal. Simple, right? Well, not in Japan. Securing a deal in this new land felt a lot like dating. There was a long courtship involved, complete with plenty of wining and dining, before any commitment could even be considered. It was like navigating a maze of social norms and cultural expectations, all while trying to maintain an air of professionalism.

One evening, I met up with three guys from Takara Standard, along with two of my NetYear colleagues, at an *izakaya*. An *izakaya* is an establishment where patrons typically go to socialize after work, where the main course is beer and sake, and the small dishes of food they serve are just there to keep you from drinking on an empty stomach.

Most of the conversation was in Japanese, and the focus seemed to be on the Takara guys trying to learn as much about me as possible. I felt a bit like a celebrity who got caught up in a scandal, with news crews firing questions at me from every direction.

"How long are you here?" "Do you have a girlfriend?" And even, "Do you have a Japanese girl on the side?"

Not once did the conversation center around our business offering. I figured they probably didn't get to meet foreigners very often, so I decided to play along. With my NetYear colleagues acting as translators in their broken English, I answered their questions in my equally broken Japanese, trying my best to recall the phrases I had been memorizing since I arrived.

One of the dishes brought out during our extended evening of drinking was something called *takoyaki*—a ball of fried dough filled with diced octopus, tempura scraps, pickled ginger, and green onion, cooked in a special *takoyaki* pan until crispy on the outside and soft on the inside. I remember everyone looking at one another as if silently asking who would be brave enough to take the first bite. The *takoyaki* looked delicious, and everything else I'd eaten up until this point had been good, so I grabbed one and scarfed it down. I had no idea what I was eating, but it tasted great. After watching me for a few seconds, everyone else reached in to grab one and started eating. Suddenly, the most senior of the Takara guys grimaced and spat a half-chewed morsel out onto his plate. The table erupted in laughter.

"Don't you like *takoyaki*?" I asked innocently, trying to suppress my own amusement.

My question only made them laugh harder, and the mood at the table grew even more jovial.

What I didn't realize was that I had unwittingly participated in the Japanese version of Russian roulette. In these *izakayas*, the cooks would sometimes place a large ball of wasabi inside one of the *takoyakis*, and whether you picked it up or not was a game of chance. If you've ever eaten wasabi before, you'll be familiar with the nostril-burning, eye-watering sensation that accompanies consuming too much of it at once. It was only a matter of time before a wasabi-filled snack landed in my hands. But I was young and more than willing to play along, and I could see they appreciated my enthusiasm for joining in the fun.

As the night went on, we found ourselves trading stories, cracking jokes, and, eventually, belting out tunes together behind the karaoke mic.

The following month, we found ourselves back at another *izakaya* for round two of our epic eating, drinking, and karaoke extravaganza. The Takara guys continued their interrogation of me, and once again, the first plate of *takoyaki* made its appearance. Just like in our first gathering, business discussions were nowhere to be found. However, the next morning, the Takara guys surprised us with a request to visit our offices later that day. They wanted to see our product in action.

When they arrived, I ushered them into our boardroom, where I witnessed a fascinating display of Japanese business etiquette. The Takara guys meticulously arranged themselves on one side of the table, with the most senior guy (the one who'd spat out the wasabi) claiming the center spot, flanked by his two colleagues. Then, the CEO of NetYear took his place directly across from the most senior Takara guy, and I sat beside him. This, I learned, was the Japanese way: The senior person from each company sits in the middle, directly across from each other, and the next most senior colleagues sit on either side in descending order of seniority, almost like a pyramid.

This pyramid structure is incredibly formal. Everyone knows precisely where they must sit because everyone is acutely aware of their rank. You know you're all going to sit on one side of the table, and you know your position relative to the boss. But the real show was just beginning. The Takara guys didn't simply take their seats, they performed a carefully orchestrated ritual. Cigarettes were placed on the table with surgical precision. Then, the business cards were arranged like a dealer's deck in a high-stakes poker game. Once everything was in order, they made themselves comfortable.

With everyone settled in, we dove into our discussions, which were entirely conceptual. I spoke at length about the impressive features of our software and asserted that the Japanese version would be as good or better than the original. It was clear the Takara guys were genuinely interested. They nodded along, asking questions here and there. But then, just like that, the meeting was over. No decisions, no next steps, just a polite "thank you" and a promise to be in touch.

Two weeks later, they invited us to a knockoff Beatles show in Roppongi, the neighborhood known for its US embassy housing and its popularity among foreigners. By this point, we were three months into our efforts to close the deal. This time, a fourth member had joined the Takara trio, and before the show, we all sat down at a bar. One of the Takara guys ordered a round of sake bombs, a cocktail made by dropping a shot of sake into a glass of beer. Several more rounds followed, each one adding a little more fizz to the evening. I had a sneaking suspicion that this might be some sort of test, a way to gauge my drinking stamina. Were they trying to see if I could keep up with their sake-bombing prowess? Was this a crucial step in the Japanese business negotiation process? I wasn't sure, but I was thankful for my youthful resilience and my liver's ability to keep up with the pace.

The following morning, they called and requested a meeting at our offices at 10:30 a.m. When they arrived, the new guy from the night before strolled in and confidently claimed the center seat, silently declaring his status as the top dog of the Takara pack. The others, now demoted in the pecking order, dutifully flanked him like loyal subjects. There was still no demo, no discussion on pricing, and no questions about when our Japanese version would be available. Our discussions remained firmly in the realm of the conceptual.

The pattern quickly became familiar: a night of drinking, a more-senior guy joining the party, and an impromptu meeting announcement. In the evenings, I'd be two or three sake bombs deep, my mind reeling at the thought of an unprepared presentation with nonexistent tech in the morning. I couldn't help but notice that these meetings were always scheduled for after 10 a.m. Initially, I found the timing a bit puzzling. Why not get an earlier start to the day? But after a few months of late-night revelry with these potential clients, it all started to make sense. It's not easy to dive into business discussions when your head is still spinning from the previous night's festivities.

It also dawned on me that all the drinking and prodding was actually a clever way of building trust. This was their method of auditioning potential business partners. First, you get to know one another in non-work situations. You bond over drinks, you belt out some karaoke tunes, and then, and only then, you sit down for a proper meeting. At each of these meetings, I couldn't help but wonder how many more hangovers I'd have to endure before they finally decided to seal the deal, or if the whole thing would blow up when they found out that the product was not yet ready. At any rate, I figured I needed a bigger supply of aspirin just to keep up with the demands of Japanese business culture.

A few weeks later, another invitation to an *izakaya* arrived. This time, a new face joined the Takara crew. The following morning, they invited us to their offices for a mid-afternoon meeting. My stomach churned with a mix of hangover and anxiety. We still didn't have our tech ready, but I was grateful for the later meeting slot. It gave me just enough time to shake off the effects of the previous night and cobble together an inspirational deck. Instead of focusing on our nonexistent product, I decided to paint a picture of Takara's future, focusing on how special and unique I thought their business could be.

With everyone strategically seated around the table, I launched into my pitch. I talked about how Takara would be the only business in Japan where customers could configure their entire kitchen or bathroom online. While their competitors were still relying on catalogs and in-store consultations, Takara would be pioneering a digital revolution in home design.

As I spoke, I could see the excitement building in the room. They would nod and look impressed, occasionally breaking into rapid-fire Japanese discussions amongst themselves. Sensing their interest, I decided to venture into more technical territory.

"Let me tell you about our technology options," I said in English. "You can either install it on your own servers and run it in your own building, or we can host it off-site for you." Then, I segued into an explanation of cloud hosting, which was a novel concept at the time. I painted a picture of a future where their entire online system could exist on computers in a distant location, accessed via the internet. They wouldn't need to worry about maintaining physical servers or dealing with software updates. "This approach could not only streamline your operations but also potentially reduce costs and allow your system to handle sudden spikes in user traffic," I added, hoping I sounded more knowledgeable than I felt.

As I spoke, I kept my ears tuned to their side conversations in Japanese. I didn't let on that by then I understood a little bit more of the language, partly because my business Japanese still wasn't great, and partly because eavesdropping was proving quite informative.

In the side conversations, I caught snippets about the *kikaku chīmu* (planning team) being needed for future talks. A junior member pressed the senior guy about the *yosan* (budget) for this project. One topic kept popping up that threw me: *sāba*. I knew it as a type of fish—blue mackerel—usually grilled whole with just a sprinkle of salt.

"How many *sāba* would we need?" one of them asked in Japanese.

"How much will our *sāba* cost?" another asked.

I sat there, nodding sagely, my mind racing. *Why are they talking about fish? I wondered. Are they planning the next dinner? Did this meeting just go nowhere?*

It wasn't until after the meeting, when I sheepishly confessed my confusion to a colleague, that I learned that *sāba* was not just fish, it was also the Japanese pronunciation of "server." I'd been hearing an English word all along, filtered through a heavy Japanese accent. And then it hit me: They were seriously considering our proposal, down to the practical aspects. They were asking, "How much should we spend on this?" and, "When can we get this up and running?" It was a good sign, even if we were still a few months away from having the software fully functional in Japanese. My hunch on selling the vision rather than the product seemed to be paying off, even though there was still no close in sight.

Two weeks later, another night of revelry unfolded, followed by yet another meeting at their offices. As I entered the room, I noticed that the group had grown. This time, six people were seated on one side of the table, and the three guys I'd initially been socializing with were now positioned further down the hierarchy. At the center sat the organization's VP, the most senior person in the room, who held the ultimate power to green-light the project. His presence signaled that we were inching closer to our goal. Would this be the moment when all those late nights and early mornings finally paid off, or would we be in for another round of conceptual discussions, demos, and relationship-building? Only time would tell.

After countless meetings, late nights, and sake-fueled bonding sessions filled with big talk and grand visions about Takara winning over the world, we finally closed the deal. With no real demo and no pretty slides with images of what the software would look like, I had just sold them vaporware. Strangely, the moment felt somewhat anticlimactic. While I had never doubted that our nonexistent product would be a good fit, the real work had been in securing each subsequent meeting, gradually building trust with our Japanese counterparts, and inspiring them to see the potential for greatness in their business.

In retrospect, I realized that the deal's success had been determined long before that final handshake. There's a certain level of tradition and formality in Japanese business culture, and by the time we reached that last meeting, the outcome was already a foregone conclusion. If they were willing to bring us that far into the process, it implied that they trusted our understanding of their needs and our ability to deliver on our promises. The final meeting was more of a formality, a ceremonial end to a journey that had been filled with cultural nuances, relationship-building, and a whole lot of patience.

## Uncharted Territory

While I can't say I gained a deep understanding of business from my time working as a salesperson in Asia, one thing I *did* develop was an extraordinary level of self-confidence, the kind that might be described as "excessive" by a normal person. This trait, I would later learn, is a consistent characteristic among entrepreneurs, regardless of their success. Indeed, it takes a person with an exceptionally high degree of self-confidence to choose the path of entrepreneurship in the first place.

Realizing I still had much to learn about business, I decided to pursue an MBA, expecting to graduate ready to be a boss. However, life had a different plan for me. For the next decade, I found myself working as a consultant at McKinsey, a global management consulting firm.

After a few years of contributing to diverse projects, from parcel delivery to wind farms and even nonprofit growth strategies, my perspective on business broadened. Each engagement built on what I had learned in business school and deepened my understanding of how large enterprises operate in practice. With this real-world experience, I was expected to step into a project-leader role and eventually specialize in an industry where I could bring in clients myself. My focus gradually shifted to the tech industry, where I developed expertise in scaling up sales and production operations. I'll expand on examples from these experiences later in the book to illustrate how big businesses approach these topics.

As I made the transition from consultant to partner, I was encouraged to focus on Fortune 100 clients, the industry leaders in their respective fields. If you specialized in the automotive industry, you'd likely work with giants like General Motors, BMW, or Toyota. In the consumer-packaged goods sector, you'd probably collaborate with Procter & Gamble or Unilever. For pharmaceuticals, your clients might be Johnson & Johnson, Eli Lilly, or Merck, and in digital media, you'd likely partner with Netflix or Amazon. Within McKinsey, these clients were referred to as "Everest clients."

At McKinsey, there was an up-or-out career path; you either made partner or got fired. To make partner in this high-performance environment, consultants had to build relationships with senior executives through their work. Working with large Everest organizations provided many opportunities to connect with potential future CEOs. By advising these rising stars, consultants could position themselves as trusted advisors throughout their careers. Along the way, they would gain exposure to various aspects of the business and connect with other advisors, expanding their team and deepening their industry knowledge.

From a practical standpoint, this often meant having up to five or six partners working simultaneously on three or four parallel projects with a single Everest client, giving consultants ample opportunities to learn and grow. McKinsey's Everest model wasn't just a path to partnership, it was their business model. It was all about acquiring clients, nurturing relationships with them, and then reaping the rewards of that customer acquisition over the long haul. As a partner, you'd spend many hours with potential clients, often with months of dialogue, before engaging in billable work. With an Everest client, you could have a two-year calendar of project work or even spawn multiple simultaneous projects. If you delivered value, that executive with a billion-dollar budget would keep coming back to you, asking for help with one problem after another.

During my decade-long tenure at McKinsey, I found myself somewhat at odds with the Everest model. The idea of being a small cog in a massive machine didn't quite resonate with me. Instead, I gravitated toward the smaller $2 to $4 billion companies that often flew under the radar of McKinsey's Everest-seeking consultants. Sure, they didn't have the massive budgets of their larger counterparts, which meant I might only help on one project a year (if I was lucky), but what they lacked in financial firepower, they more than made up for with interesting challenges and room for growth.

In my eyes, these smaller companies were the hidden gems of the business world. Many hadn't yet developed the sophistication or the internal expertise of the big players. Their problems were often hiding in plain sight, waiting for someone to come along and shine a light on them. And when you did manage to fix an issue at one of these companies, the impact was often more tangible and rewarding than tackling the same problem at a $50 billion giant.

The challenge, in addition to smaller budgets, was that these companies didn't have any experience with consultancies like McKinsey. When I started to focus my efforts on these smaller players, a few of my mentors and colleagues warned me that it was a mistake to invest my time there, and nobody was interested in helping me win work. While the other consultants were on a path to partnership with Everest clients, I was out there trying to win over business leaders who didn't know me and didn't really know what I could do.

What I could do was get a group of people excited about an idea and inspired enough to act, even when I had nothing but my words and my concepts. For me, it was about promoting a dream or a vision. I had done it once, done it again, and honed this skill throughout my career at McKinsey: "Here's the vision, and here's how we're going to improve your business." I had no tangible product, no fancy presentations. All I had were my words, and somehow, people believed that what I was telling them was possible.

Other consultants at McKinsey found my approach a bit unconventional.

"Why are you spending so much time on this smaller company that can only provide a couple of projects a year?" they'd ask. "Your goal should be to bring in $20 million or more. This company you're working with, they're only going to contribute a million and a half. You'll need to juggle a handful of these smaller clients to reach your targets. You'll never make partner that way."

But I saw things differently, and making partner was not my end goal. Instead, I wanted to forge my own path, even if it meant taking on more risk. There was something about these smaller companies that resonated with me—the people, the challenges, the chance to make a real difference. McKinsey, to their credit, gave me the freedom to pursue this unconventional approach. But they also cautioned me that I'd be largely on my own. "This isn't our standard operating procedure," they said. "And with that comes the possibility of failure."

What they didn't know was that I'd been in unchartered territory before, selling vaporware based on relationships and trust. I knew that even if I didn't succeed in the traditional sense, I'd have a fantastic experience along the way. In my mind, there was always something to be learned, regardless of the outcome.

Even when I was elected partner, I was reminded that my route was not the McKinsey playbook, entrepreneurial in nature, and that I was an outlier and taking the road less traveled. It was around this time that I began to understand that entrepreneurship meant being willing to risk failure to forge your own path to success. I became drawn to leaders with that willingness to take risks and the self-confidence to succeed.

## A Grand Vision

I had the privilege of working with one such risk-seeking leader: Tor Hagen, the founder and chairman of Viking River Cruises. Tor, a former McKinsey partner, had built a remarkable brand that catered to wealthy retired Americans, offering them the opportunity to explore various parts of Europe without the hassle of trekking across the continent and constantly changing hotel rooms. With Viking, these travelers could experience the best of Europe from the comfort of a river cruise ship.

At that time, Viking had a fleet of around forty river cruise ships, each accommodating between 120 and 200 passengers. These luxury vessels, with their signature Scandinavian design, navigated some of the world's most iconic rivers, providing travelers with unparalleled access to the heart of the countries they visited. While most of Viking's operations were focused on European waterways such as the Danube, the Main, the Elbe, and the Seine, the company also offered cruises on other famous rivers worldwide, including the Yangtze in China, the Volga in Russia, the Nile in Egypt, and the Amazon in Brazil. This global presence allowed Viking's predominantly American clientele to immerse themselves in the culture, history, and beauty of not just Europe but also other fascinating destinations around the globe.

A river cruise ship is essentially a simple yet elegant floating hotel. The main draw for passengers is the opportunity to explore cities and towns along the way. Unlike traditional cruise ships, river cruise ships don't offer an abundance of onboard activities or amenities. Instead, they provide a comfortable and convenient base from which travelers can discover new destinations. Despite their smaller size, every room on a river cruise ship has a view, ensuring that passengers can enjoy the stunning scenery as they navigate the waterways.

The beauty of a river cruise lies in its simplicity. Passengers are treated to delicious meals onboard but spend most of their time off the ship, immersing themselves in the local culture and exploring the cities they visit. It's a fantastic way to see parts of Europe in style without the need for constant packing and unpacking.

Tor's river cruises were incredibly popular, and it wasn't hard to see why. These voyages were selling out a full year in advance, which meant that travelers had to plan their trips well ahead of time. The high demand was a testament to the quality of the experience Viking provided, and it had an enormous impact on the company's bottom line. Not only was Tor's operation financially self-sustaining, but the success also allowed him to continuously expand his fleet, adding more ships to meet the growing demand.

However, at seventy years young, Tor was not satisfied with just dominating the rivers with his beautiful ships. He dreamed of conquering the seas too. We worked together on his vision to expand his fleet by building a luxury ocean vessel capable of accommodating five times the number of passengers compared to his river cruise ships. It was a bold move, but Tor saw it as a chance to take Viking to new heights, reaching a wider audience and introducing more people to the joys of cruising with his company.

Tor's vision for his ocean cruise ship was unique. He wanted to create an experience that matched other luxury cruises while maintaining the intimate, culturally rich experience that had made Viking's river cruises so popular. A ship like this would need to accommodate nearly one thousand passengers.

## Financing the Dream

The vision was intoxicating, but building an ocean cruise ship of that size would cost hundreds of millions of dollars, and the river cruise business wasn't sitting on that kind of cash. That didn't deter Tor. He had an ambitious plan in mind.

One evening, after spending the day discussing his ocean cruise vision at his European sales office, we had dinner at one of his favorite Indian restaurants in London. As the casual dinner conversation drifted back to business, I asked him the question that had been nagging at me all day: "Where is the money coming from?"

Tor smiled, his expression suggesting he had a secret to tell me. I put down my piece of naan, sensing he was about to share something big.

"Why use our own money when others are willing to give us theirs?" Tor asked rhetorically. "We can convince people to buy into our vision and then use their funds to deliver it."

I assumed he meant debt financing, like a home mortgage where you need the house to exist before you can borrow against it.

"Won't the banks be hesitant to finance a ship and a business line that doesn't exist yet?" I asked.

"The banks will be the easy part," Tor responded, dismissing my concern. "It's the passengers we need first."

He laid out his strategy: use passenger deposits to finance a portion of the initial build, then convince lenders to cover the rest when the cruise was sold out. Viking's river cruise passengers were already accustomed to placing deposits a year in advance. For the ocean cruises, however, he needed to presell an entire season two years before the ship's maiden voyage.

As I listened to Tor's plan unfold, I couldn't help but be impressed by its audacity. He intended to finance a half-billion-dollar ship for an unproven business using nothing but customer deposits and bank loans. This was exactly the kind of entrepreneurial thinking that had drawn me to him in the first place. It was bold, it was innovative, and yes, it was risky. Yet Tor had every reason to believe it would work.

Tor was essentially proposing to build a massive ship backward, starting with sales and ending with construction. As I sat there, my mind racing to keep up, I realized I was watching a master at work. Tor was playing a game of financial chess, and he was several moves ahead of anyone else. The sheer ingenuity of it all hit me: *Wow*, I thought, *this looks incredibly challenging . . . and absolutely fascinating.*

Without a physical ship, I knew he wouldn't be able to give potential customers a real-life tour of his cruise ship's amenities. But Tor was unfazed. He would create the product through catalogs and TV advertisements, complete with schedules, amenities, and prices, all before a single piece of steel had been cut. This was worlds away from my days at Blue Martini, where I was selling software to a handful of executives using PowerPoint slides, beer, and sake. Tor's version of vaporware meant convincing tens of thousands of people to pay two years in advance for a cruise on a ship that only existed in his imagination.

Tor's bold plan lit a fire for me. Here was an entrepreneur who wasn't afraid to think big. The more I thought about it, the more I realized his vision had real potential. Tor knew exactly what he was doing when it came to designing the ideal cruise experience. He had a large customer base and Viking's excellent reputation to build upon. There was definitely a viable market for this kind of luxury ocean cruise. His sales team was eager to get started, and they were just as invested in Tor's vision as I was. Tor's unwavering conviction and drive made it all feel possible.

I looked Tor in the eye and said, "I believe we can make this happen, and I want to help. I'd be thrilled to join your team and take on this challenge with you."

With that, I said goodbye to McKinsey and embarked on an exciting new journey with Tor, helping him transform Viking River Cruises into the global powerhouse that would become known as Viking Cruises.

## A Commitment to Core Principles

Working with the team at Viking to bring his vision to life, we created stunning catalogs filled with digital renderings of the yet-to-be-built ship, bringing to life imaginary passengers raising glasses in restaurants that existed only in pixels and sunbathing by pools that were still just concepts on paper. We sold the dream of luxury ocean cruises to thousands of eager travelers.

The ocean ship would still prioritize the destination, but it would have the added advantage of being able to visit picturesque ports in coastal cities that larger cruise liners couldn't access. This would give travelers the opportunity to discover some of Europe's hidden gems. There would be a variety of itineraries on offer, with various routes spanning the entire European continent. Passengers could begin their journey from the stunning fjords of Scandinavia, including Tor's hometown of Stockholm, before making their way down to the sun-drenched Mediterranean and then circling back. The ship would call at cities like Dubrovnik in Croatia, along with other destinations along the Mediterranean and Baltic coastlines.

In terms of the onboard experience, the ocean ship would feature more spacious rooms than the river cruise ships, each with its own private balcony. There would also be a wide range of onboard amenities and activities on offer, allowing guests to find the perfect balance between exploration and relaxation.

What made Tor's approach to these ocean ships truly special was how deeply personal it was. He built his business based on how he himself wanted to travel and experience the world. His vision wasn't just a business model; it was a reflection of his own beliefs about how travel should be done. And, as it turned out, there were hundreds of thousands of people who shared his perspective.

Tor's attention to detail and understanding of his clientele often surprised me. I remember questioning him about the dining arrangements on his ships. "Tor, why is every table in the dining room a six-person table? Aren't most of your customers couples?" I asked. His response was both amusing and insightful. "Sri, these couples have spent decades just sitting across the table from each other. They're on vacation. They want to talk to other people. They've been talking to their spouses for their whole lives," he said.

Tor knew exactly who he wanted on his ships: retired couples with the means and desire to explore Europe in comfort. These were people who had worked hard their whole lives, who appreciated quality, and now wanted to see Europe, discuss its history and culture over dinner, and enjoy the company of others who shared their interests.

Tor built Viking just for this set of travelers. He had no interest in appealing to young families or party-seekers. Instead of trying to please everyone, he focused entirely on creating the perfect experience for this particular group. He knew there were countless retired couples seeking exactly this kind of travel experience, yet no one was properly catering to them. He knew there were more than enough of them to fill his ships, and, more importantly, he knew exactly what they wanted because he could see himself as one of them.

At first, some of Tor's exacting standards seemed odd to me. I often found myself thinking, *That's kind of weird, but if you say so, sure.* As time went on, I began to see the genius in his vision. It was his personal connection to the product and his unwavering commitment to his ideas that really made Viking successful. And he stuck with it.

Staying true to Tor's vision paid off. Sales outpaced our projections so rapidly that we had to create schedules for a second year to accommodate eager passengers. The deposits rolled in, and with the down payment secured, we approached the banks. The fact that we had presold a year's worth of cruises spoke volumes. Tor's dream had become a proven concept with a committed customer base. The banks saw the potential, and the financing fell into place.

In the end, Tor achieved what he set out to do. Today, Viking boasts many more ocean ships in its fleet, with demand continuing to soar. It's a testament to what's possible when you stay true to your vision and refuse to let conventional wisdom stand in your way.

## The Entrepreneur's Path

Working with Tor gave me tremendous respect for his ability to envision and create something extraordinary. While Viking was small compared to its competitors, he saw this as a strength. He built Viking for a specific group of travelers, creating the kind of travel experience he knew they would want. Instead of competing with massive cruise lines, he took the time to understand his passengers and what mattered to them. Like every entrepreneur, he took huge risks, but his vision was clear; he wanted to change how his customers experienced travel. His belief in this idea won over his customers, his team, and his financiers.

My experiences with entrepreneurs were challenging some common wisdom about success. While public speakers often encourage people to dream big and tell stories about how you can achieve anything you set your heart and mind to, I was seeing something different. Most people don't have grand dreams like Tor's, and even fewer have the confidence to pursue them.

What I was discovering about entrepreneurship was that it meant forging your own path, often in the face of doubts and expectations of failure from those around you. My experiences at Blue Martini Software and McKinsey, along with working with entrepreneurs like Tor, showed me that success can be found in doing what others might consider impossible, like selling a product or service that doesn't yet exist. I saw that until you establish a track record, it is your understanding of your customers and a shared belief in your purpose that convinces others to buy into your vision, whether they are clients, investors, or team members.

I began to understand how most of us can see possibilities in our business that seem just beyond our grasp. Perhaps it's taking over the empty storefront next door or finally launching that new idea your customers keep talking about. While conventional wisdom might suggest following what the big players do, I was learning that the real opportunity lies in doing things your own way. The successful entrepreneurs I met started with the customers who already valued what makes them different. They listened to what their customers wanted. They built something meaningful, not just profitable. When they believed in their vision like Tor did, they found others who wanted to help them bring it to life. Sure, they faced challenges along the way, but that's part of the entrepreneurial journey, and even setbacks can provide valuable lessons.

The most important thing I learned was that success doesn't come from following the crowd or sticking rigidly to industry norms. Instead, I realized it often comes from being true to yourself and pursuing that one thing you've set your mind on achieving, no matter how outlandish, risky, or against the grain it might be. The entrepreneurs who let their personalities shine through their work were able to succeed where others couldn't. These observations from my work with entrepreneurs like Tor would later help shape my understanding of the three Underdog Principles.

I keep coming back to this simple truth: Anybody with the guts to take a risk has the potential to build something special. I wrote this book to remind myself, as much as to show others, that success comes from leaning on your strengths, staying committed to your vision, and letting your unique approach guide your path forward. Your unique way of doing things might just be what the market has been waiting for.

THOUGHT STARTERS

- What inspired you to start your business, and how does that initial vision align with what you're doing today?
- What makes your approach different from others you compete with, and how does this differentiation serve your customers?
- What do you understand about your customers that allows you to serve them better?
- In what ways could your business better reflect your personal vision?

*CHAPTER THREE*
# DELICIOUS AND FULFILLING

## Stubborn, yet Successful

Throughout my career, I've come across countless experts, consultants, and well-meaning colleagues eager to share their formula for success. But I've come to realize that the most successful entrepreneurs often chart their own course, tuning out the noise of conventional wisdom.

During my time at McKinsey, I had the opportunity to work with truly impressive entrepreneurs at the helm of multinational corporations. One that really stuck with me was the founder of a tech company looking to streamline his supply chain. He had built his business on a revolutionary made-to-order process. Customers could customize every little detail of their purchase yet still get their product in just days. Once an order came in, the company would build it exactly to spec and ship it straight out. This approach had landed the company in Harvard Business School case studies and earned them a reputation for having one of the best supply chains in the world.

As consultants, our job was to evaluate every opportunity for improvement, analyze data, and make transformational recommendations. We found a number of ways to help the business save costs in its supply chain. One big idea was to switch away from customizing every order and instead move manufacturing to China, preconfigure the machines, and sell them on Amazon. Hint: Everyone else in the industry was already doing it. We were confident that this approach would not only reduce costs but also maintain the high level of customer satisfaction for which the company was known.

It seemed pretty straightforward to the senior execs who worked out the details with my team. However, when we presented our findings to the founder, I realized I had totally underestimated the power of an entrepreneur's vision. His unique approach was the very foundation of his company's success. It set them apart from competitors and built a loyal customer base that valued being able to customize their machines.

"Look, I get that the market's shifting. But that doesn't mean we need to become something we're not," he said bluntly.

By suggesting he abandon this strategy and fall in line with industry norms, we were basically telling him that his vision was all wrong. It was a gut-punch moment for me. I had gone into that meeting brimming with confidence, certain we'd nailed it. After all, the math showed significant savings, and moving manufacturing to China seemed like a no-brainer at the time. But the founder's resistance caught me off guard. Months of work suddenly felt wasted.

Although his resistance to our proposal shocked me, it came as no surprise to the executives who had worked with him over the years. As we regrouped, I met with a few of those executives to better understand where I had gone wrong. They explained that it wasn't about the math or

## DELICIOUS AND FULFILLING

the idea being wrong but that our suggestion simply didn't capture his vision.

Like other successful entrepreneurs, the founder was driven by a singular vision that flew in the face of conventional wisdom. Entrepreneurs like him are the ones swimming upstream, taking risks, and innovating in ways that others might dismiss as impractical or even crazy. It's this willingness to think differently and challenge the status quo that sets them apart and drives their success.

The more I learned about him, the more I started to see this wasn't just about business; it was deeply personal. He wasn't blind to changes in the market, but he had a gut feeling about his business that went beyond market trends.

I finally got it. We couldn't just barge in and rewrite his company's DNA. Sure, we could tweak his operating practices, but the heart and soul of the business was sacred ground. So, we went back to the drawing board. Working with his vision instead of against it, we brainstormed ways to merge mass manufacturing efficiencies with the personalized, unique experience that was the hallmark of his brand.

In the end, we were able to design a proposal that aligned with his vision while still delivering the signature experience his customers expected.

That whole episode taught me something I'll never forget: Sometimes, the path a business owner wants to take isn't the one that looks best on paper. What makes sense strategically doesn't always match up with their personal vision.

I've seen this dynamic play out countless times since then. There are times when change is necessary, when an entrepreneur's way of doing things might be holding the business back. As a small business owner, it's important to recognize when you're pouring resources into things your customers don't care about or when you're obsessing over solving problems that won't really impact your bottom line.

But there are also times when focusing on your unique strengths can be the smartest business move. You don't need to capture the entire market. There's real value in being different. You don't need to blend in or follow the crowd. Often, there are plenty of customers out there who'll support you precisely because you're not like everyone else.

This lesson would come to mind years later when I met another visionary entrepreneur, Toshi Sakamaki, the owner of Yakitoriya, a Japanese restaurant in Los Angeles. Like the tech founder, Toshi had built a successful business by staying true to his vision and refusing to conform to industry expectations. His story, which I'll share in the pages that follow, is a testament to the power of passion, dedication, and the courage to forge one's own path.

But before I tell Toshi's story, let me first share with you some of my own culinary adventures in Japan.

## Bite-Sized Adventures in Japan

When I was selling software in Tokyo, I quickly learned that lunchtime was a whole different experience compared to what I was used to back in the States. In the US, lunchtime at the office was usually a social affair. We'd either grab a bite together in the cafeteria or head out as a group to a nearby restaurant. But in Japan, people had a more solitary approach. They would simply get up from their desks, leave the office, and go off on their own to enjoy their midday meal.

As I explored the streets around my office, I discovered a variety of small, unassuming restaurants tucked away between buildings. Most could only seat about eight people at a time, and they were often run by a single person. These places specialized in different types of cuisine. Some of them served udon, others offered sushi, ramen, or soba.

Since my Japanese language skills were pretty limited when I first arrived, I'd look for places with picture menus or plastic models of their dishes displayed in the shop windows (a practice they call *shokuhin sampuru*). In most of these restaurants, there was a vending machine-like device where you could choose your meal from a picture on the screen, insert your money, and collect a ticket to hand to the chef behind the curtain. The chef would then prepare your dish and serve it to you directly.

At first, I found this system a bit impersonal and mechanical compared to the more interactive dining experiences I was used to back home. There were no servers to take your order or check on you during your meal. It was only many years later, when I better understood the workings of business, that I realized that, for these small business owners, success was all about simplicity and self-reliance. By eliminating the need for front-of-house staff to handle cash and take orders, they could operate with lower overhead costs and reduced turnover. They also didn't have to worry about managing a team of employees or dealing with the challenges that come with a larger staff—like whether they would show up for work or not. By designing their businesses to run smoothly with just one person at the helm, they could focus on what they did best—preparing delicious meals for their customers.

During my first few weeks in Tokyo, I stumbled upon a little restaurant that served yakitori, a classic Japanese street food consisting of grilled chicken kebabs. The word *yakitori* literally means "grilled bird," and let me tell you, the aroma wafting from this place was absolutely mouthwatering.

Unlike some other restaurants I had visited, this one didn't have a ticketing machine. Instead, I was handed a menu and an order form with photos of each item alongside a checkbox where you could indicate the quantity you wanted. The skewers in the photos looked like the regular-sized American kebabs I was used to, so I confidently marked the checkbox with a one.

Now, if you've ever dined at a sushi restaurant, you know that the portions are often smaller than what you might expect, with one serving consisting of several bite-sized pieces. This was a lesson I learned the hard way during my first month in Japan. I actually lost about ten pounds, not because there was anything wrong with the food, but because I was still trying to navigate the menus and portion sizes. It took me a while to realize that if I didn't want to wither away, I needed to order multiple items from the menu.

So, there I was, eagerly awaiting my yakitori. When the chef brought my order to the table, I looked down to find two tiny skewers, each with just three little pieces of chicken, neatly arranged on a plate that seemed more suited for a dollhouse than a grown man's lunch. I'll admit feeling slightly insulted at first glance. However, that feeling quickly dissipated the moment I took my first bite. The yakitori was, hands down, one of the most delicious things I had ever tasted. The chicken was perfectly grilled, juicy, and packed with flavor. Those two tiny skewers disappeared in a matter of seconds, leaving me craving more. But alas, it was time to head back to the office, my hunger not quite satiated.

After my initial yakitori experience, I found myself diving deeper into the world of Japanese cuisine. While some restaurants served smaller portions that you order from a menu, I soon discovered that there were also places where the food just kept coming. One such example was *kaitenzushi*, a type of sushi restaurant where you sit at a counter and pluck plates of sushi from boats or conveyor belts that continuously circulate around the restaurant. You can keep eating until you've accumulated a towering stack of ten or more plates. Another favorite of mine was shabu-shabu, a hot pot dish where you spend a leisurely ninety minutes cooking and eating an array of meats, vegetables, and noodles to your heart's content. Once I discovered these all-you-can-eat styles of dining, my weight loss came to a screeching halt. In fact, not only did I regain all the weight I had initially lost, but I also managed to pack on an extra twenty pounds.

In Japan, tradition is everything and, when it comes to cuisine, there's often only one way to do things. Take yakitori, for example. The reason it always tastes so amazing is that every step of the process is an art form. From the way the chicken is cut (the neck is considered the best part) to the exact size and angle of each piece to how it's threaded onto the skewer, it's all done with precision and care. Before it even hits the grill, the chicken is marinated in a savory soy-based *tare* sauce, ensuring that every bite is bursting with flavor.

But the real magic happens when the yakitori meets the *binchō-tan* charcoal. This special charcoal, made from Ubame oak harvested from the mountain forests of Kishu, is considered by chefs to be the best in the world. It's smokeless, odorless, and burns longer than any other charcoal out there. It also reaches incredibly high temperatures very quickly, which is why the meat cooks fast and retains all its delicious juices.

When the marinated chicken is placed on the *robata* grill over the *binchō-tan* charcoal, something extraordinary happens. The combination of the *tare* sauce, the high heat of the charcoal, and the unique texture of the meat creates a flavor and texture that's nothing short of heavenly. Just thinking about it makes my mouth water.

But I digress.

In Japan, mastering any art or skill, including cooking, is generally achieved through a traditional master-apprentice relationship. Just as aspiring swordsmen, shoemakers, or blacksmiths in medieval times learned their trade under the watchful eye of a seasoned master, Japanese chefs have been passing down their culinary wisdom to eager apprentices for centuries.

The journey to becoming a master chef in Japan is not a short one. An apprentice must dedicate years to learning and perfecting their chosen culinary art, whether it's crafting the perfect sushi roll, grilling tender morsels of yakitori, or flipping savory *okonomiyaki* pancakes. Only after they have spent the requisite time under their master's tutelage and have demonstrated a complete mastery of their craft are they deemed ready to venture out on their own.

It's at this point that the apprentice, now a master in their own right, can take the leap and open their own small restaurant. They've earned the right to build a business around their passion and share their expertise with the world. But this privilege comes with a deep respect for tradition and a commitment to the techniques and flavors they spent so long perfecting. In their own little restaurant, they become the master, guiding the next generation of apprentices and ensuring that the art of their chosen cuisine lives on, just as it has for hundreds of years.

## Toshi's Yakitoriya: LA's Best-Kept Culinary Secret

When my wife, Crystal, and I first started our life together, we settled in San Mateo, a city in the heart of Silicon Valley in the San Francisco Bay Area. In the early twentieth century, Japanese immigrants flocked to San

Mateo to work in the salt ponds and flower industry, establishing a strong cultural presence in the area. As a big fan of Japanese cuisine, living in San Mateo was a dream come true for me, with a wide variety of authentic Japanese restaurants to choose from.

In 2013, I left McKinsey to work for Tor, and Crystal and I moved to Los Angeles with our growing family. While it was a great place to live in many ways, we couldn't help but wonder if we'd be saying goodbye to all the amazing food options we'd grown accustomed to. But during a trip to the Westside to look at potential homes, we took a break and headed down to the Sawtelle district for lunch. It turns out that Sawtelle Boulevard is a hub for the Japanese American community, known for its trendy sidewalk shops and restaurants.

As we walked along Sawtelle Boulevard, a small Japanese restaurant across the street caught my eye. The place was called Yakitoriya, which translates to "grilled bird house." It was nestled on the street-level floor of a three-story building, sandwiched between several other restaurants competing for attention on the same bustling sidewalk. Given my love for yakitori, I knew we had to try this place out once we were settled in our new LA home.

When we finally had the chance to visit Yakitoriya, it was a Friday evening, around 7 p.m. Crystal and I were excited for our date night, knowing our kids were in good hands with our babysitter. As we approached the small restaurant, the smoky aroma of grilled chicken wafted through the air, making our mouths water in anticipation.

We opened the door and stepped inside, standing somewhat awkwardly at the entrance, waiting to be seated. The restaurant was empty, but a Japanese woman with a thick accent approached us and asked, "Do you have a reservation?"

"No," I replied, glancing around at the vacant tables. "I don't."

The woman took a deep breath, scanned the restaurant, sighed, and then walked away, disappearing into the back without saying another word. Crystal gave me a look that seemed to say, "Why didn't you make a reservation?" I shrugged, wondering why we would need one when we were the only customers there.

As we waited, unsure of what to do next, we took in our surroundings. The restaurant was small and cozy, with seating for about twenty-two people. Boxes of beer were stacked haphazardly off to the side, and the floors were covered in old-school kitchen tiles. The specials of the day were printed out in English and stuck up behind the kitchen counter, where we could see the chef moving about behind a haze of smoke that emerged from the *robata* grill. While there was some artwork on the walls, it was overshadowed by single sheets of paper stuffed into plastic sleeves, bearing simple, no-nonsense statements like "You must tip 20 percent," "You must order five skewers per person," and "One drink per person minimum." It was clear that Yakitoriya wasn't trying to be a fake authentic Japanese restaurant. They were the real deal.

After a few minutes, the woman returned and said, "Okay, we can seat you." She scanned the empty seating area as if it were a puzzle she needed to solve and let out another heavy sigh.

"Sit there," she said, pointing to a table in the back corner.

I couldn't help but imagine her thought process, deciding that out of all the prime seats available that evening, she would give us the least desirable table. As we sat down, she handed us a menu—a printed piece of paper tucked into a plastic sleeve, the kind you might find in a binder. I wasn't too concerned, though. It had been a long time since I'd had good yakitori, and I was more than willing to overlook the oddities of the situation. I was there for the food.

About five minutes later, a young Japanese man, probably no older than twenty, emerged from the back.

"Would you like something to drink?" he asked.

Crystal and I ordered a beer each. Since we had already decided what we wanted to eat, we asked if he could take our food order at the same time.

"No," he replied. "I can only serve you drinks."

I glanced over at Crystal, who was as puzzled as I was, and shrugged my shoulders.

Eventually, the woman returned to take our food order. We watched as the chef moved between skewering and grilling, his movements precise and efficient.

When the food arrived, it was fantastic, every bit as good as the yakitori I'd enjoyed while living in Tokyo. We knew right then that we'd be coming back to Yakitoriya, making it a regular part of our monthly dining rotation.

The following month, we decided to return to Yakitoriya. Just like before, we walked inside, and no one seemed to notice us at first. The chef glanced up briefly before returning his focus to the grill. Eventually, Mika, the woman whom we had come to understand was his wife, hurried out and asked if we had made a reservation. Once again, I had overlooked this detail and admitted as much. As if on cue, she surveyed the empty seats and took a deep breath, seemingly unsure of how to proceed. Without a reservation, it almost felt as though we were intruding on sacred ground.

After another deep exhale, we were seated at the same table as our previous visit. The young waiter emerged to take our drinks order, followed by Mika, who came to take our food order. This time, she was a bit more communicative.

"Five skewers minimum order," she stated. "Twenty dollar minimum spend. And everybody must buy a drink."

We smiled and nodded, agreeing to her terms and conditions. We understood that the restaurant needed to turn a profit, and it wasn't a concern for us. We were there for the food, and the food was exceptional. Eating the five-skewer minimum order would be a pleasure, not a problem.

## A True Master

Born in Japan, Toshimitsu Sakamaki, or Toshi as we came to know him, moved to LA in 1984. After training under a master in Little Tokyo, he opened Yakitoriya in 2000. Since then, he has dedicated himself to serving delicious, authentic yakitori to his customers. Working fourteen-hour days without a lunch break, Toshi's sole focus is on serving his customers delicious Japanese cuisine.

In Japan, they call someone like Toshi a *shokunin*. While it simply means "craftsman" or "artisan," its deeper meaning speaks to both mastery of one's profession and an unspoken understanding of one's role in society. Walk through any Japanese city and you'll see it everywhere—the careful attention to every detail and the quiet pride in work well done, no matter how small. It's never for show or recognition. It's about mastering your craft because that's your contribution to the world. For a *shokunin* like Toshi, every detail matters, not because someone is watching, but because excellence is the only acceptable standard.

Toshi is well respected by celebrity chefs and restaurateurs. Nobuyuki Matsuhisa, better known as Nobu, who is famous for his fusion cuisine,

## DELICIOUS AND FULFILLING

blending traditional Japanese dishes with Peruvian ingredients, has been known to dine at Yakitoriya. Other high-end chefs have also come to eat Toshi's food. You might not notice them, but if you're lucky, you could spot a five-star chef sitting at the counter, enjoying Toshi's yakitori. His culinary expertise is so renowned that books have been written about him.

It's no wonder that over the course of about four years, a period when we had the luxury of leaving our kids in the capable hands of a babysitter, we became regulars at Yakitoriya, dropping by almost every month. Every single time, Mika would appear at the front and ask us, "Do you have a reservation?" Even though we consistently showed up without one, she gradually warmed up to us.

As time went on, we noticed Mika would often seat us at the bar counter (instead of the general seating area), where Toshi would be working his magic at his *robata* grill. The bar counter was a bit like the ones you find at sushi restaurants, where the chef does all their intricate work right in front of the customers seated around the counter. Toshi's bar counter had eight front-row seats to his grilling performance. For us, it was as if we'd scored a serious upgrade in terms of airplane seating. As frequent flyers, we'd gone from being squished in basic economy to enjoying the perks of premium economy. We'd gone from being invisible to being recognized.

Now, we had no clue what kind of system Mika used to decide when someone's status was due for an upgrade. It wasn't like she sent out a notification or anything. It was more a case of, "Oh, look who it is! Kazasan and his lovely wife. They're part of our regular crowd. Let's give them a prime spot." Of course, when we didn't show up for a few months for whatever reason, we might find ourselves bumped back down to regular seating, where we'd be sitting with the general crowd once again.

## UNCONVENTION

After frequenting Yakitoriya for a few years, we noticed that the young waiter had disappeared several times and that it was just Toshi and Mika running the show. We suspected that Toshi probably didn't trust anyone else to manage the restaurant besides his better half. Mika now had to serve drinks and bus tables, and Toshi would occasionally have to come out from behind the *robata* to deliver his skewers.

This change in staffing had a noticeable impact on our dining experience. We'd be seated in the usual manner, but our dinners began to unfold at a more leisurely pace. Skewers would arrive at a steady rate, but we found ourselves dining for up to two and a half hours before our final dishes were served. The absence of the waiter meant that tables weren't turned as quickly, and sometimes, they weren't even bussed until the end of the night.

But what could have been seen as a drawback turned out to be a blessing in disguise. These longer, unhurried meals became perfect for our date nights. We could linger over our meal, savoring each skewer and enjoying each other's company without feeling rushed.

Perhaps the most significant change was our increased interaction with Toshi himself. With no waiter to act as an intermediary, Toshi would bring our food to the table personally. These moments gave us an opportunity to chat with him more often, to express our appreciation for his culinary artistry, and to learn more about the man behind the grill. It felt as though we were getting a more personal, intimate dining experience, one that felt less like dining out and more like being welcomed into someone's home.

When my good friend Farrokh moved to LA in 2021, I couldn't wait to introduce him to Yakitoriya. As a globe-trotter who would hop on a plane to Japan just to indulge in fantastic cuisine, I knew he'd appreciate the restaurant, but I felt I should personally bring him there to make sure he had a great experience.

When he tasted Toshi's yakitori, he declared it the best he'd ever had, even compared to what he'd savored in Japan. There were times when we'd be sitting in the regular seating area, and we'd spot him perched at the bar counter, dining from a different set of dishes. That's when it dawned on us that he had been upgraded to the Yakitoriya equivalent of platinum status. He'd been frequenting the restaurant twice a month and was ordering every single item on the menu. And he always made a reservation. It was clear that Farrokh had cracked the code to earning Mika's approval and securing a coveted spot at Toshi's grilling station, with specially decorated dinnerware.

When the kids were a bit older, we decided it was time to introduce them to Toshi's mouthwatering cuisine. Mika glanced at us, then down at our little crew, and asked, with a hint of suspicion, "Do you have a reservation?" She kept a watchful eye on the children as if trying to gauge whether they would be on their best behavior and if they'd order enough skewers to meet her minimum requirements. Crystal joked that Mika was probably running a complex algorithm in her head, weighing the potential benefits and drawbacks of seating a family with young kids.

After a few more visits with the kids in tow, we noticed a change in our seating arrangement. Mika had apparently decided that we had proven ourselves worthy of a collective upgrade, moving us out of the regular seating area and into the family-friendly version of premium economy, closer to the action, with a better view of Toshi's grilling artistry.

Sitting at our upper-class table, we'd watch as prospective new patrons had their patience tested. One night, a couple walked in and, after not being greeted, simply sat down at a table and started staring at their phones. I thought to myself, "If I don't intervene, these folks will get the silent treatment, eventually leave, and then hammer the restaurant in an online review." I looked over at them, and before I could warn them of their fate, Crystal touched my hand as if to ask, "Why are you helping them?"

"They look like the type of people who will leave negative comments about the restaurant on social media," I explained. "And that won't be good for business."

Crystal opened up Yelp on her phone, showed me the poor reviews that were already there, and said, "Please don't embarrass us for nothing."

While the obvious lack of customer service never bothered us, any new customer unfamiliar with Japanese culture and Toshi's unique way of running his restaurant would likely visit once and never return. We witnessed this firsthand on numerous occasions. Some patrons would come in, appear dissatisfied with the experience, and never come back. Others would enter, only to walk out immediately after being asked about their reservation and being made to wait at the entrance for further instructions.

## Can This Business Survive?

When the COVID pandemic hit in March 2020, it threw the restaurant industry into chaos. For about three months, dining in was off the table, and everything shifted to takeout. I couldn't help but worry about Toshi and Mika, especially given their location in a high-rent area.

One day, I voiced my concerns to Farrokh while waiting outside Yakitoriya for our takeout orders.

"How is their business going to survive?" I asked. "They're not out there advertising their restaurant. And even if they were, how are they going to attract new customers when their service is so unconventional?"

## DELICIOUS AND FULFILLING

Farrokh gave me a puzzled look.

"Dude, you do realize they make all their money from their regulars, right?" he asked.

I returned his strange look with one of my own. "That can't be," I insisted. "How can a business thrive without actively seeking new customers? Surely they want to expand their customer base?"

Farrokh shook his head. "Look, it's not that they don't want new customers, but they want the right kind of new customers, ones that fit their style and appreciate what they offer. If a customer complains about the service, saying they didn't feel welcomed or that they weren't attended to right away, Toshi doesn't lose sleep over losing them. He doesn't need those people," he explained.

I sat with those words for a moment. After years of working with large corporations, I'd internalized their rules of success: constant growth, maximum efficiency, and endless expansion. Yet here was Toshi, operating by entirely different principles and succeeding.

Standing on the sidewalk that evening, I thought about all the times I'd watched Toshi at work. And then it dawned on me that small businesses weren't just scaled-down versions of large corporations; they operated under completely different rules. Everything I thought I knew about business success, shaped by my years in corporate America, suddenly seemed inadequate to explain how a place like Yakitoriya could not only survive but thrive. Was Toshi's success unique, I wondered, or had I stumbled upon something fundamental about small businesses? What other rules of business had I taken for granted that might not apply? There was clearly more to understand about how small businesses operated and succeeded on their own terms.

As the pandemic lockdown stretched on, both Farrokh and I continued to support Toshi by ordering takeout. While it wasn't quite the same as the fresh-off-the-grill experience of dining in, the food remained exceptional.

Even after the lockdown ended, restrictions persisted. Indoor dining was off-limits, but restaurants with outdoor seating could still serve customers. This went on for about eighteen months. With limited outdoor seating, Toshi could accommodate fewer people, but he seemed to be holding his own. The enticing aroma of chicken grilling over *binchō-tan* charcoal drew people in, and Yakitoriya remained busy. Post-COVID, Yakitoriya continues to thrive because Toshi has remained laser-focused on what matters most to him: the quality of his food.

Farrokh and I sometimes joke that Yakitoriya's unique way of treating its customers might be a blessing in disguise. If it were any different, we might never get a table!

Toshi may not be on the cover of glossy magazines, but he's undeniably a successful businessman. In an industry where customer reviews and service levels often dictate success, he dares to march to the beat of his own drum, prioritizing the creation of exceptional food above all else. He certainly doesn't lose sleep over Yelp reviews or obsess over service standards.

## Finding Your Own Way to Perfect

As a management consultant, I could easily point out areas where Toshi could improve the way he runs his business. For one, on busy Friday nights, he could bring in a waiter to help turn the tables a little faster than his standard two and a half hours. This would not only increase profitability but also allow Toshi to focus more on his true passion: grilling and cooking.

In modern-day Japan, many restaurant owners have embraced technology to streamline their operations. They might use tablets for ordering, deliver food on conveyor belts, or even have a robot deliver your drink order, all to minimize the need for waitstaff. If Toshi were to modernize with tabletop kiosks, he could potentially eliminate the need for menus, ensure that his minimum skewer order is always met, and significantly increase his table turnover. The cost of implementing such a system would likely be offset by the increased revenue from serving more customers.

Additionally, he might consider working on his restaurant's social media presence and ask people who love his business to leave reviews. He could also consider updating his decor and being more attentive to diners, which might be seen as missed opportunities or areas for improvement from a conventional business perspective.

However, every time I sit down to enjoy his incredible yakitori, I realize that there's nothing I would change. Toshi's unwavering dedication to his craft and the exceptional quality of his food are what make Yakitoriya so special. The rest, in his case, is just noise. It took me some time to come to this realization, but I've learned to appreciate the unique intimacy that Toshi has created between himself, his food, and his guests.

What sets Yakitoriya apart is the personal touch that Toshi and Mika bring to every aspect of the dining experience. They're not just cooking and serving, they're witnessing their customers' reactions firsthand. This creates a much more intimate environment than you'd find in a sleek, high-turnover establishment.

Yes, Toshi could serve more customers if he streamlined his operations. But that's not what he's trying to do. He's not aiming to feed the masses; he's creating an experience. Over the years, it's become clear that Toshi has adapted his business to suit what he truly wants, not what conventional business wisdom might dictate.

Sure, bringing in a waiter, installing new technology, or adding more tables might boost profits. But would it fulfill Toshi in the same way? Would it allow him to maintain that personal connection with his craft and his customers? I doubt it.

In the end, Toshi's story is one of a man who has discovered what he loves and has tailored his business to support that passion. He's chosen intimacy over efficiency, quality over quantity. And as long as he's able to sustain his restaurant and find joy in being the master of his craft, who am I to suggest he change his ways?

Watching Toshi over the years has transformed how I think about what makes a small business work. While my consulting brain used to focus on efficiency and growth, seeing him stay true to his vision, despite all conventional wisdom, made me look at other business owners differently. Each one has their own way of doing things that might seem unconventional but fits who they are and what they value.

Of course, not everyone can run their business like Toshi does. Most entrepreneurs face different pressures, and pure passion won't keep the lights on. I've met plenty who are brilliant at what they do but get stuck on the business side of things. They spend sleepless nights worrying about marketing or customer service while fending off countless pitches for services they're told they absolutely need.

Ultimately, if you want to be the master of your craft like Toshi, you need to have loyal customers who are willing to pay the prices you need to charge to cover your expenses and generate a profit. If you don't have that luxury, it's important to find ways to address the areas where you struggle, whether that means partnering with others or finding innovative solutions.

Fortunately, in today's world, there are countless resources available to support small businesses. From gig workers to marketing support services to accounting software and payment processing tools, there's a solution for almost every pain point.

Take time to think about what you love about your business and what you don't. Be honest about your strengths and weaknesses, and don't be afraid to seek help when you need it. Focus on what you're truly passionate about while finding the right tools and services to fill in the gaps.

- What aspects of your work bring you the most satisfaction and fulfillment?
- How do your customers experience the passion you bring to your business?
- If you could serve fewer customers but serve them exactly the way you want to, what would that look like?
- Which aspects of your business would you refuse to compromise on, even if it meant sacrificing potential profits?

CHAPTER FOUR

# ANY COLOR, AS LONG AS IT'S BLACK

## Have It Your Way

In 1973, McDonald's dominated the fast-food industry in the United States. With its iconic golden arches and classic menu items like the Big Mac, McDonald's had become a household name and go-to for a quick, convenient meal. With their rigid adherence to standardization, every burger was made the same way, with no room for customization. If you didn't want pickles or tomatoes on your Big Mac, or if you wanted extra sauce, you had to specifically request those changes.

Seeing an opportunity to differentiate themselves, Burger King decided to launch their "Have It Your Way" campaign. This bold move was a direct challenge to McDonald's one-size-fits-all approach, and it aimed to tap into customers' desire for choice and personalization. At Burger King, the customer became king. No longer would people have to settle for a burger that didn't quite meet their preferences. Whether you wanted to hold the mayo, skip the lettuce or the pickles, or add an extra slice of cheese or tomato, your wish was their command.

Burger King's "Have It Your Way" campaign coincided with a major technological shift in the restaurant industry. Electronic cash registers, the precursors to modern point-of-sale systems, were starting to make their way into fast-food joints across the country. While it might not sound like a big deal now, back then, they were a game-changer. Servers could input special requests right at the terminal. No more shouting over the sizzle of the grill or playing a game of broken telephone with the kitchen staff.

Although the new technology made it easier for servers to input special requests, it did create some additional work for the kitchen staff, who were used to a more standardized approach. However, Burger King franchisees embraced the change, recognizing the value it brought to the customer experience. Interestingly, they discovered that not every customer took advantage of the customization option. Many were happy to order their standard Whopper and move on. But for those who did want their burger their way, it made a significant difference in their overall satisfaction.

Besides being a clever marketing strategy, Burger King's "Have It Your Way" campaign represented a change in the fast-food industry, recognizing the growing importance of customer preferences and the value of offering choices in an industry where conformity had long been the norm. By giving diners the power to customize their meals and making this option central to the customer experience, Burger King not only differentiated itself from McDonald's but also created a stronger connection with its customers.

## Betting on Black

We've seen how Burger King revolutionized fast food by offering endless customization. But sometimes, the most powerful differentiation strategy can be offering fewer choices, not more. Henry Ford proved this with his famous Model T, where he offered the mass-produced vehicle in "any color, as long as it's black." During my research into ForwardLine's business cases, I discovered how one small business owner put this idea to work by taking Ford's "betting on black" approach into the twenty-first century quite literally.

The case initially caught my eye because the numbers didn't make sense. It involved a kitchen contractor who'd taken out a substantial loan to buy just one type of granite. Traditional business wisdom suggested this strategy should have failed. After all, limiting customer choice usually meant limiting growth potential.

Intrigued, I reached out to Steve, the contractor behind these unusual numbers.

Steve explained that, like most in his industry, he ordered materials only after winning a bid. At busy times, he'd sometimes experienced delays in receiving popular materials, which then led to delays in completing his projects due to the order backlog. That's when he shared with me the unusual solution he'd found to this common problem.

"Most of my clients end up choosing black countertops, especially this Brazilian granite called Ubatuba. It's got these amazing gold, gray, and green flecks that catch the light just right," he told me.

Instead of ordering granite for each job like most contractors, Steve decided to invest all his capital in a bulk order of Ubatuba slabs. "People thought I was crazy," he chuckled. "But I got such a great deal, and I knew it would let me move faster than anyone else in town."

By limiting himself to a single option, Steve was making his offering less "unique" in terms of variety. But he understood something important about his customers: A quick turnaround mattered more to them than having an endless array of choices.

At first, Steve felt almost embarrassed to tell prospective customers that they had no choice but to go with his signature countertop material. Initially, this meant turning away clients who wanted different options, but over time, he developed another approach.

"I remember the first time I had to tell a client they could have any color they wanted, as long as it was Ubatuba," he said. "But then I explained my thinking: 'Look, I'm doing this so that you can get your kitchen done on time and on budget.'" That usually got their attention, and it wasn't long before he found that his limited offering had become a selling point rather than a sticking point.

He would still offer his customers a wide range of color options but with a caveat. "Sure, I can get you that brown granite you like," he'd say, "but honestly, it'll take four to six months to come in from overseas. Or . . ." here he'd pause for effect, "I can have the Ubatuba installed in just a few weeks."

Since Steve had invested everything in his Ubatuba inventory, he had to make it work. If a potential client insisted on going with another color, he'd submit a quote he knew was too high to win. "I wasn't trying to be difficult," he explained. "I just knew exactly where I could deliver the most value."

It took me a while to appreciate the wisdom in Steve's approach. When he first told me his plan to stock only one type of granite, I thought he was making a huge mistake. After all, shouldn't offering more choices help you win more customers? But by emphasizing what made him different,

Steve found more than enough customers who wanted exactly what he offered, and he didn't waste time worrying about those who didn't. Here was another example of what made certain small businesses more successful than others—the freedom to specialize rather than generalize, to stake out their own ground instead of trying to be everything to everyone. Steve was putting the first Underdog Principle, positioning, to work.

By anticipating demand, taking an innovative approach, and building his business around efficient inventory management, Steve was able to turn a potentially challenging situation into a win-win for everyone involved. He understood that his target customers valued speed and reliability above all else, so he shaped every aspect of his service to meet those needs. "People think they want choices, but what they really want is to get their renovation completed quickly, professionally, and without any surprises," he told me with a smile. Steve's business was successful because he was leveraging another Underdog Principle: proximity—knowing what his customers really wanted because he spent time with them, listening to their concerns, and seeing their challenges firsthand.

What I learned from Steve completely changed my view on differentiation for small businesses. An unconventional approach, even one that limits customer choice, can be a powerful differentiator when you understand your market. More importantly, Steve showed me that small business differentiation can take any form, shaped by the owner's convictions about how to best serve their customers. His commitment to speed and reliability reflected his personal belief that this was the right way to serve his market. Steve proved that sometimes offering less actually sets you apart more.

While Steve wasn't concerned about other contractors copying his strategy because he knew there were plenty of customers who wanted choice, big businesses face a different reality when it comes to protecting their competitive advantage.

## Staying Ahead of the Copycats

In the years that followed the success of Burger King's "Have It Your Way" campaign, other fast-food chains were inspired to offer their own versions of customizable meals. But any innovation that's easy to imitate rarely provides a lasting edge. The challenge for Burger King now was to stay ahead in a game they had invented as competitors scrambled to catch up.

Burger King's campaign isn't the only example of a company that chose to leverage customer choice and convenience to gain a short-term competitive edge. In the world of e-commerce, online shoe retailer Zappos was one of the first to offer a 365-day, free, two-way shipping and return policy, changing how people bought shoes online. Founded in 1999, Zappos built its business on the idea that customers should feel just as confident buying shoes online as they do in a physical store. By offering free returns and a generous one-year window for exchanges, Zappos addressed a major concern: the fear of being stuck with shoes that didn't fit or weren't comfortable. This bold move paid off handsomely. Within a decade, Zappos had catapulted past the billion-dollar revenue mark.

This advantage didn't last long. This focus on customer satisfaction played a big part in Zappos's success and inspired other e-commerce companies, including Amazon, to adopt similar policies. When Amazon first ventured into selling apparel and shoes online, many potential customers were skeptical. After all, how could you buy clothes without trying them on first? How would you know if the fabric was soft or if the sizing was accurate? It seemed like a risky move for an online retailer. But Amazon had a plan. To overcome these hesitations, Amazon introduced a policy like Zappos's: Customers could buy any item and return it for free within thirty days if they weren't completely satisfied, no questions asked.

This simple yet powerful offer had a significant impact on consumer behavior. Suddenly, the risk of buying the wrong size or receiving a product that didn't meet expectations was eliminated. Customers could shop with confidence, knowing that if something wasn't quite right, they could easily send it back.

The results spoke for themselves. Interestingly, very few people actually ended up returning their purchases. The mere existence of the free returns policy was enough to ease customers' minds and encourage them to make a purchase. Online sales in these categories skyrocketed as shoppers embraced the convenience and flexibility that Amazon provided.

By prioritizing customer satisfaction and offering a safety net in the form of free returns, Zappos revolutionized the way people shop for clothing and footwear online. Amazon adopted this approach, absorbed it into its vast operation, and expanded its success by selling even the most hands-on, try-before-you-buy products in the digital marketplace. While Zappos is still around, its revenue has stagnated over the past fifteen years. Much like the idea of customizing your burger, free returns have become an industry standard. It is no longer a distinguishing feature, but an expected convenience.

These examples illustrate how initial differentiation can be quickly copied by competitors, diluting its impact. How, then, can a business ensure that its unique offering stands the test of time? This is where the MUD framework comes in.

The MUD framework tests your differentiation against three essential criteria: Is it *meaningful* to customers, *unique* in your market, and *defensible* against competitors? Let's explore what each means for your business.

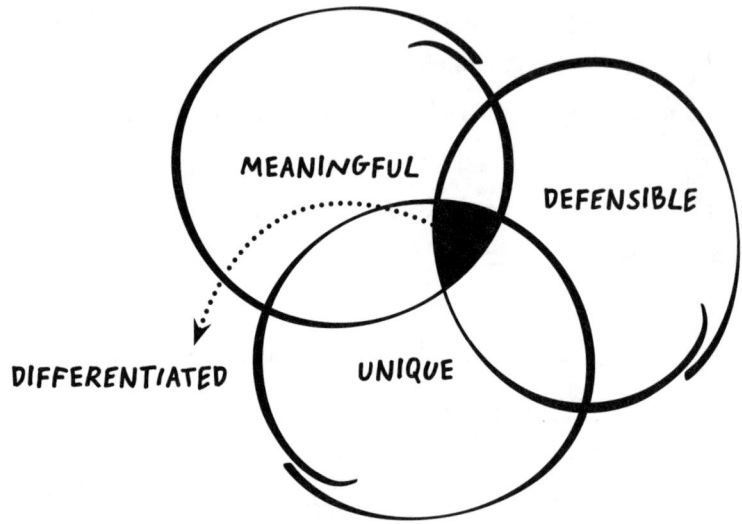

## MEANINGFULNESS (M)

Does your differentiated offering solve a real problem for your customers? If so, how well does it meet their needs? The true test is whether it has the power to sway their decision when choosing between you and a competitor.

## UNIQUENESS (U)

Look at what everyone else is offering. What do you bring to the table that others don't? This could be a single standout feature or a combination of benefits.

## DEFENSIBILITY (D)

How easily could competitors copy what you're doing? The harder it is for them to replicate or work around your unique feature, the stronger your position.

## The Advantage of Small

Big businesses have a clear advantage when it comes to differentiation through the customer experience. They've got deep pockets to fund extensive research sending out surveys, hiring data analysts, and bringing in consultants to interpret all that information. They can afford to have teams dedicated to product design, studying every aspect of the customer journey, from unboxing to everyday use. I've seen this firsthand in my consulting work with large companies. The power of data in shaping customer experience is incredible. These businesses can track how customers interact with their products, pinpoint pain points, and make informed design changes to address them. Take Apple, for example. They have the resources to invest in analyzing and understanding every aspect of the customer experience. This comprehensive approach allows them to refine and tailor the customer experience for the masses at scale.

But while this data-driven approach is powerful, it's not the only way to create exceptional customer experiences. As a small business owner, you probably don't have the luxury of dedicating this much time, money, or manpower to studying the customer experience. You're busy with day-to-day operations, including paying the bills, sweeping the floors, and taking out the trash before locking up at the end of the day. But that doesn't mean you can't create great customer experiences. It just means you need to be more creative and resourceful in your approach.

While large companies rely on extensive resources to understand their customers, your advantage comes from being closer to yours. You interact directly with your customers, see their reactions firsthand, and hear their concerns face-to-face. This close relationship, combined with your ability to act quickly on what you learn, allows you to understand and respond to their needs faster than big businesses can. These strengths allow you to create unique experiences that your customers value and that bigger businesses can't easily copy.

Here's how you can make the most of them using our three Underdog Principles:

**POSITIONING:** Your differentiation only needs to resonate with a small market. Unlike big businesses that need to appeal to a broad audience, you don't need everyone to love what you do. Big businesses often have to offer "vanilla" experiences to cater to the masses. As a small business, you have the freedom to be any flavor you want. You can focus on serving a specific niche or offering a unique experience that might not appeal to everyone, and that's okay. You can embrace this focused approach by:

a. **Considering your community:** If, like many business owners, you see your customers as a part of your community, how have you helped them feel connected? You might want to introduce them to one another or create opportunities for online interaction. You may even want to consider sponsoring or supporting an event for this community.

b. **Choosing to love it or leave it:** Don't shy away from the aspects of your offering that some customers love and others hate. When you're not trying to please everyone, you can emphasize these polarizing elements. Instead of seeing it as losing customers, think of it as refining your clientele. Letting go of the naysayers might just improve your business. For example, a countryside inn with community seating in their café has a reputation for travelers socializing with one another. They decide to lean in to this strength. They get rid of the two-top tables, replacing them with more communal seating options. They also swap out their self-serve coffee stand for a barista-served coffee bar, where guests can chat while waiting for their morning brew. Sure, they might lose some customers who prefer a quiet, private breakfast. But for their core guests, the ones who come to meet fellow travelers and swap stories, these changes make the inn even more appealing. By doubling down on what makes them special, they create an experience that their target customers will love, even if it's not everyone's cup of tea (or coffee, in this case).

**PROXIMITY:** Your close relationship with customers and intimate knowledge of your business are powerful tools for creating exceptional experiences. Big company decision-makers can't match your level of customer appreciation. When a customer tries your product, you can see their reaction firsthand. When they have a concern, you hear about it directly. This closeness can shape what you offer, providing insight into how your differentiation truly impacts your customers. You can leverage this unique advantage by:

    a. **Focusing on needs that only you can meet:** Your deep understanding of your customers allows you to solve problems others might not even recognize. If you have a physical location, remember that the entire space, not just the place where you provide your core service, is a reflection of your values. A boutique clothing store owner, for instance, might offer a glamourous fitting room experience with flattering lighting and luxurious robes because she knows it makes a difference to her customers.

b. **Extending the relationship:** Your understanding of your clients' needs might reveal additional ways to help them. A freelance web designer, for example, could feature clients' websites in their portfolio, providing extra exposure. This not only showcases their work, but also makes their clients feel special and appreciated.

**PURPOSE:** Instead of focusing only on profits like many big businesses, aim for both personal and financial objectives. Build your business around your strengths and convictions about what your customers should experience. Making your objectives personal doesn't necessarily conflict with profitability; it just makes your approach unique and difficult for others to copy. You can bring this idea to life in your business by:

a. **Emphasizing your values:** Businesses that care about more than just the bottom line can highlight what matters to them in creative ways. Instead of relying on overt self-promotion like McDonald's with their "Billions Served" signs, which often falls flat with most people, a mission-driven business could highlight things their customers actually care about. For instance, a tutoring service could place colorful charts on their walls showing how much their students' grades have improved, while a landscaper might provide a handy plant care guide after finishing a job. These simple touches show customers you're not just after their money, you're invested in their success too.

b. **Turning a loss into a win:** Sometimes, helping your customers means potentially losing immediate revenue. If providing honest, valuable advice aligns with your core values, why not embrace and showcase it? For instance, a financial advisor might proudly share stories of clients they've advised against unnecessary investments, even though it meant less commission. A home renovation contractor could highlight cases where they recommended simple repairs over costly renovations. By celebrating these moments, you're not only emphasizing your commitment to your values but also winning trust and building long-term relationships.

## Differentiation Through Experience

Big businesses recognize the value of differentiating themselves through their customer experiences. With market share, growth, and pricing at stake, they look for every advantage in designing an end-to-end experience, from the ease of ordering to the speed of delivery and even the ability to customize a product.

While big brands vie for differentiation across all aspects of the customer experience, small businesses are often inherently defined by their uniqueness. They're not under the same pressure to safeguard trade secrets. The small business advantage lies in bringing authenticity and character to their offering, which can significantly impact how their customers perceive them. For many small business owners, simply being themselves wins over their clientele, a quality that's impossible to replicate. Consequently, the idea of focusing on what you excel at seems sufficient to make your product or service stand out.

However, focusing too narrowly on what you directly control in your business, like your product or service, might lead to overlooking the broader customer perspective. A differentiated product or service inherently creates a differentiated customer experience, but the customer experience extends beyond just the product or service itself. By reflecting on your core beliefs about what your customer should be experiencing, you might realize they're not fully recognizing your efforts or that you're missing out on opportunities to create a more complete experience for them.

## Boundary Interactions

Consider a restaurant, for example. As an owner, you'd likely focus on the quality of your food. You're probably constantly asking yourself: Do we have the right menu? Are we preparing orders to my standards? Are we providing good service? Any successful restaurant owner knows that it's not just about the food. It's about offering an experience. The kitchen, the dining area, and even the bathrooms are a reflection of your core beliefs about how customers should experience your business. A spotless restaurant shows customers you care about their well-being. Friendly, attentive service makes people feel valued and welcome. The decor sets the mood and can leave a lasting impression. Even your menu plays a part, catering to different tastes and dietary needs. These elements combine to create the core experience that sets you apart from your competitors.

This core experience is critical to your differentiation and defines your business. But have you considered how customers think about the experience of your business as a whole? Continuing with the restaurant example, diners will interact with much more than just the menu, the staff, and the interior of the restaurant before and after their meal.

The location and operating hours of the business are examples of "boundary interactions" that should be considered in shaping the customer experience. A restaurant on a busy street, for example, might bring in more foot traffic, while a quieter area could offer a more relaxed atmosphere. Your opening hours can make you the go-to spot for late-night diners or early birds. These boundary areas may be out of your immediate control, but they can significantly shape your customers' expectations and overall experience.

## Purposeful Experiences

A portion of diners at a restaurant will have specific purposes and expectations for their experience. The layout of the establishment and the other patrons present can significantly impact this experience. People might come to celebrate a birthday, propose to their significant other, or conduct a business meeting. They might want a quiet spot for a private chat or to just grab a quick bite to eat. As a restaurant owner, you could choose to cater to these experiences as broadly as possible, by improving the ambiance, offering special arrangements for celebrations, adding quiet corners for important conversations, and even including a takeaway counter.

However, trying to please everyone is unrealistic. Unlike the larger players, you have the advantage of choosing which set of customers to focus on and committing to your personal vision for the experience.

## Many Ways to Be Different

Remember, people value experiences differently, and not everyone has to appreciate what you offer. As a business owner, you probably already have a good sense of how you stand out by working to your strengths and sticking to your core values. As you consider how to ensure your customers experience that differentiation, examine the boundaries of where they interact with your offering and think about the broader purpose of their experiences.

By expanding your focus to all aspects of the customer experience, you may find more opportunities to fulfill your vision and help your customers see what sets you apart.

## The Aesthetic Experience

If you're ever in LA, you might want to visit a restaurant called Mogu Mogu. This place serves up a style of noodles called *mazemen*. It's a Japanese dish that consists of noodles, sauce, and a variety of other ingredients that diners can choose to include. *Mazemen*, as it's served traditionally, is mixed by the diner before being enjoyed. Mogu Mogu has taken an experiential approach by making the diner an active participant in the creation of their meal.

At Mogu Mogu, you're not just a customer, you're the star of your own culinary show. You're handed a bowl with all the basics neatly arranged, like an artist's palette waiting for your creative touch. Along the walls are step-by-step pictorial instructions, guiding you through the art of assembling the perfect bowl of *mazemen*. As you play chef, you experiment with an array of toppings, sauces, and seasonings. Fancy a soft-boiled egg? Go for it. A splash of homemade vinegar to amp up the umami? It's all part of your gastronomic masterpiece.

What's interesting about this approach is that Mogu Mogu has turned the simple act of mixing your meal into an opportunity to appreciate its beauty. While customers could just mix up and eat their meal, the act of appreciating its aesthetics is presented as an integral part of the dining experience.

But the experience doesn't end there. Just when you think you're done, there is one final but important step: snap a photo of your creation to share on social media. After all, in this Instagram-worthy adventure, if you didn't post it, did it even happen? By transforming a simple meal into an interactive, shareable experience, Mogu Mogu has cooked up something far more satisfying than just noodles; they've served a slice of culinary stardom to every customer who walks through their doors.

Encouraging their patrons to share their experiences goes beyond clever marketing. It allows Mogu Mogu to tap into the artistry at the heart of their business and share that passion openly with their customers. Most people enjoy sharing their experiences, especially when it comes to food. By encouraging customers to document and share their self-assembled masterpieces, Mogu Mogu is creating a broader experience that extends beyond just the act of eating.

This photo-sharing moment becomes a key boundary interaction for the restaurant. It happens after the main service is over, but it's still an important part of the Mogu Mogu experience. When customers post their noodle creations online, they're not just sharing a meal, they're continuing their connection with the restaurant. This boundary interaction keeps Mogu Mogu in their customers' minds long after they've left, turning a simple meal into a memorable event that lives on through social media.

What's remarkable about Mogu Mogu's approach is that they've created an engaging experience without necessarily doing extra work themselves. They've simply highlighted what makes their noodles special and invited customers to be part of the fun.

For business owners, this serves as an important lesson: Enhancing the customer experience doesn't always mean more work for you. Sometimes, it's about recognizing what's unique about your offering and finding creative ways to showcase it. Whether it's inviting customer participation, emphasizing a special feature, or simply presenting your product or service in a new light, the key is to tap into what makes your business stand out and share that with your customers.

## The Social Experience

Another way of extending the reach of your product or service is through the social experience. This can be a key part of the overall customer experience, depending on your business type.

Some services are purely transactional. People want to get in, get what they need, and get out as quickly as possible. But for others, the social aspect is a big part of what keeps customers coming back. Take barbershops, for example. For many people, a haircut is just a chore to tick off their to-do list. They want it done well, and they want it done fast. But then there are barbershops that have become local institutions. When you walk in, you know the barber, you recognize many of the other customers, and you're there for more than just a trim. These barbershops have tapped into something powerful. They understand that for their regulars, the haircut is almost secondary to the experience of being there. It's about the conversations, the sense of community, and the chance to catch up on local news or debate the latest sports results.

Some of the savviest barbershops take this even further. When I lived on the north side of Chicago, my barbershop would ask, "Bears or Bulls?" when I booked an appointment. They organized their schedule around their customers' different sports interests. On Mondays and Tuesdays, the talk is always about the NFL, Wednesdays and Thursdays are for the NBA, and Fridays it's back to football. By managing their schedule this way, they create a tailored experience for each group. Customers know they'll be among like-minded individuals, ready to dive into passionate discussions about their favorite sports.

This approach extends far beyond barbershops. Any business where people gather can build this sense of belonging. In fitness centers, where the same members show up day after day, friendships form naturally. People start looking forward not just to their workout, but to catching up with the regulars they see each morning. We saw something similar at Jonah Zimiles's bookstore, [words]. His annual Where's Waldo hunt became a town tradition, bringing families together each summer. By getting involved with Maplewoodstock, the town's two-day music festival, and opening their space to community groups, [words] became woven into local life. When COVID hit and [words] was struggling, their community stepped up, organizing online fundraisers to help the store survive. That sense of community, those relationships between customers, can make all the difference in whether a business thrives or just survives.

The social experience extends into the digital realm too. Just as Mogu Mogu created its unique dining experience and encouraged its diners to share their photos of their meals online, boutique hotels and other businesses have found ways to build community through social media. They might invite you to Instagram your beautifully plated meal or your stylishly decorated hotel room. Some businesses even go as far as to say, "Don't forget to snap a pic before you dive in!" While this might seem like a marketing ploy, it's actually tapping into how many customers naturally behave today. By encouraging this behavior, these businesses are making their customers feel comfortable being part of a shared experience.

## Leaning into Differentiation

As a small business owner, it's easy to make assumptions about what customers expect or value. You've likely found success by delivering what you believe to be most important. However, it's not uncommon to overlook aspects of the experience that matter more to your customers than you realize. The extended experience you offer might only meet industry standards rather than reflecting the higher standards you demand for your core offering.

By understanding what makes your business special and which aspects of your offerings customers truly appreciate, you can emphasize these strengths through your customer experience. Embracing this differentiation allows you to double down on what's working but also highlights areas where you can scale back or improve things that customers don't value as much.

When you look closely at how your core beliefs shape the whole customer experience, you might find new ways to add value. You may even realize you've been focusing on the wrong things. Just remember, what you think is important might not always be what your customers care about most.

## Unboxing an iPhone

Think about the last time you received a package in the mail. If it arrived in a plain, nondescript box with little to no branding, you might not have thought much of it. But if that package was carefully designed with thoughtful touches like branded tissue paper, a handwritten note, or a thank-you card, it probably made a much more positive impression.

With this in mind, think back to the early 2000s before smartphones revolutionized the mobile industry, when the thrill of getting a new mobile phone only began once you'd wrestled it free from its packaging. You'd be greeted with a jumble of items—a quick-start guide, a manual, and a bunch of plastic or Styrofoam bits holding everything in place. Most of these would end up in the trash. It seemed like manufacturers were more focused on ticking boxes than creating a great customer experience. They'd include every possible accessory and instruction, trying to anticipate every user's needs, regardless of whether most people would ever use them. The result? A cluttered, confusing unboxing experience that left you feeling overwhelmed rather than excited. And after wading through all that, you'd still be left to figure out the setup on your own.

Then Apple came along and changed the game. They turned unboxing into an event, a seamless, feel-good experience that's almost an art form. If you've ever bought an Apple product, you know exactly what I'm talking about.

Let's start with the packaging. Apple transformed what was once an afterthought into something truly luxurious. Pick up an iPhone box, and you'll notice it's compact, sturdy, and has a satisfying weight to it. It's a far cry from the flimsy cardboard boxes of old. Open it up, and you'll find only the bare essentials inside. Apple has stripped away almost everything unnecessary. They looked at all the stuff people typically tossed out and thought, *What if we make the box itself do the job?* Their designers decided to use thicker cardstock with cleverly designed air gaps, creating a package that feels substantial but is still light enough to ship economically.

But Apple didn't stop at the unboxing experience. They've put a lot of thought into simplifying the setup process too. When you first switch on your new iPhone, you'll find the battery is already partially charged.

After all, the first thing you want to do is turn on your new phone, right? From there, on-screen instructions guide you through the entire setup process: connecting to the internet, backing up data from your old phone, and restoring it to your new one. It's all laid out in a don't-make-me-think-too-hard kind of way.

By focusing on these details, Apple has transformed what used to be a mundane process into a memorable experience. They've shown that every interaction a customer has with your product, even before they start using it, is an opportunity to impress and delight.

This approach to customer experience goes beyond just phones or tech products. It's a lesson for any business: look at your product or service from your customer's perspective. What can you simplify? What can you improve? How can you turn a routine interaction into something special? Remember, you're not just selling a product or service, you're selling an experience. And that experience starts the moment your customer first interacts with your brand, whether it's walking into your store or office, visiting your website, or simply opening a box.

Apple's meticulous attention to the unboxing experience shows how much they value those boundary interactions. They've turned the simple act of opening a box into an event, recognizing that this moment, while not part of the core product, plays a huge role in shaping how customers feel about their purchase. By designing this boundary interaction so carefully, Apple starts delivering on its brand promise before you even power up your new device. It's a clever way to extend their influence and set the stage for a positive experience with the product itself.

## Styrofoam Boxes or Disposable Dinnerware?

During the early days of the COVID lockdown in 2020, I found myself relying on restaurant takeout for the first time. At the same time, restaurants that had always relied on dine-in service were scrambling to figure out how to put their food in a box. For many, it was the only way to keep their doors open and their kitchens running.

One evening, while driving home with takeout from a local Chinese restaurant, a car cut me off, and I slammed on the brakes. Luckily, most of our family's dinner stayed in the bag, but inside, it looked like a wok had exploded. The resulting blend of noodles, sauces, and soups was a disappointing meal. At least my fortune cookie's message was on point: "Good things come to those who wait."

The following Friday, I ordered from a Thai restaurant I'd been wanting to try. The food arrived in flimsy Styrofoam boxes stuffed into a thin plastic bag that was already tearing. The pad thai had shifted sideways by the time I reached my kitchen counter, the sauce had leaked everywhere, and the spring rolls were crushed beyond recognition. Two takeout disasters and one very fragrant car interior later, I started paying a lot more attention to how restaurants packaged their food.

Some restaurants seemed to assume their responsibility ended the moment food left their kitchen. Others had clearly thought through the whole journey, from providing stable containers that could survive sudden stops to including proper utensils for eating at home.

The noodle place down the road had mastered the art of takeout. They quickly figured out that noodles and broth needed separate containers. Their food came in sturdy, compartmentalized containers, neatly packed in a branded bag with proper handles. They separated hot and cold items and tucked in a handwritten note thanking me for my ongoing support. They'd considered every aspect of getting this food home and enjoying it.

A local Japanese restaurant elevated the experience further, switching from generic supplies to containers that matched their minimalist aesthetic. Each order included proper chopsticks instead of splintery wooden ones and a small origami creation. Their prices went up slightly, but the experience justified the cost. By recognizing that their packaging was a key boundary interaction—their last chance to impress their customers before the meal was enjoyed at home—they found a way to extend their dining experience beyond their restaurant and into our living room.

I hadn't considered any of this when ordering takeout. Like most customers, I didn't consciously think about container types or whether my food would stay properly separated. I didn't realize I wanted my noodles packaged separately from the broth or that a sturdier bag could make my drive home less anxiety-inducing. I never thought about whether I had the right utensils at home, and, apparently, neither did some restaurants, who assumed everyone kept a drawer full of chopsticks. The restaurants that took care of these details, ensuring I had everything needed to enjoy their food properly, quickly became my go-to choice.

If packaging is part of your business and you're wondering whether investing in better materials is worth the cost, that's understandable. Your brand might be built on simplicity or affordability, and that's perfectly fine. Whatever experience you choose to deliver, make sure it's intentional. Your customers won't always know to ask for sturdy packaging or special touches that make their experience smoother and more enjoyable. But when you provide these details, they notice. These small, deliberate choices can turn a good experience into a great one and keep your customers coming back for seconds.

## Stick to Your Mugs

While analyzing ForwardLine's business cases, I found many examples of small businesses struggling to balance staying true to their vision while running a viable business. One coffee shop's file particularly caught my attention. Initially, our funding consultant had advised against the loan, questioning the value of their business case. Yet months later, we'd ended up funding them, and they maintained a strong relationship with ForwardLine for years.

Curious about what had changed between the two decisions, I pulled up the recorded call. I listened as the owner, Shannon, explained her vision to our funding consultant. "People thought I was crazy to open a coffee shop just because I loved making latte art," she said. "Other cafés in the area are focused on churning out quick cups of coffee, but our team is committed to creating an experience for our customers, even if it means a longer wait.

During that call, Shannon explained that their dedication to artistry came with its own challenges. Her shop had become known for these mini masterpieces, but her team was struggling to keep up with the morning crowd. Most customers were simply snapping a plastic lid on their paper cup and rushing out, drinking it down on their way to work.

"It's frustrating to watch all that artistry go unnoticed," Shannon sighed. "The team puts such care into each design. But I understand. The lines are too long, and I'm losing the morning customers who just want their caffeine fix."

To ease the stress on her baristas and keep the lines moving, Shannon was considering limiting the artistic lattes to dine-in ceramic mugs only. But she knew she'd disappoint the customers who specifically came for these foam masterpieces, even if they were taking them to go.

"Just this morning, I saw another perfect latte shot pop up on Instagram. One of our regulars had captured every detail of the art, right down to the way the light caught the foam swirls. It's moments like those that remind me why we do this," she told the consultant. "These photos end up all over social media, and people come here specifically for the designs they've seen online."

Despite her success, Shannon was wrestling with a dilemma: how to keep both the art lovers and the morning rush happy without compromising what made her café special.

"You're right," the consultant agreed. "It doesn't feel right to force your customers to stay in the café just to experience what makes you special."

Shannon wouldn't make that trade-off. Without the extra revenue from handling more morning rush customers, she couldn't justify the investment in new crockery.

When I reviewed her second file, created several months after that initial call, I was surprised to see that she'd returned with what appeared to be the same plan. However, after examining the business case more closely, I noticed she was projecting better returns with a lower investment. Intrigued by what might have changed to make such a difference, I decided to reach out to her.

First, I checked her coffee shop's social media presence to see if her customers were still as engaged as she described. What I found led me to make a few double taps of my own. Her feed was filled with stunning photos that captured the essence of her brand, from baristas pouring intricate latte art to bustling crowds lining up each morning. The comment sections were filled with customers raving about both the coffee and the artistry. In one recent post, she'd even hinted at plans to upgrade her crockery to better reflect her shop's unique style.

Encouraged by what I saw, I gave her a call. After introducing myself and explaining my interest in her business's journey, Shannon was eager to share her story.

"We used to have this huge challenge," she explained. "We had two very different types of customers: our morning rush who just wanted their coffee quickly, and others who came specifically for our latte art. I knew I had to find a way to serve both without compromising either experience. Then it hit me, what if we let customers choose? If you're in a rush, then you can simply opt out!"

She explained her new system. The regular to-go lattes now came without the special artwork, keeping the morning line moving. But she added a new option: a special wide-mouth paper-cup latte where her baristas could show off their skills. This simple menu change had transformed her business.

"Now everyone gets what they want," she told me. "The morning rush flows better, and we get to focus our creative energy on customers who actually care about the art. Plus, we're still creating those Instagram-worthy moments," she explained, her pride evident even over the phone.

Shannon's approach embodied the third Underdog Principle: purpose. Instead of following the big coffee chain playbook of maximizing efficiency at all costs, she'd found a way to honor her artistic vision while building a sustainable business.

Shannon's story taught me an important lesson about small business differentiation. When you start a business, you have a vision of offering something special. Along the way, you might find yourself needing to make some trade-offs to serve different types of customers, but that doesn't mean abandoning your vision. What matters is remembering why you started, including the passion you wanted to share and the unique experience you wanted to create. Your distinctive offering doesn't need to appeal to everyone, but it needs to matter to enough customers to build a viable business. Like Shannon, you can find creative ways to stay true to your vision while meeting different customers' needs.

## How to Find and Embrace Your Authenticity

Small businesses, by their very nature, are differentiated, each one offering something unique in their market. They also have the freedom to focus on what makes them different, whether that's product or service, their geographic reach, their operational approach, or the types of customers they serve. The businesses that succeed are often those that embrace their differentiation rather than trying to be everything to everyone.

Here are four areas to help you uncover and leverage the Underdog Principle of positioning:

## Decide on What Sets You Apart from Your Competitors

- What is unique about your offering and overall customer experience?
- Does this differentiation pass the MUD (meaningful, unique, difficult to copy) test? In other words:
  - » Does your offering address a real need?
  - » What makes it stand out from others?
  - » How easy would it be for competitors to replicate?

- Do at least a portion of your customers recognize that your business offers something special compared to your competitors?

Let's revisit our Mogu Mogu example to see how a small business can leverage its unique strengths. Mogu Mogu recognized the artistic appeal of their unmixed noodle bowls but understood that their customers might need a little encouragement to fully appreciate its significance. By highlighting what made their offering special, they educated their customers to value this uniqueness too.

Mogu Mogu went beyond traditional restaurant concerns like ambiance, music volume, and lighting. They enhanced the dining experience by:

- Emphasizing presentation as an important part of the experience, guiding customers on how to assemble and showcase their dishes.
- Reminding customers that aesthetics and enjoyment of the meal were both important, naturally resulting in more photogenic meals.
- Actively encouraging photo-taking during meals, making it a normal and expected part of dining there.

This approach extended Mogu Mogu's influence on the customer experience beyond the restaurant walls. Customers continued to engage with the brand after their meal through shared photos and social media conversations. These customer-shared photos and comments serve as free advertising, attracting potential new customers to the restaurant.

## Check the Boundaries of Your Product or Service in Relation to Your Customer's Overall Experience

At what point does your customer first interact with your business? Is it when they walk through your door, or does it start earlier, perhaps when they're browsing your website or reading reviews online?

When does that interaction end? Is it when they leave your store, or does it continue after they've used your product or service?

Are there any aspects of your customers' journey that you've overlooked because you don't consider them within your control?

Consider the entire journey your customer takes with your business, from parking at your location to how you package their order. Does every aspect of the experience meet your standards?

We've probably all been there, walking into a dimly lit mechanic's waiting room, the air thick with the smell of motor oil and the soundtrack of clanging tools in the background. Eying the sad, stained couch, you can't help but wonder if you'll catch something just by sitting down. It's a far cry from the plush, welcoming lounges at the big car dealerships, where the smell of fresh-brewed coffee and the hum of high-speed Wi-Fi make you feel inclined to linger.

For many mechanics running their own shops, that waiting area is an afterthought. The only thing that's neat and tidy is their well-stocked toolbox. Their focus is on tackling those tough problems under the hood, not worrying about customer comfort. Whether it's an hour for a quick repair or a full day for more extensive service, there's a good chance their customers will opt to come back later rather than stick around.

But what if one of those mechanics took a page from the big car dealerships and freshened up their space, adding some comfortable seating and accessible, high-speed internet? Instead of needing to find a ride back home or to the office, the customer might choose to stay and get some work done, catch up on the news, or just relax for a bit. This isn't about over-the-top, BMW dealership–level luxury; it's about recognizing that the waiting room is an extension of the service and a chance to make a lasting impression. If customers feel genuinely comfortable, even eager, to spend time there, they're likely to assume the mechanic's work is just as impressive as their attention to the overall experience.

What is the "waiting room" in your customer's journey with your business? This isn't just about physical spaces; it could be your website, your booking process, or even how you handle phone calls. Every interaction point is an opportunity to enhance the customer experience. Is there a neglected touchpoint that needs some TLC? Before making changes, think about your specific clientele. For a mechanic, should the waiting room cater to busy professionals who need to stay productive or frazzled parents who'd appreciate a kid-friendly corner? For an online business, is your website easy to navigate, and does your checkout process offer clear shipping information and secure payment options? For a restaurant, is your online reservation system user-friendly, and does your voicemail provide clear, helpful information when you're closed? Identifying these preferences and upgrading accordingly is key. Look at what the big players in your industry are offering, and tailor your own waiting experience from there. What small touches could transform a necessary interaction, whether in person or online, into a welcomed and memorable experience?

## Test to Make Sure Your Offer Supports Purposeful Experiences

What are the most common reasons your customers need your offering? What problems are they solving with your product or service?

Beyond the actual purchase, how do your customers interact with your business? Consider their journey from first contact to their after-sales experience. What challenges do they face before, during, and after using your product or service?

Is there post-purchase support, educational content, or help finding complementary services that customers could benefit from?

Are there opportunities to enhance their experience at any of these touchpoints, even if these enhancements don't directly generate revenue?

Think about Steve, our resourceful contractor with the one-granite-fits-all approach. He understood his customers' entire journey, from their initial search for a contractor through to the completion of their kitchen renovation. He recognized that speed and reliability weren't just about the installation itself; they mattered at every step, from the first showroom visit to the final cleanup. By building his business around these priorities, he created an experience that aligned with what his customers valued most.

While his competitors offered more flexibility, Steve found that plenty of customers preferred his streamlined approach. By committing to what he did best—delivering quality Ubatuba granite countertops quickly and reliably—he created a clear, consistent experience that set him apart in a competitive market.

## Leave Your Signature

- Is it easy to identify your personal touch in what you deliver to your customers?
- How do your customers experience that personal touch?
- What aspects of your offering do customers remember most?
- Is there anything about your offering that customers might want to share on social media?
- How can you make customers feel proud of their purchase and want to tell others about it?

Think back to our Apple example and how the company invested in its unboxing and setup experience. They didn't just focus on delivering a high-quality phone to the customer, they considered the entire journey.

Let's look at some of the questions Apple might have asked when designing the experience at this stage of the customer journey and how they addressed each challenge:

- **What happens when customers first receive the box?** Apple made its packaging sleek and appealing, turning the act of opening the box into an event.
- **What's the first thing customers see when they open the box?** Apple made sure the phone was beautifully presented, with everything else neatly tucked away.
- **How do customers start using the phone?** Apple made sure the phone had enough charge to turn on immediately, eliminating the frustration of waiting to use a new device.

- **How do customers set up their new phones?** Apple created a user-friendly setup process with clear, step-by-step instructions, making what could be a daunting task feel simple and intuitive.

By addressing these details, Apple extended its influence beyond the phone itself. They designed a memorable experience from the moment a customer receives the package, through the setup process, and into the early days of phone use.

This approach can be applied to many businesses. For instance:
- A CPA could deliver annual tax returns in a high-quality, branded binder, including next year's quarterly estimated tax payment forms prefilled.
- A car dealership might provide a tire pressure gauge, a guide to dashboard warning lights, and the maintenance schedule, along with their service department's contact information.
- A hair salon could include a style-care kit with a schedule and simple tips for maintaining a new hairstyle between appointments, along with reminders to book the next visit.

By adding your personal stamp to your product or service, you elevate the customer experience beyond the ordinary. These thoughtful touches can transform satisfied customers into loyal fans who return time and time again.

## THOUGHT STARTERS

- What is it that makes your offering different from that of your competitors?
- How would you describe the core group of customers that values your positioning the most?
- How could you better communicate what makes your offering special?
- Are there ways to improve or highlight the customer experience at the edges of your offering or to better address that set of customers?
- How can you make the impression you leave on your customers more unique and longer lasting?

CHAPTER FIVE

# EVEN A HOLE IN THE GROUND HAS VALUE

## The One-Hundred-Dollar Slug

My friends David and Carolyn were hosting a celebration for their son, who'd just been accepted to the University of California, Santa Cruz.

As I walked into their backyard, my eyes were immediately drawn to a couple of the most exquisite-looking cakes I'd ever seen. One cake, in particular, caught my attention. It was an uncannily lifelike representation of a banana slug, UCSC's quirky mascot. The attention to detail was exquisite, from the slimy sheen of its skin to the perfectly formed antennae. I'd never seen anything like it in any bakery.

"Wow, these are incredible. Where did you get them?" I asked David, pointing to the cakes.

David rolled his eyes dramatically. Carolyn, noticing our exchange, walked over to join us. "We got them from a teammate's mom. She does custom cakes, and she uses only organic ingredients."

"What am I missing?" I asked David, who suddenly had a rather pained look etched on his face. "Why aren't you excited about these amazing cakes?"

David let out a deep sigh. "You know these cakes are over one hundred dollars each, right?"

I nearly choked on my punch. "One hundred dollars? For a cake?"

"Yeah," said David. "My bank account is still wincing."

I glanced back at the cakes with newfound respect, and a touch of sticker shock. "Well, I guess I'll be savoring every crumb of my very small slice then."

Suddenly, we found ourselves in an impromptu discussion about cake pricing.

"Look, this woman is creating edible art. I know for a fact that you'll never find cakes like these at Whole Foods or the local bakery. She's carved out a unique niche for herself," I said.

David nodded reluctantly. "I get it, but one hundred dollars for a cake? Who's going to pay that?"

"Apparently, plenty of people here on the west side of LA," Carolyn laughed, playfully digging David in the ribs. "Remember when I tried to book her? She was booked solid for months. She did us a favor to squeeze these in."

David chuckled. "Well, I guess when you think about it, one hundred dollars for a cake is a drop in the bucket compared to what we'll be paying for tuition. Maybe it's just part of the college experience package now."

While helping myself to a second slice of cake, I thought about the baker's pricing strategy. At over one hundred dollars per cake, it seemed unlikely she was selling hundreds every month. When she initially determined her pricing, she could have gone the route a number-crunching accountant might suggest, perhaps just above the forty-dollar price of a similar, premium, all-organic cake at Whole Foods, and kept herself frantically busy.

But our cake maker saw a different opportunity. She recognized that for certain customers, the perceived value of her unique, beautifully designed, organic cakes was much higher. By pricing her cakes at over one hundred dollars apiece, she lost customers like David who didn't value her artistry, but found those who did.

"You know, if making beautiful, unique cakes is what she loves, building a business around it makes logical sense. Sure, she might need to stay focused on wealthy clients in West LA to stay in business, but she might even be able to price higher if she wanted," I said.

David raised an eyebrow. "You think people would pay even more?"

"For something this unique?" I shrugged. "Possibly. There are no other options for cakes like these. She's not just competing with Whole Foods, she's created her own market."

"Oh, she definitely charges more, David," Carolyn said with a wink. "We got the friends and family discount. Can you imagine what she'd ask for a celebrity's order?"

Driving home that evening, I thought about our discussion from a broader perspective. Big corporations approach pricing scientifically, running complex analyses to find the perfect balance between profit and market share. They obsess over their competition, always calculating how high they can push prices before losing customers to rivals. But here was this baker playing an entirely different game. She wasn't trying to compete with supermarket bakeries or capture every possible customer. Instead, she'd built her business around serving clients who truly understood and valued her artistry.

This concept of perceived value, what customers believe something is worth in a specific situation, is more common than you might think. We encounter it every day, often without realizing it. Sometimes, it shows up in surprising places, like when we're willing to pay a premium for a simple bottle of water.

## The Value of a Bottle of Water

Imagine you're out and about, running errands on a hot summer day. You're thirsty, and suddenly, you spot a vending machine offering a chilled can of Coca-Cola for $2.50. You know you could get that same can for a fraction of the price at the grocery store, maybe a dollar or even sixty cents. But in that moment, when you're parched and craving something cold and refreshing, the value of that single can of Coca-Cola is far greater than the price tag suggests; it's a small luxury you're willing to pay a premium for. This is the power of perceived value—the value that a product or service has in a consumer's mind based on their subjective perception rather than its intrinsic value.

Coca-Cola's strategy of being "within arm's reach of desire" brilliantly taps into this concept. It's not just about the drink itself; it's about having that ice-cold can of Coke readily available when you want it most. This strategy extends beyond soft drinks, though. Let's consider another everyday example: bottled water.

In many parts of the world, including the US, you'll find vending machines selling bottled water for two to four dollars, often right next to a free drinking fountain. Surprisingly, many people choose to buy the bottled water instead of using the fountain. Why pay for something you can get for free, especially when it's essentially the same product?

The answer lies in the subtle but powerful factors that shape our perception of value. Bottled water offers convenience—you can take it with you, sip it at your leisure, and not worry about finding another water source later. There's also a perceived sense of cleanliness and safety with that reassuring sealed cap. These factors combine to create a value that, for many, justifies the cost.

What's fascinating is that most consumers are aware that a lot of bottled water is simply filtered tap water, not some exotic spring water from a remote mountain source. Yet, people still buy it. They're not just paying for the water, they're paying for the convenience, the perceived quality, and the peace of mind it brings.

## Garbage Economics

The concept of pricing for value, as illustrated in the bottled water example, extends far beyond consumer goods. It's a principle that applies across various industries, even in sectors we might not immediately associate with sophisticated pricing strategies. The bespoke baker in West LA reminded me of some work I did for a landfill on the west side of another city.

I'd learned from the many pricing projects I'd worked on that the key to setting your price was understanding the value of your differentiation. This particular project opened my eyes to how differentiation doesn't have to be glamorous to command a premium price. Who would have thought that a giant hole in the ground could have its own unique value? Yet it does, and it all boils down to understanding what makes each site stand out from the rest.

The west side landfill project was a small part of a larger effort to help a corporation improve pricing at its many landfill sites across the country. The corporate group oversaw the overall strategy, but each landfill could set its own prices based on local market conditions. Our team wasn't alone; there were other consulting teams working with different landfills to help them set better prices.

I was leading a team that covered one region's landfills while other teams worked in different parts of the country. We treated each landfill visit as its own small project. Before diving in, I called up my colleague Michele, who'd already started similar work in another region.

"Does every location really need an on-site visit?" I asked Michele, hoping there might be a shortcut.

"Sorry, buddy," she replied. "Each site is unique, and we need to be there in person."

"Well, that's not so bad. At least they'll have offices we can work from," I said, picturing a proper building.

Michele laughed. "Don't get too excited. We're talking about trailers, basically metal boxes with a desk and some paperwork. Not exactly luxury accommodation, but it's where we need to be. All their data is kept on-site, plus we have to measure truck timing and do other local research."

Accepting that site visits were unavoidable, I shifted focus. "I've worked on pricing projects before, but usually for unique or differentiated offerings. What's so special about these landfills?"

"The business model for each of these landfill sites is pretty simple," Michele explained. "Garbage collectors charge city residents for waste pick-up and disposal. Then, they pay the landfills by the ton to dump that waste. Our job is to figure out how much more valuable our landfills are compared to the alternatives."

"And what makes one landfill more valuable than another?" I asked.

"It's location," she said. "Getting trash to the site is expensive. We need to price each site so that nearby garbage collectors still find us the best option, even at a premium."

"Won't we lose customers who are farther away?" I asked.

"That's actually part of the strategy," Michele said. "The garbage collectors that are farther away are already using other landfills. If we get this right, we can charge more to the customers who are already choosing us, and most will stay because we're still their best option."

## No Better Options

Michele's warning about the trailer office helped set my expectations for the first site visit to the west side landfill. Our workspace was exactly as she had described (and almost comical in hindsight)—a metal box perched on the edge of a trash dump. We weren't counting on having access to the client's networks, so we came prepared with pocket Wi-Fi, cutting-edge technology at the time. Just getting IT to approve these mobile units felt like we were asking for something from a sci-fi movie.

Our landfill was one of only two near the city center. Ours was on the west side, thirty miles out, and our competitor's site was on the east side, fifty miles away. The extra distance to our competitor's site meant garbage trucks had to drive an additional forty miles round trip. That difference was valuable once you added up all the costs: drivers' wages, wear and tear on the trucks, fuel, time lost on the road, and other operational costs.

But distance wasn't the only factor. Each landfill was licensed to handle different types of waste. Sometimes, a garbage company would drive the extra miles if our site could take materials their local landfill couldn't.

Speed mattered too; no garbage company wants their trucks and drivers sitting in line at the dump site. Every minute spent waiting is money lost.

We needed to figure out exactly what these differences were worth to each garbage collector. That meant digging into every cost: how much they spent on gas, what they paid their drivers, how quickly their trucks wore out, and how efficiently they could complete their routes. It was like putting together a giant puzzle, but once we had all the pieces, we could see the true value of our landfill, even the parts that weren't obvious at first glance.

At this site and others, my team spent endless hours in those trailers, often working fourteen-hour days. We pored over local maps and tracked how long it took trucks to arrive and unload their waste. Most days were spent hunched over spreadsheets and mapping tools, calculating distances and drive times. We dug into every detail, from how much the trucks weighed to current gas prices. For each landfill, we researched the local garbage companies to find out which ones employed union drivers and what wages they were paying. We even scoured newspaper listings for job postings to gather information on local labor markets. This was before the days of Indeed or easily accessible online job boards. It was old-school, labor-intensive work, but it was the only way to get the granular, local data we needed to understand the true cost savings and value proposition of each site.

Interestingly, I found that landfills are a lot more organized than I would have expected. And they didn't stink as much as I had imagined. The real challenge wasn't working out of a trailer all day; it was finding food or something fun to do in the evenings. After all, landfills tend to be placed far away from people for good reason.

# EVEN A HOLE IN THE GROUND HAS VALUE

After running all the numbers for the west side landfill, we discovered something interesting: Being closer to the city meant a significant cost saving for the garbage collectors, in some cases, more than ten dollars per ton. Armed with this information, we sat down with the landfill manager to present our findings.

"We aren't looking to bring more waste into the landfill," I explained. "What we're suggesting is pricing that would make collectors to the east of the city stick with your competitor at their thirty dollars per ton while keeping your city and western customers coming here, even at forty dollars per ton."

One of my team members jumped in. "Even at the higher price, it's still cheaper for these companies once they factor in all their transportation and operational costs."

The landfill manager looked skeptical. "I don't see how we can raise prices without losing customers. Nobody likes paying more."

I pulled up our analysis on screen. "Let's look at each of your customers. With these new prices, can any of them find a better deal elsewhere?"

We walked him through the math, showing him how we had looked at everything from the garbage collector's perspective. Finally, it clicked, and he summarized it perfectly: "At this price point, we can improve margins and not lose any customers because they just don't have better options."

Like all our site managers, he implemented and tracked the results over time. We wanted to know if they kept their customers, how much waste still came in, whether the garbage companies raised their own prices, and what the competition did. A few months later, we got our answer: The west side landfill hadn't lost any business. In fact, their competitors had raised their prices too.

The west side landfill's success wasn't unique. At site after site, we saw how carefully calculated price increases led to better profits without losing business. Competitors usually followed our lead, knowing they too could charge more without losing their loyal customers. The ripple effect continued; the garbage collectors passed these costs on to their customers, who saw their monthly bills tick up by a few dollars. Few people complained. In fact, most simply accepted that paying a little extra for garbage disposal was just a fact of life.

It might not be the most glamorous industry, but these landfill owners are shrewd businesspeople. They understood what we were showing them—that customers will pay more for convenience when it saves them money in the long run.

What started as our site-by-site analysis evolved into a broader solution. Another team developed a "playbook" so that all their locations could apply these pricing principles. The detailed work we'd done paid off handsomely. Even small improvements in pricing at each site added up to tens of millions of dollars in additional profit across the company.

A landfill taught me an important lesson about value, though not the one you might expect. The west side landfill succeeded not just because they understood their value, but because they understood their market. Their location defined who they were best positioned to serve—west side garbage collectors—and they built their business around these customers' specific needs. They didn't waste resources trying to attract every garbage collector in the city.

This same principle holds true for small businesses everywhere. Whether you're operating a convenience store selling bottled water or running a landfill, your pricing strategy comes down to two things: focusing on the customers you're naturally positioned to serve best and understanding exactly what they value. That's what gives you the power to price with confidence.

## Pricing for Differentiation

Thinking back to the baker and her one-hundred-dollar slug cake, I wondered how many small business owners truly understand the value of their differentiation. Many hesitate to raise their prices, fearing they'll lose customers. Yet, in doing so, they might be overlooking significant value they could unlock in their business.

Understanding your differentiation starts with a simple question: Where else can your customers find what you're offering? If there's a well-known competitor pricing a similar product at a certain level, ask yourself if your offering is superior enough to command a higher price. And if others in your market are pricing lower than you, don't automatically assume you need to match them. You might just have discovered the true value of what sets you apart.

When you offer something truly unique, you're not just competing on price anymore. The baker understood this intuitively. She knew her artistic, organic cakes offered something customers couldn't find elsewhere. This gave her the confidence to price according to the value her customers perceived.

Your pricing strategy becomes a powerful tool once you understand the dollar value of what sets you apart. But remember, you don't need to capture this entire value through higher prices. Instead, you can choose how much of this benefit to share with your customers.

## Using Pricing Concepts to Value Your Differentiation

The goal of pricing strategy is to ensure your customer gains value beyond the price they pay. To understand this better, let's explore some fundamental concepts of pricing.

When pricing a transaction, there are three key elements to consider: the *cost* of producing your product or delivering your service, the *price* you charge your customers, and the *benefit* your customer receives from that product or service. For any business, understanding the relationship between cost, price, and benefit will help make informed pricing decisions.

Let's break these terms down:

- **COST:** What you spend to produce your product or provide your service
- **PRICE:** What you charge your customers
- **BENEFIT:** The value your customer receives from your product or service

We can use two simple formulas to understand these relationships:

- Your Business's Profit = Price minus Cost
- Your Customer's Excess Value = Benefit minus Price

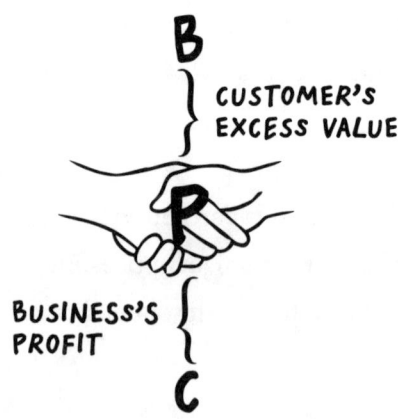

To gauge the value of your differentiation, compare the benefits you and your competitors create for your customers. If you've successfully differentiated your product and created real value, your benefit should outweigh the competition's, at least for some of the market.

Big businesses typically set their price between their cost and the customer benefit. If their product stands out from their competitors, they might price above the market rate.

As a small business owner, figuring out and putting a dollar value on your differentiation doesn't necessarily mean raising your prices. The price you set affects which customers choose your business and how much profit you make. In the end, it's up to you to decide what feels right for your business and your customers. Knowing the value of your differentiation helps you decide how to share the created value and with whom.

## The Contractor Who Was Just That Good

Several years ago, I worked with a general contractor named Max who needed help with his business case so he could attract financing. In the US, general contractors handle a broad range of construction-related tasks. These professionals often earn substantial annual revenues, ranging from hundreds of thousands to over a million dollars. As the primary contact for clients, they manage the entire project, outsourcing specific jobs to various specialists, like electricians for electrical work and plumbers for plumbing tasks, and hiring day laborers to handle basic tasks like digging.

The contractor's profit model is based on adding a small margin to the overall project cost. It's a generally accepted practice in the industry. There's a markup on the labor they employ and manage and a markup on the materials supplied, such as kitchen or bathroom countertops, bathroom fittings and cupboards, and large appliances like stoves and ovens. The contractor often doesn't add much to these material costs because they're likely getting bulk discounts from suppliers. This is savings that individual customers can't access.

This economic model creates an interesting dynamic. In a market where clients often compare multiple bids, contractors are more likely to win bids if they can complete the job with the right amount of labor at a competitive price. However, their profit is directly tied to the project's size; bigger jobs mean better earnings. It's a constant balancing act between keeping bids competitive and maximizing their profits.

In the contracting world, it's a bit of a numbers game. Most clients see a finished project as pretty much the same, no matter who does it. So they shop around, trying to get the best deal possible. It's like they're trying to squeeze out every bit of value (customer profit) they can.

This puts contractors in a tight spot. They're always walking a tightrope between keeping their bids low enough to win jobs and high enough to actually make money. It's no surprise that many end up focusing on cutting costs wherever they can just to stay in the game.

## Understanding Max's Figures

I had Max's project list and revenue plan in front of me when we started our phone call. I had some disappointing news to deliver.

"Max, I've got some concerns about the financing side of your plan. Investors and lenders are going to be worried about your revenue." I paused, then added, "Most of the contractors I work with have revenues in the millions. Lenders tend to back off when a business asks for more than what its revenue suggests it can handle."

Max, in his northern Massachusetts accent, replied with some confusion: "But I'm not asking for more than a few months' worth of income. It's really just a bridge."

I realized there was a gap in my understanding. Max was looking for a short-term loan to cover project expenses, which amounted to about 15 percent of his annual revenue.

"Oh, I see," I said, trying to clarify. "So you only need a portion of the funds described in your plan?" I asked, plainly misunderstanding his point on income.

"No, no," Max insisted. "I need it all. And we've got more than enough cash flow to pay it down in a few months."

I took a moment to think. For many contractors of Max's size, the amount he was asking for would be a whole year's income. Contractors, especially general contractors, typically earn much smaller margins. If a contractor is making $500,000 a year and wants to borrow $50,000, most lenders would be hesitant. Why? Because for a contractor, that $500,000 in revenue might only translate to about $50,000 in profit. Given this reality, it was important that Max built a strong business case that supported how he would benefit from and be able to repay the loan.

Realizing Max wasn't quite grasping my point, I tried a different approach. "Let me put it this way, Max. If you were running a restaurant with $500,000 in annual revenue and wanted to borrow $50,000, a lender could probably feel pretty comfortable lending you that amount. For a restaurant, $500,000 of revenue typically produces an income of $150,000. The lender would see that you make enough profit to pay back the loan without breaking a sweat."

I continued, trying to drive my point home. "But Max, you're not running a restaurant; you're a contractor. In your industry, you'll probably need more than a million in revenue to earn enough income to comfortably pay off a loan like that."

There was a pause on the line, and then Max's voice came back, a mix of confusion and frustration. "Did you even look at the tax returns I sent you?"

I felt a familiar twinge in my gut. I've been wrong before, and it's never fun to get called out. I flipped through the documents in his file, searching for Max's tax returns. Had I missed something important?

"Let me take another look at those returns, Max," I said.

Upon properly reviewing his financial records, I was surprised to find that despite taking on significantly fewer jobs and having much lower overall revenue compared to his competitors, his profit margins (and therefore his take-home income) were significantly higher than other contractors doing the same type of work. Looking closely at his invoices, I noticed that he was pricing his labor and materials slightly higher than his competitors. However, what really stood out was the markup he added for his project management fee, which was significantly higher than the industry standard.

## I'm Priced What I'm Worth

Given that he had such a satisfied customer base, I reckoned that he could easily take on additional work to increase his revenue. When I suggested this, Max said he couldn't, which surprised me. His response provided an interesting insight into his business philosophy.

"You know, the construction industry has gotten a bad rap for delays and missed deadlines. Clients are often frustrated by projects that drag on forever. A lot of contractors make their money by taking on multiple projects, hiring day laborers for each project, and then spreading their time across those projects," he explained. "I work differently. While my overall price might be similar to other contractors, I structure it differently. I only hire a small number of low-cost laborers because, most of the time, I use my own guys. I don't take on a large number of jobs because it spreads us too thin. Instead, I focus on fewer projects, but I charge more for our time, and I dedicate more of my personal attention to each one. This way, I can deliver better-quality work and ensure that projects are completed on time."

Max's approach was a bit different from the industry norm. He looked at his business and realized he was bringing something special to the table. Instead of trying to match what everyone else was charging, he decided to charge more. While this might sound risky, Max became really good at explaining to his clients why his services were worth more.

He pointed out a key difference in his approach when potential customers queried his higher estimates.

"Many contractors plan for mistakes and have labor on standby to correct them," Max explained. "They work on an estimate-then-bill basis, not a fixed cost. They provide initial estimates, but the final bill can often be higher. Especially when you're working with inexperienced labor, you've got to anticipate at least one serious mistake that could make the job unprofitable if you don't account for it."

He continued, "Other contractors build in a buffer to their estimates to cover potential fixes or additional work. But I avoid this by doing most of the work myself. I'm not paying extra for mistakes to be fixed, and I don't need to bring in additional labor to clean up at the end."

This strategy had clearly paid off. Max recognized that he was the one creating value, and priced his services accordingly. By dedicating more of his own time to each job and ensuring projects were completed on time and within budget, he was able to create more value for his clients. He became comfortable with the idea that he would lose some potential customers who didn't fully understand or appreciate his pitch. In essence, he chose to share less of the "customer profit" with clients, knowing it meant he'd win a smaller percentage of bids. But the bids he did win were more profitable, allowing him to maintain a full schedule despite taking on fewer projects.

Max excels at selling his value to his customers. He's a business owner who understands the benefit of his differentiated approach and has the confidence to charge for it. Max is able to price his projects higher than his competitors because he communicates the benefits of his approach clearly, and his customers understand it. As he put it, "When I put that time into the project, the value is there for my customers. And I'm selling that value." This strategy allows him to do less work in terms of volume but make more money. And it showed in his numbers. His take-home income was substantially higher than other contractors doing similar work.

## The Value of Reputation

Not every business owner can pull out a spreadsheet and calculate the exact dollar benefit they bring to their customers. Most look to industry standards or what similar businesses charge. But when you offer something different, you need to know what that difference is worth. The gig economy, for example, might seem overly commoditized at first glance—a space where everyone's offering the same service. But look closer, and you'll see plenty of ways to stand out: your track record, how you present yourself, your pricing strategy, and especially your ratings. These all shape how potential clients see your value.

Take Uber drivers, for instance. They're motivated to earn those coveted five-star ratings, but the real power lies in strategically leveraging those ratings. A driver with consistently high ratings might gain more flexibility in choosing their routes or have a higher likelihood of securing rides.

With other freelance worker platforms, service providers operate in highly competitive, transparent marketplaces where differentiation can be challenging. These platforms often push service providers into specific commodity segments, where price becomes the primary competitive factor. While there are opportunities to use media and content to highlight one's differentiation, the search and listing features on many platforms can make it difficult for gig workers to truly stand out.

Many of these platforms include rating systems and transparency features, which are great for consumers as they can easily compare providers based on their star ratings and choose the one that offers the best price for their desired level of quality. Gig workers understand the value of these stars. For example, a consumer might opt for a provider with a 4.5-star rating at a lower price point, while someone else may be willing to pay more for a 5-star provider.

From a consumer's perspective, the platforms provide a window into a freelancer's track record, and that transparency is powerful. When browsing through profiles, you can see how many gigs someone has completed and their overall rating. If they've got a solid 4.5 stars and a couple dozen jobs under their belt, you can be a little more confident that they're likely to deliver quality work.

For freelancers, those ratings are like gold. They're motivated to go above and beyond to earn those five-star reviews because they know it's going to help them land more gigs down the line. But pricing? That's where things get tricky.

Freelancers have to find that Goldilocks price—not too high to scare away potential clients, but not so low that people question the quality of their work. Take book formatting and layout design, for example. You might see one freelancer starting at fifteen dollars and another at ninety-five dollars. Both seem way too low for the amount of work involved, right? But here's where the transparency comes in. That ninety-five-dollar freelancer has a thousand jobs and a 4.9-star rating, while the fifteen-dollar one has just twenty-three gigs and the same rating. Suddenly, you've got a lot more context. You start to understand why someone might pay a premium for the more experienced pro. Their perceived value is much higher.

You can actually put a dollar value on those star ratings. I discovered this when my team at ForwardLine needed to hire a programmer through a freelance platform. Like many businesses post-COVID, we were watching our costs carefully. I asked one of our analysts to find someone who could code the changes, with the caveat that they should be affordable but highly rated. Our analyst saw this as a chance to put my theory on differentiated pricing to the test. Looking at the programming listings, we found prices ranging from eighty to two hundred dollars. Each listing showed the freelancer's completed jobs and their average rating. As you might expect, the higher prices came from people with 4.9 or 5.0 ratings and lots of work experience. After analyzing the data, we found something interesting: Among highly experienced programmers, the difference between a 4.8 and 5.0 rating was worth about twenty dollars, or 10 percent of the price.

But not everyone priced themselves at the top of their range. One programmer caught my eye. His experience and ratings matched the best, but his price was twenty-five dollars lower than similar freelancers. When our analyst reached out for a quote, he asked about this pricing strategy. The programmer's answer made me want to hire him immediately.

The programmer explained that his lower price brought in more project requests, allowing him to cherry-pick the most interesting ones. He only chose projects where he could learn something new and was confident the client would be so happy they'd leave both five stars and tips, more than making up for his initial discount. His approach opened my eyes to something I hadn't considered: Small business owners can use pricing strategically to achieve goals beyond just maximizing profit.

It's important to note that raising prices isn't the only option for gig workers with high ratings. They have a choice. Some might decide to keep their prices competitive and simply take on more work, leveraging their high ratings to stay consistently busy. Others might choose to raise their rates, attracting clients who are willing to pay more for perceived higher quality. And some, like our programmer, might deliberately price below market to create opportunities for growth, learning, or simply more enjoyable work.

If you're a freelancer, your reputation is everything. Even if you can't control the market rates, you can control the quality of your work and the relationships you build with clients. And when you've got a good reputation, you might be surprised at how much people are willing to pay for your services. Take the ninety-five-dollar freelancer, for example. They're not scaring away clients with that price point; they're attracting the ones who value experience and reliability. And that's the secret sauce in the gig economy. It's not always about being the cheapest. It's about knowing and enhancing your perceived value to customers and sharing that value in a way that's best for you.

## Standing Out in Standardized Markets

Many businesses operate in marketplaces where prices are largely dictated by external factors, leaving little room to set their own prices. For example, in regulated industries like utilities or telecommunications, government agencies often set price caps or determine rate structures, limiting companies' ability to freely set their own prices. In other industries, prices are often driven by the marketplace, and participants must conform to these predetermined rates to remain competitive. In such cases, business owners may feel that they have little to no control over their pricing, as they are essentially price-takers rather than price-setters.

Healthcare providers, in particular, are expected to offer a certain standard of care at a predetermined price. Insurance providers often determine the prices doctors and dentists charge, limiting their ability to set their own rates for visits and procedures. This might suggest that there is no room for pricing flexibility or creating incremental value. However, just like Max in the contracting world, some healthcare practitioners find ways to differentiate themselves and create additional value for their patients.

Doctors and dentists often deal with high patient volumes and packed schedules. It's not unusual for patients to call or drop in with non-emergency issues, hoping to be seen right away. Typically, these practitioners have to turn such patients away and ask that they schedule a proper appointment instead.

However, some innovative healthcare providers have found a way to accommodate patients who need more flexibility. For example, they might offer premium scheduling options, setting aside specific days where they compress their schedule to fit in last-minute or urgent appointments. This approach is particularly appealing to patients with busy or unpredictable schedules, such as business professionals or frequent travelers.

Taking it a step further, some providers offer services that go well beyond standard care. They might provide pick-up and drop-off services for elderly or mobility-impaired patients or even make house calls for certain treatments. By offering these additional services, even within the constraints of standardized care, these practitioners create extra value for their patients that sets them apart from other practices.

For small businesses in highly regulated or standardized industries, the key is recognizing what sets you apart and understanding its value. This doesn't necessarily mean charging extra for additional services. Instead, it's about acknowledging the unique aspects of your offering and deciding how to leverage them.

Whether you choose to share this value through additional fees or absorb the cost to attract and retain customers is a personal business decision. Regardless of your choice, remember to communicate this value to your customers. If you opt for premium pricing, clearly explain the additional benefits customers receive. If you offer extra services at no charge, ensure your customers understand the unique value you provide compared to your competitors.

Like Max, identify what sets your service apart, understand its value, and determine the most effective way to convey that value to your customers. This approach can help you stand out, regardless of industry constraints.

## Parking Lot Economics

Small business owners often need to find quick, intuitive shortcuts to determine their value proposition. I witnessed this firsthand during an unexpected economics lesson at a sports event in downtown Los Angeles.

A few years back, a long-standing client gifted me a pair of Lakers tickets. My wife wasn't interested in watching the Lakers take on the Knicks, so I decided to turn it into a father-son outing.

As we exited the freeway into downtown LA, we spotted signs for Lakers game parking. "Fifteen dollars," my son pointed out a lot in the underpass. "Aren't you going to park?"

"Dude," I said. "That's six blocks from Staples Center, and it's pretty sketchy down there."

We kept driving. A block later, it was twenty dollars. Another block, it was twenty-five dollars. My son, curious now, asked, "How much is it to park at the arena?"

I eyed a small lot nearby, probably only space for thirty to forty cars but filling up fast. "Tell you what, I think it's close enough here that we don't have to find out." I pulled in and dug into my wallet for twenty-five dollars.

As I handed over the cash to the attendant, curiosity got the better of me. "How do you guys decide on your prices?" I asked.

"We keep an eye on what the other lots are charging," he grinned, handing me my change. "Plus we factor in the event, how many people we think are coming, even the weather. Tonight's a big game, and the weather is clear, so people won't mind the walk. But if it was raining, we'd probably bump the price up a bit," he winked.

His explanation got me thinking about how businesses, especially smaller ones, approach pricing. They don't have the massive budgets of corporations like Coca-Cola or teams of consultants to research their competitors. Instead, they rely on market signals, intuition, and ideas borrowed from others who seem to be doing it right.

As we walked toward the arena, I noticed how the parking options varied. The official venue parking structure loomed ahead. Its convenience came at a premium, sometimes up to a third of the ticket price. But all around us were less-formal options: small lots with attendants waving flags, offering lower fees for those willing to walk a block or two.

I pointed this out to my son. "See how the price drops the farther you get from the arena? It's all about what people value most." I paused, then added, "Why do you think some folks choose to pay more to park closer?"

He shrugged. "I guess they're lazy and don't want to walk?"

I nodded, considering his answer. "That might be part of it. But what about people who can't walk far? Or families with little kids?"

He thought for a moment. "Well, maybe some people don't feel safe walking through places they don't know at night, especially if they're only saving a little money. For them, paying fifty dollars at the arena lot instead of twenty-five dollars across the street might feel worth it." He grinned. "If Mom was here, she'd make you park at the arena for sure."

I couldn't help but chuckle. "You got that right."

As we neared the arena, the buzz of the crowd grew louder. The aroma of sizzling bacon-wrapped hot dogs wafted from one of LA's famed street carts, making our mouths water.

"And if Mom were here she probably wouldn't be excited about us spending our parking savings on a couple of those dirty dogs," I added.

My son grinned. "Yeah, this is pretty cool. Getting to grab a hot dog and check out the city like this."

"That's another perk of our parking choice," I said, nodding toward the hot dog cart. "We get to soak in this pregame atmosphere."

My son took a big bite of his hot dog, savoring the flavor. As we walked, I added, "You know, those small lot owners are pretty clever too. They're constantly adjusting their prices based on what's happening around them. They think about everything—the type of event, how many people they expect, even the weather. It's all about guessing what people will value most at that moment."

"Like the guy back there mentioned about the rain?" my son asked, his mouth still half-full. "I thought he said that he just copied what the guys across the street do."

"Oh yeah, that's right."

We continued our scenic route to the arena, taking in the sights and sounds around us. As we joined the throng of fans entering the stadium, I realized that the small lot operator had indeed found a shortcut to pricing. He wasn't crunching numbers, poring over weather forecasts, or researching game schedules. Instead, he'd found a way to quickly determine his unique value in any situation with just a glance down the street.

## Share the Value You Create

The three Underdog Principles—positioning, proximity, and purpose—play a big role in understanding and sharing the value you create. They shape not only how you differentiate your business but also how you determine your pricing strategy. Your positioning helps you connect with customers who truly value what makes you unique. The proximity you have with these customers, those everyday conversations and relationships, helps you understand and convey that value in ways that feel authentic. And your purpose guides how you balance profit with what matters most to you and your business.

Don't be afraid to charge for your uniqueness, but be ready to explain why you're worth it. Remember, how much of your added value you decide to share with your customers through your pricing is up to you. It's about finding a balance that feels right for your business and your customers.

## Determining the Dollar Value of Your Differentiation

Unlike big corporations, your edge as a small business isn't in scale or brand recognition; it's in being different. Your strength lies in offering something personal and unique. Plus, you have the advantage of market focus. To capitalize on this, you must first recognize what sets you apart. For some businesses, this comes naturally and intuitively. Think back to the parking lot operator. He didn't need a fancy analysis, he just looked up and down the street, saw where he fit in both in terms of location and competition, and priced his spot accordingly.

But for many small business owners, pinpointing their real competition takes some work. Let's stick with our parking lot analogy for a moment. To figure out your block, compare the uniqueness and quality of your offer to others serving similar customers. Look at the prices of businesses that provide comparable levels of attentiveness, service, and quality. That's a good starting point for understanding your value. Remember to factor in the travel distance for your customers. How easy or difficult is it for customers to choose your business over others? If your offering is more convenient or requires less effort for a certain group of customers, that alone can set you apart.

Just like our parking lot operator who glanced down the street to gauge his competition, you need to look at your neighbors. The competitors down the street who offer similar products or services have already put their pricing into the market. What are they charging? Don't worry if their prices aren't posted on their buildings or listed on their websites—you've probably lost work to or won business away from these businesses anyway. Your customers, like the sports fans choosing where to park, will know both the prices and the perceived value of these other options. You'll likely need to work backward from your competitor's prices and consider how your product or service differs. This process will help you understand the added value you provide.

When you know what others in your neighborhood are charging, you can decide which features are more beneficial to your customer and which are less. The value of this benefit may be as obvious as the difference between the best and worst on your list, but it's not always that simple. Remember that not every customer values your differentiation or your benefit in the same way. Thinking back to our parking example, a family with small children might place a much higher value on a nearby spot than a group of young adults would. This is where the first Underdog Principle, positioning, comes into play.

Determining your positioning means identifying and targeting the customers who would value your offer the most. This approach allows you to set your prices more confidently based on the value you provide to your ideal customers. Just as our parking lot operator focused on game-day customers willing to pay for convenience, you need to identify your core market. In cases where you offer multiple unique features, each with its own value but not all equally important to every customer, try to assess each one separately. For instance, a local coffee shop might offer organic beans, a cozy atmosphere, and expert baristas, much like how a parking lot might offer proximity, security, and easy exit. Different customers might value each of these features differently. The benefit of having a focused market is that you can cater to the group (or groups) who value these features the most.

## Communicating Your Value

Imagine you're at a farmers market, surrounded by stalls selling fresh produce. One stand catches your eye. Their tomatoes look just like everyone else's, but they're charging double the price. You're about to walk away when the vendor starts chatting with you. He tells you how the farmer uses a special organic fertilizer, hand-picks each tomato at peak ripeness, and delivers them straight from the farm every morning. He explains that this special treatment results in tomatoes with more antioxidants and vitamins, fewer nitrates, and a better overall flavor.

The vendor understands a key principle: It's not just about having a great product; it's about helping customers see its value. The shoppers who value higher nutritional value will gravitate to these tomatoes, while those looking for a deal will move on. As a small business owner, you have a unique advantage that bigger businesses often lack: the ability to engage in personal conversations with your customers every day. These interactions give you a unique window into their needs and show how your product or service meets them. This is the second Underdog Principle, proximity, at work, and it's a powerful tool for smaller businesses.

Once you've identified what sets your business apart, the next step is to ensure your potential clients recognize it too. After all, if you're working hard to build a strong reputation yet hesitate to communicate your value, potential clients may not fully appreciate it. Since people perceive value differently, it's up to you to highlight what makes your offering special.

Your pricing strategy depends on how well your customers understand the benefits of your differentiation. Clearly communicating your value proposition is essential, especially if your prices are higher than your competitors. Help your customers see what makes your offering unique and why it's worth the investment. If they believe they can get the same offering elsewhere, or simply don't see the value in your differentiation, they're likely to opt for the lowest price. Positioning yourself as a unique solution, however, gives you more flexibility in setting your prices.

Take Max the contractor, for example. He conveys his value most effectively through one-on-one conversations with his clients, showing them why his approach is different. In contrast, gig workers often rely heavily on star ratings to signal their worth. Your method of communication should align with your industry and target audience. If face-to-face interactions are your strength, lean into them. Otherwise, consider how your branding, online presence, or physical environment can reflect your unique qualities. Your website, office, or storefront all send messages that influence how customers view your business, and these elements can speak volumes about the quality and value of what you offer.

Interestingly, one of the most powerful signals of value is your price itself. A higher price tag often suggests premium quality or expertise. If you decide to position yourself alongside the big players, you might want to consider how you'll demonstrate that you belong in that category, whether through branding, customer testimonials, or the overall experience you offer.

As a business owner, you might adopt a philosophy similar to Max's: providing better value by dedicating more time to your clients than your competitors do. This kind of strategy can help build a strong reputation, which, in turn, may give you the confidence to charge higher prices. When you effectively communicate your value, you'll often see this reflected in customer feedback. Reviews like "I enjoyed working with this guy; he was worth the price" not only justify your pricing but also strengthen your reputation.

Remember, communicating your value isn't just about justifying your pricing, it's about conveying the benefits your customers perceive. Your strong customer orientation, developed through your daily interactions, helps you understand why your customers see value in your offering. This allows you to communicate your value with confidence and authenticity.

## Sharing the Value

Now that you've identified the specific value of your differentiation and feel confident communicating it, it's time to decide on your pricing strategy. This can be daunting for small businesses that rely on every customer they have and are concerned about driving them away by raising prices. Remember, your mission objective as a small business owner doesn't always have to revolve around maximizing profits. You have choices in how you use the value you've created.

Think back to our vendor at the farmers market with his premium tomatoes. He knows his organic, hand-picked fruit is worth more than the average tomato. Organic tomatoes go for $4 per pound at Whole Foods, while conventional tomatoes sell for $1.50. Our vendor offers his tomatoes for $3 per pound. Yes, that's twice what conventional tomatoes cost, but it's actually a dollar less than his closest competitor. He's not leaving money on the table; he's giving his customers a premium experience without breaking their whole paycheck.

Prices act as a secret language in the market, signaling more than just cost. They help customers gauge quality and uniqueness while also communicating the value you're offering. The challenge is ensuring your pricing is telling the right story about your business. Price too low and you might undermine your offering's perceived value; price too high and you could scare customers away. The key is finding a balance where the benefit to your customer aligns with your profit in a way that's sustainable for both parties.

One approach is to start with your full value and then consider strategic discounts. This framework allows you to think about which customers or services should receive discounts and which don't need them. You can offer different prices to customers who value your benefits differently. If you have a high transaction volume, you might even test various price points to see which types of customers truly value your differentiation. In testing, you're trying to figure out what your price could be, not necessarily what it should be.

The amount of value you share with your customers through pricing depends on your specific business dynamics. Is it difficult to acquire customers? Do you have a lot of capacity? If acquiring new customers is challenging, you might want to share more value to encourage loyalty and repeat business. On the other hand, if you easily attract customers but have limited capacity, you might lean toward holding on to more value through higher prices.

Ultimately, your customers will decide whether to accept your pricing or not. As a business owner, you need to identify which customers you want to attract and ensure there are enough who value your offering at your chosen price point. If there's excess value, you can decide how to allocate it, whether by sharing it with your customers, investing in your business's future, or improving your work-life balance. For instance, you might choose to offer slightly lower prices in exchange for the freedom of choosing projects you enjoy or customers that you like working with. This is where the third Underdog Principle, purpose, comes into play: Your pricing decisions shouldn't just reflect the value of your offering but also align with what matters most to you and your vision for your business.

- What aspects of your offering would your highly satisfied customers say they value most when comparing you to competitors?
- In your current pricing model, what portion of value do you keep versus share with your customers?
- Are there customer segments that don't understand or appreciate the extra value you offer, and how might you reshape their perception?
- If you were to change how much value you share through your pricing, how would that impact your long-term vision for your business?

## CHAPTER SIX
# MEET ME WHERE I AM

### Just-in-Time Marketing

My travels once took me to Castroville, Texas, a small town just outside of San Antonio, to meet a potential investor. With no hotels in Castroville at the time, I booked my stay on the outskirts of San Antonio, in Medina Valley.

Arriving at the hotel early in the afternoon, I hoped for a quick check-in. Instead, I found myself fifth in line for the front desk. Never one to pass up a chance for conversation, I noticed the guy in front of me had no bags.

"Planning a short stay?" I asked.

He turned, smiling. "No, actually, I'm here to promote my restaurant."

He introduced himself as Jorge and shared his story. His Castroville eatery thrived on local patrons, but out-of-towners often missed it, opting for his competitor's place right off Highway 90.

"Their food's no good," Jorge said, his nose wrinkling at the mention of his competitor.

"Makes sense," I said. "Those highway spots know their customers rarely return. Where is the incentive to even try?"

Jorge's eyes lit up. "That's just it," he said. "I refuse to compromise on the quality of my food and service. But reaching those out-of-towners who'd appreciate that? It's tough."

He went on to explain his online struggles. When potential customers searched for Castroville restaurants on platforms like Yelp or Google Maps, his place didn't show up. Larger restaurants from San Antonio were paying to appear first, even for searches in his town.

"I searched for my own restaurant in my own city, and I'm being shown places fifteen miles away!" he told me, throwing his hands up in frustration.

Tech giants like Google and Yelp are hardly going to be concerned about this situation. They're making money from their paying advertisers, leaving small-town business owners like Jorge in the lurch. But Jorge wasn't about to throw in the towel. Instead of spending a fortune on online advertising to compete with the big players, he got creative. He decided to piggyback off local businesses that were most likely to interact with out-of-town visitors.

"I come to hotels like this one, and I give away free meals to the front desk staff," he explained.

His strategy was to target locals who interact with visitors, including hotel concierges, pharmacists, and other local business owners. These locals, who know and love their town, could then recommend his restaurant to travelers.

"I love my restaurant and my town," Jorge explained, his eyes shining with pride. "I want people to know about it. So I'm out here, sharing that love with the people who can represent our town. When visitors talk to them, my passion for this place is shared authentically."

After that conversation, I didn't need to consult Yelp for my dinner plans that evening.

Jorge's timing was strategic. He knew that the afternoon front desk staff fielded most of the dinner recommendations from hotel guests who were just settling in and starting to think about their evening plans. By building relationships with these staff members, Jorge found a way to reach potential customers at exactly the right moment. He sought out people who knew and loved their town, just like he did, turning them into unofficial brand ambassadors. Rather than fighting algorithms and paid ads, he connected with real people who could genuinely vouch for his restaurant when it mattered most. The cost of covering someone's dinner once made more sense than paying for endless clicks that might not convert. Now, when out-of-town visitors ask for dining recommendations, his restaurant is top of mind.

You might be wondering: Does this mean you should track down every potential customer right before they're about to make a purchase and personally pitch your product or service? Probably not. But it should get you thinking about how to get in front of your prospect at the right time.

While Jorge's timing with hungry travelers proved effective for his restaurant, different businesses require different approaches. Sometimes you need to plant seeds years before you see any results. I saw this in action when I worked with a company in the industrial manufacturing sector.

## Rubber, Years Before It Hits the Road

Guiding customers to your business just as they are making a decision can be pretty powerful. Understanding when and how those decisions are made is a key part of any business's marketing strategy.

I once worked with a company that manufactured engineered rubber hoses for hydraulics and other complex applications. Their products were expensive, but they were high-quality with good profit margins.

I had been tasked to find ways to improve profitability across their different sales channels. They made good money selling their hoses through distributors: They simply had to produce the hoses in the required lengths with the necessary connectors, and the distributors would handle orders and shipping. The margins were high, and we found we could probably take them higher.

Their direct business, however, told a different story. Here, the company sold to original equipment manufacturers (OEMs) that produce construction equipment and other heavy machinery using hydraulics. This channel presented several challenges: margins were razor-thin, marketing expenses were high, and the costs associated with supporting these demanding large customers were substantial.

As my team brainstormed opportunities for profit improvement across the two channels, a pattern emerged. The OEM business consumed far more resources and people than the distribution side. Puzzled by this mismatch, I met with Patrick, the executive responsible for the group, in our small team conference room.

"Let me show you something," Patrick said, walking to the whiteboard covered in our diagrams and idea trees. He pointed to the stick figures I'd drawn to represent customers outside a distribution center. "See these folks? Their decision to buy our hoses was made years before they got to this point."

He moved his finger to another part of the board where we'd mapped out the OEM price-quoting process. "This is where the real decision happens. Right here."

Patrick's explanation shifted my perspective entirely. The direct-to-OEM business, despite its low margins, was actually the backbone of their entire distribution model. Without their rubber hoses being designed into the original equipment, no one would seek them out for replacements or spare parts through distributors.

"So, how do you get your hoses designed in?" I asked. "Your marketing budget is substantial."

Patrick smiled. "We don't waste money advertising hoses and connectors to the masses. We go straight to the source—the engineers who design the equipment."

He described their approach in detail. Their design engineers would regularly visit large manufacturers, but not to sell. Instead, they would teach.

"We host technical seminars, showing their engineers how our products can solve specific problems. Things like how our adaptive resistance features and specialized connectors help build better hydraulic systems," Patrick explained.

"But it goes beyond presentations," he added. "Our engineers spend weeks working alongside their teams, helping solve broader system-design challenges. We become partners in their process."

"You're essentially offering free consulting," I observed. "That must be expensive."

"It is," Patrick acknowledged. "But building those relationships with design engineers is crucial. We're not just selling them hoses, we're helping solve their broader system-design problems. When they understand why our product is the best technical fit, we become their standard."

"And once you're the standard . . ."

"Exactly. The sales follow naturally." Patrick gestured to our earlier diagrams. "That's why timing is everything. We invest in highly skilled professionals who can engage meaningfully with other experts early in their design process. Yes, it's costly. Yes, it might take years after finalizing the equipment design before we see meaningful revenue. But by then, the decision to use our hoses is locked in."

"And that drives your distribution sales?"

"Right. Once our hoses are designed into the equipment, maintenance teams know they need our specific product for replacements. That's when they go to distributors. It's a long game, but it works."

Watching Patrick explain their strategy, I realized something important. Their biggest challenge wasn't in the engineering of their products—they knew their hoses were top quality—it was convincing potential buyers of their product's value at the right time.

While some businesses can go to market with broad campaigns, this one was playing a longer game. They were building relationships with the people who would drive decisions down the line—the engineers designing tomorrow's equipment. Each seminar, each consultation, and each problem solved together was laying the groundwork for future sales.

This approach doesn't look like traditional marketing; it helps to illustrate the most important aspect of any marketing effort. Instead of blasting messages to everyone, hoping something sticks, it's about finding the real influencers or decision-makers when they're still working out their own solutions. Both Jorge and the rubber company understood this; they just operated on different timelines. Jorge found a way to reach travelers right when they were looking for dinner recommendations, while the rubber company connected with engineers years before purchases would be made. It all comes down to knowing who to talk to and when.

## The Customer Decision Journey

Knowing when and where to connect with prospective customers is something businesses often take for granted. Stepping back to evaluate how you are influencing your customers today can help you improve marketing effectiveness and better promote what sets your business apart in the future. My favorite framework for thinking about influencing your customers is just as useful for a one-person startup as it is for a Fortune 500 company: the customer decision journey.

Think of the customer decision journey as a road trip. Just like how you don't suddenly decide to drive cross-country without some planning, customers don't make their buying decisions in a neat, linear fashion. They don't just walk into a store or click "buy now" without going through a process.

This journey has several stages, and the information customers use to make decisions could come from anywhere—a friend's recommendation, an online review, a random social media post, or even an offhand comment overheard at the grocery store. Understanding each stage can help you identify the most impactful (and cost-effective) moments to reach your potential customers.

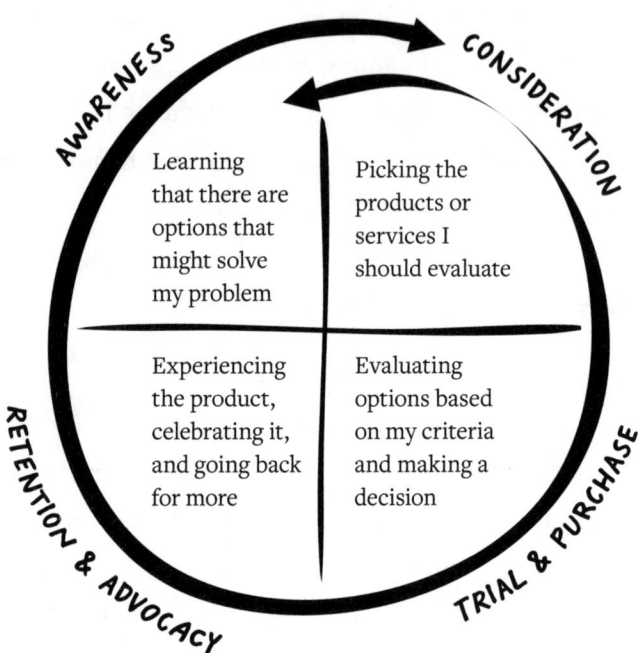

Let's break it down using an example we're probably all familiar with: buying a car.

I grew up in Detroit, the heart of the American auto industry, so cars have always been a big part of my life. But even if you're not a gearhead, this analogy should help illustrate the customer decision journey in a way that's easy to grasp.

## AWARENESS: LEARNING THAT THERE ARE PRODUCTS OR SERVICES THAT MIGHT SOLVE MY PROBLEM

Motor manufacturers know most people (historically, at least) will buy a car once every two or three years. Yet, you see car ads all the time. Why? Because they're playing the long game.

It's probably happened to you: You're cruising down the freeway, not even thinking about buying a new car. Suddenly, you spot a billboard showcasing the latest model from a well-known manufacturer. Or you're flipping through channels, and there it is again, a commercial featuring a ruggedly handsome guy driving a pickup truck through mud.

These car manufacturers are not telling you about the horsepower or the miles per gallon or even how much the car costs; they're selling you a lifestyle. "Buy our car," they're saying, "and suddenly you'll have a full head of hair, a supermodel spouse, and kids who actually want to spend time with you!" It's all about making you aware of their brand and associating it with positive feelings.

This is the awareness stage. Car companies aren't expecting you to rush out and buy a car right then and there. They're betting on the fact that when you do decide to buy, maybe months or even years down the road, their brand will be locked into your brain.

## CONSIDERATION: PICKING THE OPTIONS I SHOULD EVALUATE

Now, let's say your trusty old clunker starts making sounds like a heavy metal drummer is trapped under the hood. Suddenly, those car ads you've been seeing aren't just background noise anymore. You're actually paying attention; you've reached the consideration stage.

This is where the local car dealers come into play. Remember Mel Farr Superstar, the football hero turned car salesman extraordinaire in Detroit? His ads, like many others we see today, were focused on consideration. They're all about creating a sense of urgency, often promoting deals that were about to expire or limited-time offers that you just couldn't miss.

These ads typically focus on things like "Sign and drive your car off the showroom floor by the end of the month, and you'll get $500 off!" or "Get 0% financing if you come in this month!" Of course, that 0 percent financing isn't really free. Someone's paying for it, but as a customer, it sounds like a great deal.

These ads are trying to kick you into gear, to get you thinking, *Hey, maybe I should check this out before the deal expires*. They're creating that sense of urgency to move you from just being aware of the brand to actively considering a purchase.

But consideration doesn't stop at the ads. You've made it to the dealership. You're walking around, you find your dream car, and then you hear the magic words: "Would you like to take it for a spin?"

The test drive is a big deal, especially for something as complex and expensive as a car. It's one thing to see a vehicle on TV or in a brochure, but it's a whole different ballgame when you're actually sitting in the driver's seat, feeling the steering wheel in your hands, and trying to figure out how to adjust the mirrors without looking like a complete doofus.

## TRIAL AND PURCHASE: EVALUATING OPTIONS BASED ON MY CRITERIA AND MAKING A DECISION

You've fallen in love with the car. The new car smell has gone straight to your head, and you're ready to sign on the dotted line. This is the moment of truth—the purchase stage. It's where all the previous steps culminate in a decision.

Sometimes, a small business can put too much emphasis on this part of the journey because this is the only time they are with their prospective customer. If the other parts are done well, however, this step could be pretty simple.

For the dealership, this is the payoff for all their marketing efforts. You're walking in there with years of baked-in subliminal messaging. If you're a man, it's all about being rugged, handsome, and free because apparently, nothing says "masculine" like a shiny new car. You know there is a special deal that's going to expire soon (and has been expiring soon for the last six months). The sales guy can probably see it on your face and hear it in the questions you're asking. For you, it's the exciting (and perhaps a little nerve-racking) transition from prospect to owner. The endgame is you driving off the lot in your new car, with a mix of pride, excitement, and hopefully not too much "Did I really just do that?" running through your mind. Don't worry, that feeling fades . . . right around the time of your first car payment.

## RETENTION AND ADVOCACY: EXPERIENCING THE PRODUCT, CELEBRATING IT, AND GOING BACK FOR MORE

Once you've bought the car, the journey isn't over; it's just beginning. The car company doesn't want you to buy just one vehicle from them; they want you to be a customer for life.

This is where the real relationship-building begins. Every service appointment, every maintenance check, and every interaction shapes your experience and ultimately influences whether you'll choose them again or recommend them to others. Premium dealerships especially understand this. They'll lavish attention on their customers with personalized gifts and exclusive event invitations. It's a carefully orchestrated reminder that you're not just someone who bought their car, you're part of their community. Happy customers become their most powerful advocates, influencing friends and family long before they're even thinking about their next car purchase.

While big businesses like car manufacturers have the resources to invest heavily in every stage of the customer decision journey, the landscape looks quite different for small businesses. Most business owners don't have the luxury of multimillion-dollar ad campaigns or decades of brand recognition and, therefore, need to be more strategic about where and how they engage with potential customers. Let's shift gears and look at how small businesses can apply these concepts to their own customer acquisition strategies.

## When Awareness Is Half the Battle

After my time with Viking Cruises, I joined a company called Tax Credit Co., where I started gaining real hands-on experience helping small business owners. The company focused on helping all kinds of businesses claim federal and state tax credits that were available but often overlooked. While I had joined to grow the business across all service lines, one stood out as particularly interesting: the employment tax credit service.

In the United States, our tax laws are notoriously complex, many of them written by lobbyists primarily working for large corporations. One such complicated law is the Work Opportunity Tax Credit, commonly known as WOTC. This credit allows businesses to reduce their tax liability if they hire individuals from certain groups, such as former prisoners, minorities, or people who have been on welfare, and retain them for a specified period.

To illustrate how this works, let's consider a restaurant owner. Say you hire about sixty people annually to keep your restaurant running, with each employee staying an average of six months. If twelve of these waiters and waitresses were previously on some form of government support, and they worked for you for six months, you could be eligible for roughly $500 in tax credits per person. When you do the math, that's $6,000 in potential tax savings.

Many small businesses don't know about WOTC, and those who do often find it too complex to bother with. Small business owners are usually too busy running their day-to-day operations to worry about claiming tax credits. On top of that, they need to gather specific information when they hire someone new, which adds extra work. For a business with just a handful of employees, all this paperwork might not seem worth the effort, especially when the potential savings are relatively small.

This is where Tax Credit Co. saw an opportunity. The idea was to help small businesses navigate these complex regulations so that they could access benefits that larger companies routinely exploited. Tax Credit Co. would handle all the paperwork on behalf of small businesses, integrate it with their payroll systems, and split the resulting tax savings. My vision was to automate all the paperwork and documentation and build enough scale that we could deal with the different government entities in bulk.

To reach that scale, though, my sales team had to do extensive outreach to small businesses that weren't taking advantage of these potential tax credits and bring our company's service to their attention.

Eager to understand the process firsthand, I spent a lot of time talking to these small business owners and learning about their decision-making processes and specific challenges. Through these conversations, I began to grasp the complex and unique problems that small business owners face.

These entrepreneurs wear many hats. They're not just CEOs, they're also the janitors, receptionists, accountants, and HR managers all rolled into one. Between all these roles, their attention is constantly pulled in different directions. They're juggling so many responsibilities that it's hard for them to focus on any one thing for too long.

Our sales team would call small business owners with a pitch that went something like this: "As a business owner, are you aware that the government might owe you around $6,000? By hiring people who were on unemployment, you're entitled to this money by law."

Every sales rep understood and believed in the value of the service we offered. They had all seen success with their customers firsthand. On each new call, team members would picture striking gold with their pitch. They'd imagine the business owner exclaiming, "Wow, really? I could use $6,000!" and closing the deal right there. Unfortunately, it never quite played out that way.

Looking at it from the perspective of our customers, our calls and emails were actually received more like: "Greetings, esteemed business owner. I am a Nigerian prince with a generous offer of $6,000. Simply provide your social security number and those of all your employees, and I shall arrange the transfer post-haste." I have a friend of Nigerian aristocratic lineage (not quite a prince) who grimaces every time I use this example. Sorry, buddy!

The irony was we were offering a fantastic product. My team was essentially selling free money, albeit with a catch—it required substantial paperwork to claim the credit. But that's where we came in, handling all the bureaucratic heavy lifting. All the client needed to do was share their payroll information with us.

However, we quickly learned that generating awareness of a great product is not enough. We needed our customers to be interested in being educated first. Imagine this scenario: I'm telling you I can get you $6,000, I'll handle most of the work, and all you need to do is trust me with some sensitive information. Now, put yourself in the shoes of the small business owner, juggling countless responsibilities and probably fielding numerous sales calls. Would you have the time or inclination to verify the legitimacy of this offer? The offer sounds too good to be true, so you question the messenger.

The business owner doesn't have a ton of time and has to make a simple decision: Should I continue this call or not? Common wisdom dictates that there's no such thing as free money, and since business owners often received our calls out of the blue, it was hardly surprising that many were skeptical of our seemingly too-good-to-be-true offer.

Reflecting on this through the customer decision journey framework, I realized that we were trying to solve too many steps in the journey on that first call. Our business owner didn't even know that these tax credits existed; we needed to focus on solving that piece first.

Our new first-call script was focused solely on educating business owners about the different tax credits available to them, the legislative history behind them, and the kinds of challenges small businesses face in getting the credits they deserve. We'd leave the discussion there and prompt the business owner to do some independent research to decide if it was worth pursuing on their own or reaching out to us if they wanted help.

We weren't really ending the discussion to leave these prospective customers in the lurch; we were confident that we were the best of the three options we presented: let the government keep your money, spend countless hours wrestling with complicated government paperwork to get the money yourself, or call us when you're ready for help.

This two-step approach worked well, thanks to the genuine value of our service. Half of our effort in selling was just tackling the lack of awareness. With that hurdle out of the way, we gave our target customers breathing room to complete their journey. For me, it was the perfect example of how even an unbelievably good product doesn't automatically fly off the shelves.

With a new approach to introductions and a focus on awareness, our sales took off. Revenue from the small business tax credit side of our operation grew rapidly—we're talking a tenfold increase over two years. The business continued to scale, expanded into new employment tax credit programs, and was eventually acquired by a much bigger firm.

## Dancing Her Way to Purchase

While big businesses can invest heavily in awareness campaigns, small businesses often need to be more creative. You might not have deep pockets for widespread advertising, but you can still find clever ways to get your name out there.

While reviewing ForwardLine's business cases, I came across an interesting file for a dance studio in the San Fernando Valley. The owner, Annette, had applied for financing to expand her space, but what caught my attention was that she had answered "none" to the question about her marketing plans. Investing all her capital in an expansion project without having a marketing plan seemed risky. It usually doesn't work out well. Yet, Annette had grown the business steadily while she paid back her loan. Had she somehow cracked the code on customer acquisition without breaking the bank? Curious about how she'd filled all that new space without spending money on marketing, I decided to pay her a visit.

"Tell me about how you bring in new students," I said during my visit.

Annette smiled. "We don't really do marketing, if that's what you're asking."

"No marketing at all? How does that work?"

"Our existing students are our best ambassadors," she said proudly. "They have friends, they go to school, they spread the word about our classes."

I was impressed. Annette was tapping into the awareness that already existed in her community rather than trying to create it from scratch. All she had to do was encourage her students to spread the word, and make it easy for them to do it.

Her favorite marketing trick was awarding sew-on patches to students as they progressed through different stages of their training. The logo for her studio was a silhouette of her mother, who was also a dancer. The kids took pride in earning these patches, and Annette kept a sewing kit and iron at her studio to ensure the badges were proudly displayed on her students' backpacks. Those patches sparked curiosity among classmates, leading to questions about the studio.

"But seeing a pretty logo isn't enough to get someone to sign up," I said. "When do these potential dancers actually make that decision?"

Annette explained that her performances were the real turning point. These seasonal shows were both her greatest joy and biggest source of anxiety. She had her students post flyers at their schools and even created a friendly competition around selling tickets to friends and classmates. Now, with the expansion, she could accommodate more than double the audience, giving even more potential students their first glimpse of what her studio could offer them.

As friends and classmates witnessed the grace of dance, some would ask themselves, "Could I do that?" Annette knew she had to catch those fleeting thoughts. Her solution was "golden tickets," offering a free first lesson. These tickets gave potential customers a risk-free taste of her studio's magic. She even armed each of her students with a ticket, encouraging them to invite a friend of their choice. This way, Annette turned her current students into recruiters, spreading the joy of dance through their own networks.

What made Annette's approach so effective was how naturally it guided potential customers through their decision journey. Her students became walking billboards, creating awareness with their patch-adorned backpacks. Her performances sparked genuine interest in dance, leading children and parents to consider lessons. And her golden tickets transformed curiosity into commitment by letting newcomers experience the magic firsthand.

Annette had nailed all the key steps in the customer decision journey simply by pursuing her passion for dance. She hadn't invested heavily in traditional marketing, but her expanded studio space became the perfect stage for inspiring new generations of dancers.

The customer decision journey breakdown gave us an opportunity to brainstorm each piece independently and sparked our creativity. We explored alternatives to what was already working for her. For instance, we asked: Could patches be complemented with other branded items in the school halls? What about T-shirts and pullovers? Might parents be willing to sport a bumper sticker or magnet on their cars?

We weighed the cost and scope of each investment. Annette poured a ton of effort into her seasonal performances, and while they made a big splash, we wondered if their value could be stretched further. What if she recorded shows for giftable DVDs or shared snippets on social media, reaching those who were unable to attend in person? The production costs would be minimal compared to the work already going into the performances, but the potential reach would be significantly greater.

We also looked beyond the dance world for inspiration. Taking a cue from car dealerships, we considered adding expiration dates to her golden tickets. Would a deadline nudge more people to act? Car dealers always have a promotion; it just changes every month. For Annette, she could mix it up too, maybe offering free dance shoes instead of always offering a free lesson.

Annette was particularly excited about extending her performances' reach through video and social media. It was a perfect example of getting more value from existing investments—taking something she was already doing well and finding new ways to make it work harder for her business.

Driving back to my office that day, I couldn't help but smile. While others poured money into Google ads or coupon sites, hoping to draw people through their doors, Annette had tapped into her close relationships with her students to build her business. Because she knew her students personally, she understood exactly where in their journey to create the right experiences to win new students over. She'd found a cost-effective way to bring new students on board by leveraging proximity, turning her existing relationships into a powerful network for growth.

## The Real Cost of Finding Customers

When many small business owners hear the term "marketing," they think of traditional channels such as pay-per-click advertising that charges for every website visitor, premium listings on review sites, or discount platforms that take hefty cuts of each sale. But investing in marketing isn't just about paying for advertising. It's about finding the right customers, helping them understand what makes your offering special, and giving them reasons to choose you—and to keep choosing you.

Paid advertising can be expensive and will most certainly eat into your profits. Pay-per-click advertising, for example, might drive traffic to your website, but those clicks add up fast, especially when they don't convert to sales. Review sites like Yelp and Trustpilot charge premium rates for featured listings without guaranteeing results. Discount platforms like Groupon might bring in customers, but they're taking up to 50 percent of your profit on every sale. And online marketplaces like Amazon and eBay claim around 20 percent of every transaction.

Many of the small businesses I interacted with during my time at ForwardLine were like Annette: They spent little to no money on traditional marketing, relying instead on word-of-mouth and organic growth. While Annette was proud of the fact that she wasn't using traditional marketing channels to grow her studio, she was still investing time and energy in growing her business through her patches, her performances, and her golden tickets. She just wasn't thinking of these investments as marketing costs, or what we call customer acquisition cost (CAC).

Big businesses have gotten pretty good at calculating these costs. They know exactly how much they spend on advertising to get one customer through the door. This helps them focus their marketing dollars where they work best. But, as a small business owner, how do you know if your marketing efforts are paying off when you can't track every customer like an online business can? This becomes especially challenging when you can't guarantee a fixed profit margin on every sale.

This raises some important questions that many small business owners often overlook: What is the real cost of acquiring a customer? In your own business, how much are you really investing in finding and keeping your customers? More importantly, are these investments working for your business? To answer these questions, we need to start by understanding your true CAC.

## The Cost of Acquiring the Customer

To calculate your CAC, take what you spend on sales and marketing over a specific time period and divide it by the number of new customers you acquire as a result of these efforts. While this might sound simple, the costs of acquiring customers are often spread across many different activities. Beyond obvious marketing expenses like advertising, you need to consider all acquisition-related costs, from your sales team's salaries to the commissions paid to lead-generation services. Understanding your true CAC means looking at everything you invest in bringing customers through your door.

Think back to Annette's dance studio. She thought she wasn't spending on marketing, but when we looked closer, we found costs everywhere:

- Materials and time spent making patches for backpacks
- Organizing and hosting performances
- Maintaining her website
- Printing golden tickets for free trials

We identified three main ways students discovered her studio:
1. Through current students sharing patches and golden tickets
2. By attending performances

3. From website visits and phone calls

By dividing the total cost by the number of new students gained, we calculated the real cost for each path:

- Student referrals: About $500 a year in patches and time, bringing in eight new students ($63 each)
- Performances: $2,000 per show, attracting five new students ($400 each)
- Website: $100 yearly hosting fee, leading to three new students ($33 each)

The numbers told an interesting story. While performances cost more per student, these students often stayed longer and brought siblings. The website brought in new students at minimal cost. And the student referral program provided steady growth at a reasonable cost.

Looking at these numbers sparked new ideas. Could Annette reach more potential students by recording her performances on DVD? Could she invest a little in online advertising, given how well her website was already working? Sometimes the path with the highest customer acquisition cost can still be worth the investment if those customers prove more valuable over time.

While Annette's studio offers one example of calculating CAC, every business needs to consider its own unique acquisition costs. When calculating your own CAC, start by listing all the ways customers find your business. The costs might surprise you:

### A restaurant might need to consider:
- Prime-location rent and signage costs
- Review-site fees and food photography
- Delivery app commissions
- Marketing team salaries and agency fees
- Costs of promotional events and tasting menus

### A contractor (like a plumber or electrician) might look at:
- Vehicle signage and branded uniforms
- Online directory listings and website costs
- Sales team commissions and salaries
- Lead-generation service fees
- Marketing materials and local advertising

### A retail store might track:
- Shopping center lease premiums for foot traffic
- Social media advertising spending
- Sales and marketing staff salaries
- Promotional event costs
- Local community sponsorships

This kind of analysis can help you answer some important questions in your own business when calculating your CAC:

- How much are you really spending to acquire customers, and are those investments paying off?
- Which marketing channels are bringing in your most valuable customers?
- Are there organic or low-cost sources of customers that could benefit from more attention?

- Where could additional investment yield better results?
- How can you adjust your approach to attract the right kind of customers for your business?

You don't need exact numbers; rough estimates work fine. The goal is to understand where your efforts are paying off and where they might need adjusting. Understanding your true customer acquisition costs puts you in control of how—and how much—you invest in growing your customer base. Sometimes, spending a bit more in the right places can lead to significantly better results.

## Juice That Isn't Worth the Squeeze

I learned just how important it is to track what you spend on acquiring customers when I watched those costs balloon at my venture in HR tech. I'd seen how small businesses struggled with hiring. Without the right tools and resources, these businesses often brought people on board who didn't stick around. While there were services to help them find candidates, business owners didn't have the time to review every resume. This led to poor hiring decisions and high staff turnover, creating a costly and time-consuming cycle of constant recruiting and training.

To address this issue, my colleague Tom and I founded Talytica, a combination of "talent" and "analytics." Like many entrepreneurs, we started the business with a product that solved a real problem for a specific type of customer, one that the right customer would gladly pay for. We knew going in that if the cost of getting the customer's attention exceeded the product's value, the business would struggle, no matter how good the product was.

Our goal was to help businesses make better hiring decisions by analyzing applicant personality tests against historical employee data. By examining a company's payroll and hiring information, we developed algorithms that could predict how long a new hire was likely to stay based on the business's historical performance. We discovered fascinating insights about employee retention, like how different personality types could succeed in the same role and how having multiple people vouch for an applicant during a reference check was consistently linked to longer retention.

Our main product was a simple personality test coupled with customized algorithms that could be used to predict job fit and longevity in a particular role. As we worked with early customers, we added more features based on their feedback: math skills assessments, attention-to-detail tests, automated phone screening, and reference checks. We designed everything to integrate smoothly with a company's existing recruiting processes.

We priced our product to be accessible, from a few hundred dollars a month for basic tools like reference checks or phone interviews to several thousand for the fully integrated algorithm-based recommendations. While the higher tier was pretty pricey for small businesses, it was significantly less than what larger companies typically spent on recruiting. More importantly, we could demonstrate that our recommendations saved more than the product cost through reduced turnover and better quality hires.

We invested heavily in developing the product and hired smart, experienced (and expensive) salespeople to bring it to market. After two years, we had a working product and several happy customers. However, we faced an unexpected challenge: The cost of acquiring new customers was far higher than we'd anticipated.

The problem wasn't our product or its price. The real issue was the complexity of the sales process in larger companies. To make a sale, we needed to convince multiple departments, including finance, HR, legal, operations, and more, that our algorithms were both effective and legally sound. Even though I was good at sales and wasn't drawing a salary as a founder, it still took me months to close deals. When we hired salespeople to scale up, they were expensive and even less effective at closing deals than I was. This lengthy process meant our entire business model was broken. We needed more salespeople to close fewer deals, driving our customer acquisition costs far higher than planned. I'd learned the hard way that even a great product can fail if the cost of acquiring customers, whether in time or money, exceeds what you can earn from them.

This realization forced us to rethink our entire approach. We had a product that worked and customers who loved it, but we couldn't sustain the resources needed to sell it. Reluctantly, we decided to scale back our ambitions to bring affordable AI into recruiting. We reduced our focus on marketing the fully integrated portion of the solution and shifted our attention to the simple tools that needed less explanation. After all, everyone understands what a reference check and a screening call are. The revenue was lower, but we no longer needed a large, expensive salesforce.

This experience taught me a meaningful lesson about the importance of understanding both your product's value and the full cost of bringing that product to market. While Annette had focused her time on the right parts of the customer journey, making it easy for interested students to try a class and letting her performances naturally spark desire, we, on the other hand, were spending enormous resources just trying to get customers to understand our offering. Even with a great solution that customers loved, we were putting our energy in the wrong place, making our acquisition costs unsustainable.

For other entrepreneurs, this highlights the importance of thoroughly researching your target market and understanding their decision-making processes before investing heavily in product development and sales. Sometimes, a great product isn't enough; you need to ensure that you can effectively and efficiently reach your market with your solution.

## A Solution for a New Mom's Problem

Expensive customer acquisition is a common challenge for startup founders. I've made it a habit to ask entrepreneurs about their growth challenges, which led to an interesting conversation when I met Amy at a digital marketing seminar. She had designed an innovative baby bag, born from her own struggles with back pain after giving birth to her first child. Working with experts, she developed an ergonomic, multifunctional bag with a special strap for comfortably holding baby essentials. The design allowed a parent or caregiver to carry the baby and all the necessary paraphernalia without causing back issues. She'd even secured an endorsement from an orthopedic physician for her invention.

Driven by her own experience, Amy wanted to help as many new mothers as possible avoid the back issues she had endured. She had been selling her product online through her website and Amazon. She told me that her early success stemmed from getting her product featured on blogs focusing on new-mom challenges. She'd shipped samples and organized giveaways to persuade a few popular "mom bloggers" to promote her product. Interest was high, and it was evident that the benefit to those moms outweighed the price she was charging. With a growing base of satisfied customers and plenty of positive online testimonials, Amy was poised to expand her operations.

But expanding beyond her initial success proved challenging. While blogs had helped her sell directly to consumers, getting attention through other pay-per-click advertising on Facebook and Google was an expensive way to market her product. Often, this bag was a one-time purchase, and she had to spend as much (if not more) on advertising as she made in profit margin. She needed to find other avenues to reach a wider audience.

## Exploring Market Opportunities

Having learned from my Talytica experience about the true cost of educating potential customers, I recognized similar challenges in Amy's situation. Like us, she was dealing with a product whose value wasn't immediately obvious. It needed explanation. She considered several routes to market, each with its own customer acquisition hurdles.

One option was to approach big-box retailers like Walmart or Target. These stores could provide the volume she needed, but they were hesitant to take chances on items without a proven track record. Convincing a buyer at one of these retailers would likely require more than just positive reviews from mom blogs. Moreover, selling to these retailers meant sacrificing profit margins, though Amy reasoned that the exposure might be worth it. More people would see, touch, and understand what her bag could do, potentially leading to more sales.

For Amy's specific product, retail made sense, but she needed to be strategic about which retailers to approach. Given that her product targeted a specific buyer (parents), she thought a big-box specialist baby shop might be the ideal route.

Another option Amy considered was increasing her presence on Amazon. But this presented its own challenges. She wondered if anyone was actually searching for "ergonomic, multifunctional baby bags" on the platform. It seemed unlikely. A general search for "baby bags" would yield hundreds, if not thousands, of options to scroll through.

Shopping on Amazon is vastly different from a brick-and-mortar store where customers can physically interact with products. Online shoppers rely heavily on search results, and Amy's product struggled to stand out. Few people specifically searched for baby bags with back pain solutions, forcing her to continue to rely on expensive pay-per-click ads on Google and other platforms.

Even the advertising itself posed challenges. How could she capture attention in a single image or headline? A smiling mom with a baby and the bag? A mom holding her back in pain? Should she lead with "Do you have back pain?" Her product's benefits were too complex to explain in a simple ad. Her most effective keyword phrase was "postpartum back pain," but the cost per click was too high to generate profitable sales.

When Amy investigated the high cost of these keywords, she realized she was facing an even bigger challenge: She was competing against established brands in the baby product industry. This wasn't just about finding the right sales channel, it was about breaking through in a market dominated by big players with deep pockets.

## Facing Industry Giants

Many innovative products exist that could genuinely benefit consumers, but often people don't even realize they have the problem these products solve. In Amy's case, how many new parents are aware that poorly designed baby bags could cause back problems? It's unlikely that many are thinking, *My life would be so much better with a multifunctional ergonomic baby bag.*

Making matters more challenging, established brands like Gerber, Huggies, Pampers, and Enfamil strategically target new mothers with free samples. While still in the hospital, a new mom receives a hefty care package filled with products from these brands. Days after the baby's born, these and other companies start mailing samples directly to her home. For these corporations, this practice is worth every penny, even when repeated multiple times. They're all vying to ensure that new parents are aware of their products. For instance, formula companies want to establish themselves as a viable alternative to breastfeeding, sending out small packets of formula in the hope that, at some point, parents might decide to buy.

To understand Amy's challenge better, it's worth looking at the typical experience of new parents, especially mothers, in the weeks following childbirth.

There are many things a mom believes are possible before her baby arrives, thanks to the well-meaning advice of other parents. "Breastfeeding is easy!" they say, or "Cloth diapers will save you a fortune!" But when that bright-eyed mom finally gets home with her bundle of joy, reality sets in faster than a diaper leak at 3 a.m.

Suddenly, those rosy beliefs start to crumble. She discovers her own reality, and it's nothing like what everyone told her. Breastfeeding might feel more challenging than expected, and those cloth diapers? Well, they're giving her a crash course in laundry management she never signed up for.

As she navigates this new world where every baby seems to come with its own rulebook, she concludes that either parenting has changed dramatically since everyone else had kids or every baby is uniquely designed to keep parents on their toes.

Enter the big brands. They're right there, ready to offer solutions for every unexpected challenge. "Struggling with breastfeeding? Our formula is the next best thing!" "Drowning in laundry? Our disposables are here to help!" They're capitalizing on this uncertainty like seasoned pros.

It's easy to see why these companies invest so heavily in capturing new parents' attention. Once they've connected with that sleep-deprived new mom or dad, that parent is likely to stick with their products for the long haul.

In the end, Amy wasn't able to convince any major retailers to stock her product, nor could she bring her digital marketing costs down. How could she when every baby product company was competing for new parents' attention? The established brands could afford to spend more on ads because they were banking on years of future sales from these parents, not just a one-off purchase.

Amy was facing an existential challenge: Unless she found a different way to reach new customers, her business wouldn't survive. Like Talytica, she had a product that solved a real problem, but the cost of reaching those customers was threatening to sink the entire venture.

## Amy's Pivot

A few years later, I bumped into Amy at another event. I asked her how things were going.

"A lot has changed since we last talked," she said. "I spent months brainstorming ways to market the bag without spending a fortune. I thought about reaching out to more mommy bloggers, trying to get a feature in baby magazines, and generating more word of mouth. But even our satisfied customers were having a hard time convincing others to buy it. It's not the kind of thing that comes up naturally in conversation. 'Hey, have you thought about your back pain when carrying a baby bag?' It's just not an easy sell."

"But then I noticed something interesting," she continued. "Our customers weren't finding us by looking for baby bags at all. They would start by googling back pain solutions, finding articles about postpartum pain everywhere. And somewhere in those search results, they'd come across the mommy blogs featuring my bag. That's when these moms would realize that maybe their back pain was actually coming from their regular baby bag. Suddenly, my solution made perfect sense to them."

"Interesting," I said. "You weren't really competing in the baby products market at all. You were actually in the back pain solutions space. What did you decide to do with this new information?"

"I decided to pivot," she said. "Instead of wasting money trying to market the bag to every new parent, I focused my spending where it was actually working and began reaching the moms who were already searching for back pain solutions. We've expanded our product line to include a posture corrector, a maternity belt, and a back brace. We have chair cushions, shoe inserts, and herbal pain remedies in the cards for next year, all geared toward postpartum back pain."

"Smart move," I said. "It sounds like you've created a niche market for yourself."

"It's working well," she said. "When someone searches for help with back pain and finds us now, we can offer them whatever solution fits best. Maybe it's the bag, maybe it's a support brace, or maybe it's one of our herbal remedies. And I can justify spending more on search terms because we're more likely to convert the click into a sale."

Once again, here were the Underdog Principles at work. Amy had found her edge through positioning, focusing specifically on moms with back pain rather than trying to reach all new parents. What impressed me most was seeing how her purpose, helping other mothers avoid back pain, combined with her intimate understanding of the problem, led her to reach customers more effectively than if she'd focused solely on selling her product.

By understanding exactly where her marketing spend was most effective, she stopped competing with established brands for general awareness and instead focused on expanding her offerings to customers who already understood the problem she was solving. This approach not only reduced her customer acquisition costs but also increased the lifetime value of each customer.

## Walking Your Customer's Journey

As a small business owner focused on growth, you know you need to spend money to bring in new customers. But have you considered exactly when your potential customers make their buying decisions?

Many small business owners concentrate their efforts on the most visible parts of the customer decision journey, like when customers are actively considering options or are ready to make a purchase. You might be placing ads on Google, hoping to catch someone's attention during their search. Or, you might be thinking, *I'll get my next customer by telling them about how great my product or service is when they call or walk into my place of business.* While these are important moments, they're just one piece of your customer's decision-making process. Without understanding the full journey, you might miss the critical moments when customers actually make their decisions, or find yourself competing in spaces already crowded with other businesses vying for attention.

So, how do you reach potential customers at the right moment? How do you make them aware of your offering and what's unique about you without breaking the bank?

## Map the Journey Your Customers Take

Before walking through each stage, it's helpful to visualize the path your customers take from first recognizing a need to making a purchase. This mapping process helps you identify where and when to best reach them, and how to do it cost-effectively.

Awareness: Start by looking at the problem your business solves through your customers' eyes. This might be as simple as "I need a quality place to eat" or as complex as "I need my 5,000 psi hydrostatic drive to be rated for both high and sub-zero temperatures." Think about when and how your customers first realize they have this problem. If you're not there, what information or influences are around them in that moment?

Now, imagine you're there when they recognize this need. What would you tell your potential customer about your solution? What would you say to show them your solution is exactly what they're looking for? The way you'd explain it probably highlights what makes your offering unique and what customers should value most.

Consideration: Put yourself in your customers' shoes. How would you go about solving your problem? What information would you be researching? This perspective helps you understand whether your business even shows up in their initial search for solutions.

Look at how customers currently find your business. It might be through foot traffic, word of mouth, or online listings. Which of these channels best helps you explain why your solution is the right choice?

Trial/Purchase: Look at what matters to customers who are weighing their options. What criteria do they use to make their final decision? This could be as simple as convenience or availability, or it might involve detailed comparisons of cost, quality, service, and support.

Match these criteria against what you offer. Do your strengths align with what matters to your customers the most? Are they overlooking features that would make you their obvious choice? What aspects of your offering are hardest to communicate?

Remember that different customers often find you in different ways. By mapping out these common paths and understanding each stage, you can focus your time and money on where they'll have the biggest impact.

## Assess Your Acquisition Funnel

Every business has a path that leads customers from first hearing about them to making a purchase. Think of it as a funnel with many potential customers at the top that narrows as people move closer to buying until a smaller number become paying customers at the bottom.

With this acquisition funnel in mind and your customer decision journey mapped out, let's look at what you're spending at each stage to bring in customers. Don't worry about matching your cost analysis exactly to the customer decision journey stages. Focus instead on where you can track concrete numbers, such as how many clicks your ads get or how many trials convert to sales. Look at both the cost of each action and how many customers move from one stage to the next. This is what is known as conversion rates.

Other things you might track could include:
- How many people request quotes
- How many quotes convert into sales
- What percentage of social media clicks convert to website visitors
- How many website visits become phone inquiries

For each stage, wherever you can measure both your spending and your results, you'll be able to calculate a cost per unit. This could be your cost per click, cost per quote, or cost per lead. For example, if you spend $500 on Google ads and get one hundred clicks to your website, your cost per click is $5. Along with these costs, measure your conversion rates to the next stage. If ten of those one hundred clicks request quotes, your conversion rate from click to quote is 10 percent.

Then ask yourself:
- Where in the customer's journey does this marketing investment have an impact?
- What do these numbers tell you about your business's strengths?
- Where could you improve your results in this area?

Think back to Annette's dance studio. By analyzing her numbers, she discovered that her website brought in leads at a low cost, while her performances, though more expensive, attracted long-term customers. Understanding these patterns helped her make smarter decisions about where to invest her marketing budget.

## Align Your Principles with Your Customer's Journey

The success of your customer funnel comes down to how you leverage your positioning, proximity, and purpose. Here's what we saw in the stories we covered:

**POSITIONING:** Having a well-defined customer base can make your marketing more effective with certain audiences. Take Jorge and his small-town restaurant. While he wanted to attract out-of-town visitors, he specifically wanted those who valued quality dining. He found that his most effective marketing channel was through locals who understood and could recommend great restaurants, making his investment in building relationships with hotel staff particularly powerful.

**PROXIMITY:** Knowing your customers well means understanding what motivates them to take action. Annette recognized that seeing dance performances was often the turning point in a potential student's decision journey. This insight led her to find ways to share these performances with a wider audience through recordings, social media, and larger venues.

**PURPOSE:** Sometimes, focusing on the problem you want to solve rather than conventional business metrics can reveal unexpected opportunities. When Amy took a step back and analyzed how effective her marketing was, she discovered she was already reaching the people she most wanted to help—those dealing with postpartum back pain. This led her to expand her product line to serve these customers even better, rather than trying to reach a broader market.

## Move Investments to Where They Matter Most

Understanding where your marketing dollars work hardest helps you make smarter decisions about where to invest. Here's how to use your CAC analysis to adjust your strategy:

- **Focus on What Works:** Look for stages in your funnel where you're getting better results at lower costs. The rubber hose company discovered that investing in engineering support during the design phase locked in years of future sales. Where could your business double down on what's already working well?

- **Fix What Doesn't:** Identify places where conversion rates are low or costs are high. Sometimes, the issue isn't your product or service, it's how you're communicating its value. At Tax Credit Co., we improved our results dramatically once we realized our first contact needed to focus on awareness rather than selling. Are your messages aligned with where customers are in their journey?
- **Find Hidden Opportunities:** Look for underutilized basic touchpoints like how you handle incoming calls or whether your website presents your business professionally and makes it easy for customers to take action. Many businesses don't realize they need to verify and manage their listings on Google Business, Yelp, and other platforms where customers might find them. Beyond claiming these profiles, actively managing your online reputation by responding to reviews, encouraging happy customers to share their experiences, and addressing concerns professionally, can significantly impact your success. Small investments in these areas often yield surprising returns.
- **Stay True to Your Purpose:** Let your purpose guide your decisions at every stage of the customer journey. Invest more in channels that bring you the customers you really want to serve. Consider reducing investment in areas that bring business that doesn't align with your personal goals. Like Amy with her back pain products, sometimes focusing more narrowly leads to better growth.

- When do your customers first realize they need your offering, and what steps do they typically take before deciding to work with you?
- What aspects of your offering should be emphasized at each stage of your customer's journey?
- Are you investing enough in the right channels or touchpoints to showcase your value to potential customers?
  - Are these investments attracting the type of customers you're best positioned to serve?

## CHAPTER SEVEN
# MORE THAN A MILE IN MY SHOES

### Airplane Anxiety

Over the years, I've spent more time in airports than I care to admit. I've also racked up more frequent flyer miles than I care to count, and let me tell you, the thing I value most about traveling isn't the free upgrades and fancy lounges or the promise of future trips. It's the simple joy of getting from point A to point B without wanting to pull my hair out. While free upgrades are nice, they pale in comparison to the sweet relief of touching down at your destination on time, with your luggage intact and your patience still (mostly) in reserve.

This philosophy has led me to develop a bit of an aversion to connecting flights. Each layover is like adding another roll of the dice, another chance for Murphy's Law to kick in. But sometimes, you don't have a choice, like the time I needed to get to Sioux Falls in South Dakota for a meeting with a potential business partner.

## UNCONVENTION

To get to Sioux Falls from Los Angeles, I had no option but to take a connecting flight. As I booked my ticket, I could feel my blood pressure rising with each click. One connection. Two different planes. Twice the opportunities for something to go wrong.

The morning of my flight, I found myself at LAX, my mind racing through its usual preflight checklist. Will the security line be a nightmare? I've paid for Clear to speed things up, but this is LAX we're talking about. Better safe than sorry, I thought, as I arrived with time to spare. Good thing, too. The family in front of me apparently thought bringing their entire beverage collection through security was a brilliant idea. As I watched the TSA agent patiently explain for the umpteenth time that, no, those couldn't go through, I felt a wave of relief wash over me. That Clear membership was already paying dividends.

Next on my worry list: the dreaded overhead bin space race. Would there be room for my carry-on, or would I be forced to check it at the gate? Thankfully, my airline status usually gets me on board before the bin space becomes prime real estate. Still, I speed-walked to my gate, positioning myself strategically in the boarding line.

Once on board, carry-on safely stowed above, I allowed myself a small sigh of relief. Sure, we could still run into mechanical issues, traffic congestion, or weather delays, but those were out of my hands. I've learned the hard way that you can't control everything in air travel, no matter how much you'd like to.

The first leg of the journey went smoothly. We even landed on time. But I knew better than to celebrate too early—I still had a connection to navigate. As we taxied to the gate, I found myself doing mental calculations. Would we be departing from the same terminal? If not, how much of a sprint would I be in for? Luckily, I had almost an hour between flights. No need to channel my inner Usain Bolt, but a brisk walk wouldn't hurt.

I made it to my next gate without breaking a sweat, feeling pretty good about how things were going. The plane to Sioux Falls was already there, and passengers were few. But as I approached the gate, the universe decided to remind me who was really in charge.

"Sir, I'm afraid your bag won't fit in the overhead compartment on this aircraft," the flight attendant said, eyeing my carry-on like it was some oversized monster.

I looked past her into the cabin, and my heart sank. Three seats per row. Of course. If I'd known this leg was on a puddle jumper, I might have packed a bit lighter.

Having your bag taken at the gate is like a minor form of torture for frequent flyers. Not only does it mean extra time wasted at the baggage claim, but it also opens up the possibility of your luggage deciding to take an extended vacation without you. But what could I do? I handed over my bag, trying to channel my inner Zen master.

Just as I was getting comfortable, I noticed the gate agent and flight attendant huddled over the manifest, stealing glances in my direction. Great. Now what? Did they lose my bag already? Had I somehow ended up on the no-fly list between gates? I caught their eye, and they quickly looked away. Nothing suspicious about that at all.

I took a deep breath. Whatever it was, it was out of my control. Maybe they were just admiring my impeccable choice of travel attire. Or maybe I'd be shopping for new clothes in Sioux Falls tomorrow. I hear they have great malls in South Dakota.

The flight itself was uneventful, which in my book is the best kind of flight. As we began our descent into Sioux Falls, I braced myself for potential bad news about my bag. But hey, at least we were landing on time.

When the plane pulled up to the gate, I noticed an airport agent boarding and then having a hushed conversation with the flight attendant. She handed him something, and once again, they both glanced my way. At this point, I was convinced my bag had not only gotten lost but had somehow managed to insult the airline's CEO in the process.

*It's fine*, I thought. *I need some new clothes anyway.*

I stood up, ready to face whatever travel disaster awaited me. But as I walked toward the exit, the gate agent approached me with a smile.

"Mr. Kaza?" he asked, confirming my identity. "Congratulations, you've become a million miler!"

He handed me an envelope from the flight attendant. Inside was a card signed by the entire crew—all three of them—thanking me for flying a million miles with their airline. Then, he proudly presented me with a plastic bottle of champagne, undoubtedly the finest vintage available on our flying minivan.

I smiled and thanked them, but inside, I felt nothing. A million miles isn't a celebration; it's a sentence served. It's countless hours spent sardined into metal tubes, eating mediocre food, and praying for on-time arrivals. My million miler story isn't the worst I've heard, but it's hardly a tale of luxury and excitement. In fact, I've yet to meet a frequent flyer whose million miler moment made them feel all warm and fuzzy about their airline of choice.

Don't get me wrong, I appreciate the gesture. But after a million miles, you start to see through the veneer of these loyalty programs. They're not about relationships or appreciation. They're about locking in repeat business at the right price point. A plastic bottle of bubbly isn't going to make me choose a more expensive or less convenient flight. I've got million miler status on two airlines now, and I still wait until the fourth boarding group to get on the plane for either one. It's just another transaction in a long line of transactions dressed up as a relationship.

As I stood there, plastic champagne in hand, I couldn't help but wonder how airlines managed to convince millions of us to pledge our loyalty over a few miles and the occasional upgrade. The story, as it turns out, goes back further than you might think.

## The Airline Loyalty Revolution

Back in the day, booking a flight meant a trip to your local travel agency. These middlemen chose which airline you flew, pocketing commissions from the airlines for selling seats. This setup had a downside for airlines. Travel agencies, being businesses themselves, would sell tickets that made the most sense for them and maybe for the passenger, but not necessarily for the airline.

Then, in 1979, Texas International Airlines shook things up. They asked themselves: What if we could make our customers choose us, not just whichever airline the travel agent suggested? Their answer? The frequent flyer program. The idea was simple: fly with us and earn miles. The more you fly, the more you earn.

It was a win-win: For the airline, they simply took the money they were paying travel agents and started giving it back to their customers as rewards. For frequent travelers, these miles became valuable currency, encouraging them to stick with one airline.

The strategy worked so well that Western Airlines followed suit with a similar program the next year, as did most other airlines in the decades that followed. Today, these programs have evolved into complex systems of tiers and perks. The more you fly, the better your treatment from priority boarding to free upgrades.

If anything, I was a living example of this strategy's success—a million miles flown, always choosing the same airline even when it wasn't always the most convenient option. That plastic bottle of champagne might not have impressed me, but it was living proof of how these programs had me wrapped around their frequent flyer finger.

This shift allowed airlines to cut out the middleman in a big way. Sure, travel agents were still booking flights, but now customers had a reason to book directly with the airline. Did this mean cheaper flights? Not necessarily. In a competitive industry like air travel, prices tend to level out as everyone copies successful ideas. But it did give airlines a direct line to their customers, allowing them to build stronger relationships with them. They could now communicate directly with their passengers, understand their preferences better, and tailor their services accordingly.

By focusing on their most valuable customers and offering them something unique, airlines transformed their business model. They turned anonymous passengers into repeat customers and, in doing so, created an entire industry around customer loyalty. But in redefining the relationship between businesses and their customers, they also redefined the word loyalty itself, turning what was once a form of faithful allegiance into nothing more than an indication of repeat purchases.

## Starbucks's Strategy for Repeat Sales

While airlines focus on ensuring their customers choose them the next time around, Starbucks has an innovative approach to encourage repeat purchases: They stimulate new demand. Let's look at how they've taken the loyalty concept and given it a caffeinated twist.

Starbucks faces a common challenge in the food service industry: uneven traffic throughout the day. Their stores are buzzing in the morning with office workers grabbing their cappuccinos and lattes, but come early afternoon, the crowds thin out.

Often, they're rolling out new products, maybe a refreshing cold drink or a tempting dessert. The challenge is generating awareness and trial of these new offerings. To tackle this, Starbucks came up with a clever strategy. They started handing out coupons to their morning customers for two dollars off, but only valid later that same day.

At first glance, it might seem odd. Why give a coupon to someone who just bought coffee? But think about it: They're solving two problems at once. First, they're boosting afternoon sales, making better use of their staff and space. Second, they're encouraging customers to try new products that they might not usually order. And third, who better to influence than the people who are already loyal to your brand?

But Starbucks isn't just thinking about individual customers; they're banking on the power of social influence. When you return to the office with your coupon, you're likely to mention to your coworkers that you'll be heading back to Starbucks later after lunch to try their new caramel vanilla swirl iced coffee. Suddenly, your two-dollar coupon turns into a group outing.

What Starbucks has done here is shift the focus from repeat customers to repeat purchases. Not only are they building a community of loyal customers, they're actively driving more consumption.

## Not Just Points and Prizes

Starbucks, the airlines, and other big businesses with loyalty programs are focusing on a measurable outcome: repeat purchases. In doing so, they are able to make profit-oriented tradeoffs on investing in their programs. At its core, these businesses are offering customers an incentive to choose their otherwise undifferentiated product over that of their competitors. It's designed for the customer to see each purchase as an investment that they can redeem in the future. The catch, of course, is that the investment can only be cashed in with the same business.

But points and miles aren't the only way companies create these relationship-specific investments. Take Sam's Club and Costco, for example. They require customers to purchase a membership to access their discounts. Buying in bulk often becomes the best way to save more than the membership costs. Amazon employs a similar strategy with Prime. Once customers have paid that annual fee, they're much more likely to default to Amazon for their online shopping needs.

The basic principle behind these loyalty programs is that through their points, they make the customer's investment tangible. Every point earned, every mile flown, and every bulk purchase made reinforces the value of sticking with that brand. It's a constant reminder that your loyalty is paying off.

However, this game isn't just for the big players. While independent operators might not have access to the structured customer data, marketing dollars, and complex software systems that make traditional loyalty programs tick, they're not out of the loyalty-building game. In fact, their size can be an advantage, allowing for more personalized, creative approaches to building and maintaining customer loyalty.

Whether you're a multinational corporation or a corner coffee shop, the principle remains the same: create value for your customers that they can't easily find elsewhere and give them reasons to keep coming back. The tools might differ, but the goal of building lasting customer relationships is universal.

## Relationship-Specific Investments

Airlines share updates and regularly show customers how many miles they've earned. Like all other loyalty point programs, they ensure their customers see how much has been invested in the relationship. But how does a small business without a fancy website and monthly account statements remind its customers of the relationship that they're building?

For some small businesses, just recognizing a customer's face is more than any big business could do. The human brain can generally remember a thousand faces or more. But it's hard to recall how many times someone has visited, what they last ordered, or even just match the right name to that face. For any business that's dealing with more than a handful of customers, relying on memory alone won't cut it. Customer relationship management (CRM) software, or CRM features embedded in another system, would be a good first step.

Whether in memory or in software, having a list and tracking how much your customer has invested in you is a prerequisite for making that investment tangible to them. If you're not awarding points on every purchase, here are a few creative examples I've seen of small businesses making investments tangible:

- **Wearable Progress:** Remember Annette, the dance instructor I mentioned in Chapter 6, who gives her students sew-on patches to represent the different dance styles they've mastered? These visible symbols remind her students of their achievements and are a symbol of their achievements to their peers. It's the same principle behind the color belts used in martial arts.
- **Public Recognition:** At Yakitoriya, I felt valued when I was seated close to the master. But when my friend Farrokh was served with a specially decorated plate, it was clear he was a VIP. Even though I didn't understand the significance of that plate at first, Farrokh knew he had earned some serious bragging rights.
- **Subtle Reminders:** Our dog groomer cleverly uses her CRM software to add a personalized line to her receipts. Ours is: "Grooming Momo since 2018." This simple touch reminds us not only of our long-standing relationship, but also reassures us of Momo's comfort and subtly encourages customers like me to keep bringing her back.
- **Account Balance:** A business broker I know checks his prospect database when sending out annual Christmas cards. In mine one year, he wrote: "On average, my clients look at twenty different businesses before they pull the trigger on the right one. You and I have looked at ten together so far. We're halfway there!" When I asked what he says when the count exceeds twenty, he grinned and said, "I change it to 'You're above average, my friend, but be patient, and we'll find something together.'" It's a clever way of reminding me that all the time spent researching businesses,

attending meetings, and performing due diligence isn't wasted effort. Instead, it's a necessary part of a longer journey that will eventually lead to finding and purchasing the right business.

## Rewards Are Better Than Discounts

The second component of loyalty programs involves offering something valuable that's exclusive to repeat customers. While discounts, free sessions, or complimentary items are common, not every small business can afford to give these away regularly. You can, however, get creative. Your customer-oriented approach means you understand your customers' needs better, especially after working with them over time.

Without sacrificing price or profit margins, you can enhance the experience for your loyal customers in innovative ways. Here are examples of how small businesses have created value through exclusivity and priority treatment:

- **Exclusive Options:** A barbecue joint known for its smoked brisket would sell out of its famous burnt ends within hours after opening each day. They decided to keep it on the weekend menu for newcomers but made it an unlisted special during the week. This way, their regulars could still order the coveted dish while weekday newcomers were none the wiser, creating a sense of exclusivity for loyal customers.
- **Priority Access:** A popular nail salon known for its eye-catching designs often found itself swamped with one-time customers booking for special occasions. They solved this by requiring new customers to book their appointments months in advance. For their loyal regulars, however, the salon kept a few slots open and even provided a separate phone number for last-minute bookings,

ensuring their most valued customers always had access to their services.

- **Special Choices:** A lawncare provider offering a weekly or biweekly service was consistently adding two or three new customers to his customer base each month. He assigned each customer a day of the week to balance the workload among his two-man teams. While new customers didn't get to choose their service day, he accommodated their preference for morning or afternoon service. His longer-term customers, however, always got their preferred time and could request to move their service day, rewarding their loyalty with added flexibility.

While these incentives are great for encouraging repeat business and word-of-mouth recommendations, they don't automatically translate into emotional loyalty. Consider frequent flyer programs: I might consistently choose to fly with a certain airline, but it's solely for the points. It doesn't mean I'm emotionally invested in or will ever advocate for that airline. My relationship with them remains purely transactional.

To move beyond these transactional relationships and build genuine connections, businesses need to focus on earning their customers' trust.

## Trust: A Two-Way Street

During my time in Asia, I developed a deep appreciation for the power of relationships in sales. While relationships matter in all aspects of business everywhere in the world, as an inexperienced engineer, I initially struggled to understand how simply showing up once a month to share a few beers and sing karaoke with a potential client could eventually lead to them spending a million dollars on my software. Yet, beer and karaoke turned out to be the common thread in every success I experienced in Japan. What started as confusing cultural practices became valuable lessons about trust-building that would shape my entire approach to business relationships.

Anyone with experience in sales will tell you that trust is a key ingredient in winning over a customer. Trust with vendors, staff, and other stakeholders is equally critical for any meaningful accomplishment. Pretty much every notable success I've had in my career was due to having built trust in an important relationship. Conversely, a lack of trust contributed to some of my failures.

Early in my career, I thought that building trust was about showing people what I was capable of and proving I could get the job done. After one particularly painful failure, Nick, a good friend and fellow partner at McKinsey, helped me understand what went wrong, giving me a whole new perspective on trust in the process. Here's what led up to that discussion.

As a new partner in McKinsey's Silicon Valley office, working with businesses that had never used McKinsey before, I felt I had to prove that on any given topic I was the most knowledgeable and capable person they'd met. In this particular lost opportunity, I believed I had accomplished just that, but the client still chose a competing firm because he trusted that firm's partner more than me, even though my experience and insight made me well suited to address his needs. I described in detail to Nick each of my meetings and all the effort I took to get to know my client.

"I thought we had done a great job with our meetings and proposals," I said. "I took his team for dinner, and we even got his secretary a gift for setting up our roundtable sessions," I explained. "In fact, over that same dinner, he acknowledged that we had the smartest and most capable team he'd met. Why would he choose to work with someone else on this important problem? Could it be that I didn't build enough trust with him?"

Nick smiled. "Well, trust isn't just about dinners and gifts."

"Are you saying there's more to it?" I asked, feeling somewhat confused. "Should I have learned a secret handshake?"

Nick chuckled. "Not exactly, but you're close. You're missing one critical component of trust: intimacy."

"Intimacy?" I echoed, half-joking. "Are we still talking about business here?"

He laughed. "Yes, we are. Trust has components, and intimacy is a key one."

"Wait, trust has components?" I asked.

"Yes," he said, taking on the tone of a professor explaining a scientific equation. "There are four components, and understanding how they combine is what really matters."

## The Trust Equation

Nick, eager to help me grow as a partner, gave me a copy of David Maister's book *The Trusted Advisor*. Maister's work introduces a formula that breaks down trustworthiness in professional relationships. The equation goes like this: Trustworthiness equals the product of credibility, reliability, and intimacy, divided by self-orientation (or interest).

$$\text{TRUST} = \frac{\text{C} \quad\quad \text{R} \quad\quad \text{I}}{\text{S}}$$

**C** — CREDIBILITY — THEY KNOW THEIR STUFF
**R** — RELIABILITY — THEY ALWAYS DELIVER
**I** — INTIMACY — I FEEL SAFE WITH THEM
**S** — SELF-ORIENTATION — THEY'RE FOCUSED ON MY NEEDS, NOT THEIRS

Let's unpack each piece of this formula to see how it played out in my lost opportunity:

**SELF-ORIENTATION:** This is about how much you're in it for yourself versus the other person. The more self-oriented you are, the less trustworthy you seem. Salespeople have a colorful term for this: commission breath.

In my case, I was careful not to come across as too pushy or self-serving in this situation. Our proposal centered on the client's needs, showing that I was fully committed to helping them succeed. By all accounts, they seemed to get that.

**CREDIBILITY:** This is all about whether people see you as believable and that you are capable of doing the things that you say you can do. In other words, can you walk the talk?

With this prospective client, I had hammered home my expertise and track record. They knew the McKinsey brand and its reputation, and they had access to industry references to back us up. I figured I'd nailed this in nearly every interaction.

**RELIABILITY:** This is all about consistency. Can your clients count on you to follow through every single time?

I showed up punctually, maintained professionalism, and responded promptly with useful information or tweaks to our approach. I figured I'd proved I was dependable, available, and engaged.

**INTIMACY:** Here's where it gets personal. It's about being open, understanding, and even vulnerable with the people you are trying to impress.

This is where I missed the mark. My prospective client had never finished college and had built a business that the big players had ignored for years. I waltzed into his offices with my MBA, representing a firm known for catering to industry giants. Whatever preconceived notions he might have had about know-it-all McKinsey partners, I confirmed by harping on about my credentials.

Nick's key takeaway from applying Maister's formula to me was that if any of the top three factors—credibility, reliability, or intimacy—are missing, you can kiss trust goodbye. I failed to open up about myself or show even a hint of vulnerability. To my lost client, we might as well have been from different planets. In retrospect, it was easy to see why he didn't feel comfortable choosing me as a partner despite all my experience and insights. Instead of coming across as smart and thoughtful, I probably seemed arrogant and aloof.

That message hit home hard, forcing me to reassess my entire approach to building client relationships.

## *Takoyaki* Roulette and Sake Bombs

While reading Maister's book, I evaluated many of my career experiences, including my days in Japan, through the lens of the trust equation. I thought about how each component of the formula played a role in building the trust necessary to close deals, win over teammates, and deliver on projects.

Take my experience with Takara Standard, the company that manufactures customized bathrooms and kitchens under their brand System Kitchen, which I recounted in Chapter 2. Those late nights of sake bombs and karaoke weren't just about having fun, they were about breaking down walls and challenging preconceived notions about one another.

The term "intimacy" in Maister's equation might raise eyebrows, but in this context, it's really about finding common ground. I realized that when the Takara team fired off personal questions, and I played along, we weren't just making small talk—we were building a foundation of trust. They were looking for common ground, and we found it together over pitchers of beer and plates of *takoyaki*.

Now, you might wonder why this matters to a small business owner. When it comes to advocacy and retention, small businesses can leverage their unique positioning, proximity, and purpose to build trust in ways that bigger businesses often struggle to match. Here's how:

**POSITIONING:** As a small business, you can build more credible relationships with your customers through a clear market focus and differentiation. These often go hand in hand. For instance, imagine a motor mechanic who specializes in vintage models. Their tightly defined market (vintage car owners) and clear differentiation (expertise in older vehicles) make their skills more relevant and believable to their specific customers than a general auto shop. A smaller customer base also allows you to be more available and responsive. These aspects of reliability are critical for cultivating customer loyalty.

**PROXIMITY:** Big businesses often struggle to connect on a personal level. As a small business owner, you have the unique opportunity to share more of yourself and learn more about your customers in return. This personal touch can build a level of trust that larger corporations simply can't match.

**PURPOSE:** While big business decisions tend to be transparently based on profit, small businesses can afford to come across as much less self-oriented and more mission-driven. When you openly share your passion and purpose, customers see beyond the profit motive. This authenticity often resonates more deeply than any corporate mission statement.

## From Trust to Advocacy

Building trust with prospects provides benefits far beyond closing deals. I've always coached my sales teams to develop this trust before making "the ask." When a prospect trusts you, they're more likely to be candid about why they might not be ready to commit. This foundation of trust also opens the door for other asks. And when handled well, even these requests can strengthen the relationship.

To illustrate this, let me share a story about Mike, a body shop owner who discovered the power of trust in gathering online reviews.

A distracted driver, a red light, and Crystal's crumpled front bumper brought me to Mike's door. We needed a body shop, and, with several in the area, I suggested she check their Yelp reviews first.

"If they're not at least 3.5 stars, keep looking," I said, thinking about one of the things I learned at ForwardLine. Our underwriters had seen too many fly-by-night body shops come and go. Poor reviews often signaled deeper problems.

Mike's shop had a 4.9-star rating. His customers filled the review pages with detailed stories about their experiences, describing how he'd guided them through stressful situations with patience and understanding. With reviews like these, visiting his shop was an easy choice.

After he finished walking us through the repair estimate, I asked Mike what made his shop stand out. His response came without hesitation: "My customers."

Like many small business owners, Mike understood that reviews could make or break his business. He'd started with the usual approach: a sign in his waiting room asking customers to share their experience online. It brought in two or three new customers each month, which helped offset the occasional negative review from prospects who questioned his pricing.

Then, the landscape changed. Insurance companies became more sophisticated in steering customers toward their preferred repair shops. While California law prevented them from directly pushing customers away from independent shops like Mike's, they could truthfully state that their preferred shops could provide authorized quotes while independents could not. This simple statement was enough to plant seeds of doubt.

Mike watched with growing frustration as his negative reviews began echoing the insurance companies' doubts about independent shops. Potential customers who balked at his quotes would leave reviews questioning his pricing, repeating the same concerns the insurance companies had planted. When these negative reviews started gaining prominence, he knew he needed a better strategy. He began by explicitly asking for reviews when customers picked up their vehicles. While this brought some improvements, the timing wasn't ideal. Many customers, eager to get back to their day, would drive off the lot with good intentions but never follow through. Despite matching the preferred shops in cost, and often exceeding them in efficiency, Mike's business continued to suffer.

The breakthrough came when Mike began taking the issue personally. He started appealing to his customers during the initial quote, sharing openly about his challenges with online reviews. He explained how his actual customers gave him five-star reviews, while his negative reviews came from people who had never stepped foot inside his shop. He would conclude these conversations with, "If you choose me, I promise you'll agree with those five-star reviews. And after I deliver for you, you'll promise me that you'll write me another one."

The results were impressive. By opening up to his customers, Mike was building trust from the very first interaction. Then, by following through with accurate cost estimates and delivering quality work on schedule, he proved both his credibility and reliability. The combination, together with the intimacy he'd established early on, created a strong foundation of trust. By the time he asked for a review, customers were not only willing but eager to help. His review count skyrocketed, and his rating climbed to 4.9 stars.

Sharing your personal story or business challenges with your customers can feel a little risky; after all, it might make them question your stability or competence. Understanding the trust equation will help you recognize where to improve your credibility, how to better demonstrate your reliability, when to increase your intimacy, and what you have to do to reduce self-orientation. The trust you build as a small business owner is your most valuable asset. It opens doors to all sorts of asks, from closing the deal to referrals to repeat business. It took me years of observing successful small businesses to understand not just how they built trust but how they actively used it to grow.

Every repair at Mike's shop reinforced his purpose—showing that independent shops could outperform the corporate "preferred" networks. Though most would never need another repair, they wanted his shop to survive. Each review they wrote helped ensure other drivers would find their way to his door rather than settling for the insurance companies' choices. Your customers will do the same for you when they connect with the deeper purpose behind your business, and you're not afraid to ask for their support.

## Owning Your Customers

Not every business owner needs to create a loyal customer base, but most understand that repeat customers make business better. The work takes less effort to win, offers better margins, and, in general, flows more smoothly due to the shared history. It can also be more personally rewarding.

From a purely economic standpoint, repeat customers should be more profitable since you don't need to spend as much to acquire them. They've already completed their journey with you once and value what you offer.

Some small businesses, however, have grown dependent on third-party services to find their customers, paying substantial fees or commissions in the process. If your business relies on these platforms for most of your work, you're probably well aware of the costs involved. These platforms offer three main services: marketing your business to potential customers, facilitating secure transactions, and providing some level of mediation if things go south. While these aren't low-value services, the associated fees can significantly eat into your profits.

Online brokers, lead aggregators, service marketplaces, or food delivery sites might justify their fees for first-time customers by doing the work of finding and educating prospects. The problem is, with many of these services, you pay the same acquisition cost for a loyal customer as you do for a new one. Once you've proven your value directly to your customer, continuing to pay these fees feels like throwing money away.

Even worse, these services can hijack your customer relationships. Take restaurants using Postmates or DoorDash. What seems like a quick way to increase your orders and grow your customer base can backfire when regular customers who used to order from you directly switch to using the app. Suddenly, you're losing a big chunk of each sale to platform fees, even from customers who would have ordered from you anyway.

So, how do you get people to come back to you directly, if not the first time, then the next time? Small businesses face increasing challenges as they compete with larger platforms for their own customers. While these platforms may spend more on attracting attention, they haven't built any trust or personal connection with their customers.

Bringing a customer back isn't about convincing them to need you again; it's about being the first business they think of when that need arises and making it easy for them to find you. Restaurants provide a perfect example of this principle in action. If you're a restaurant owner making use of online delivery platforms, it's important that you actively manage your online strategy. Without proper management, you can watch your margins be cut in half, or worse. The solution isn't avoiding delivery platforms entirely but rather building your own direct channel to customers. This means investing in your own website with an integrated ordering system and then making sure customers can easily find it. Your web address should be on every receipt, menu, and takeout container. Your social media profiles should link directly to your ordering page. And when customers Google your restaurant's name, your website, not a delivery platform, should be the first result they see. Without this infrastructure, your regular customers might default to services that add little value while consuming up to 15 percent of your revenue.

Staying top of mind is especially challenging in competitive marketplaces, where client relationships often feel fleeting. Yet, even in these environments, you can transform one-off gigs into lasting connections by focusing on delivering value and building trust.

## One-Off Gigs to Trusted Relationships

In today's digital world, you can get almost any job done online. Whether it's creating a piece of art, writing code, developing marketing materials, or even getting consulting advice, you don't need to shake hands or even know the real name of the person you're hiring. These independent contractors are often referred to as gig workers. They are freelancers who take on temporary jobs, usually in the service sector.

A few years ago, I decided to give my executive team a special end-of-year gift. My idea was to commission a personalized cartoon that would capture how our team had overcome a particularly challenging year. I wasn't looking for a Rembrandt, but I wanted something meaningful.

I turned to Fiverr, an online marketplace for freelance services. Like other platforms, Fiverr displays the usual trust signals, including five-star ratings for credibility and job completion numbers for reliability. But these metrics only tell part of the story. It's hard to trust someone to get your vision right when all you have is their screen name and a few data points.

After browsing through several portfolios, I narrowed my search to three artists. I sent each one a brief, but one in particular, an artist in India going by the screen name Mazzi888, stood out immediately. She responded with a flurry of questions, showing genuine curiosity about why I wanted this artwork. Her enthusiasm for the project won me over. Here was someone really trying to understand what I wanted to achieve.

Over the next two weeks, Mazzi888 and I exchanged messages through Fiverr's system. Half the conversations weren't even about the artwork. We discussed my teammates and shared stories about working with large teams. When she delivered the final piece, complete with thought bubbles and quotes, it was exactly what I'd hoped for. And all for just $125.

The artwork arrived as a zip file through Fiverr's portal, along with a feedback questionnaire on her letterhead. I filled it out and emailed it back. This was our first direct communication outside the Fiverr platform. She responded the following day, saying she'd enjoyed the project and asked if she could add me to her mailing list for future work.

Her response piqued my curiosity. When I asked what prompted her to reach out directly, Mazzi888 explained that she only did this with clients she enjoyed working with and saw potential for repeat work. The term "repeat work" stuck with me.

When I asked her how lucrative working through Fiverr was, she told me that while the platform helped her find new customers, it took a substantial cut of her earnings. Of the $125 I paid, Mazzi888 received just $70, and this was for twelve hours of work. Even in Mumbai, where she lived, making just over $5 an hour wasn't sustainable.

Mazzi888 had figured out how to use platforms like Fiverr and Upwork strategically. She'd accept work that earned her a small margin but connected her with clients who appreciated her work and with whom she enjoyed working. By getting to know her clients more personally, she invested in the intimacy that's required for building trust—trust that she could then confidently leverage to move relationships off-platform, where she could earn more while offering better rates to her clients.

This approach has paid off. She's largely moved away from Fiverr, growing her business through direct connections and referrals. She still keeps in touch, sending two or three emails a year asking if I need any work done. If I want to unsubscribe, I can, and she's lost nothing. But she's built a list of people who know her work and might need her services again.

Mazzi888's story is not unique to freelancers. The principles of building direct client relationships and reducing platform dependency apply across many industries. To see how this plays out in a different context, let's look at the highly competitive trucking industry.

## Trust in Trucking

Many business owners who operate in marketplaces where suppliers look alike believe they have little control over customer loyalty. What they may not realize is that by investing in developing trust, they can gain some control over the consistency of the demand for their services. Building deeper relationships with select buyers gives them access to steady work and opportunities outside the marketplace where competition is less intense or where they can charge for additional services and value that are not typically offered in the primary marketplace.

The trucking industry operates in an equally competitive but sometimes less transparent marketplace than the gig economy. Think of it as the offline version of getting off-platform.

The trucking industry connects shippers (companies with goods to move) with carriers (trucking companies or independent truckers who handle the transportation) through a complex web of relationships. Owner-operators have several avenues for finding work: They can sign up with brokers to hear about jobs, or they can check load boards (online marketplaces where shipping companies post available jobs). Most experienced truckers will tell you that these middlemen offer a quick way to stay busy but no way to make a sustained living.

In the trucking world, without direct relationships, most of your work comes through load boards or brokers. These arms-length tools play an indispensable matchmaking role, connecting a vast market of carriers with lots of potential jobs from shippers. In today's logistics landscape, owner-operators can't ignore them entirely.

Traditionally, brokers succeed at matchmaking by leveraging great information systems, solid relationships with shippers, and a network of reliable carriers. They work closely with shippers to negotiate the best rates and ensure that the carriers selected are capable of delivering on time. Often, brokers hunt for the cheapest option or dictate prices to the truckers they select, leaving these business owners in a challenging position with limited control over their rates and job selection. If you're just another name on a broker's list, you'll end up competing for low-rate jobs.

Load boards have digitized what brokers traditionally did, making the marketplace even more commoditized. These platforms put even more emphasis on rates when determining who gets the job. With more shippers participating and a wider carrier network, truckers taking jobs from load boards often end up working with shippers once and never seeing them again.

Truckers wanting to earn enough revenue to maintain their vehicles, pay their bills, make a living, and possibly grow their business or take time off occasionally need something more—they need relationships. The question is: How do you transform from being just an ID number in a spreadsheet or a screen name on a load board into a trusted partner with shippers or brokers who look out for your interests?

It turns out that brokers understand value beyond rates, and they carefully track which truckers they can trust. They maintain detailed internal data about their carriers. When they monitor commercial driver's license (CDL) expirations, renewals, and business license statuses, they're measuring credibility. By keeping detailed records of things like miles driven, adherence to schedule, or even how courteous they are with their shipping partners, they have a measure of reliability. These aren't visible ratings on a website, but they carry as much weight as public ratings in the gig economy.

While not as transparent as the ratings on gig platforms, these internal evaluations work like a hidden five-star system. Smart truckers who recognize the importance of these ratings and work hard to perform well and build solid relationships with brokers are more likely to receive high ratings, leading to more job opportunities and potentially better rates.

But are credibility and reliability enough? Without a personal relationship, you're still just an ID number or a screen name. Most truckers get off-platform through the people they deal with directly at the shipping companies or brokers. By taking repeat work with a shipper over time, you get to know the right people and can build the personal relationships that enhance your reputation for being reliable and on time.

A shipper who trusts you will try to keep you busy, offering steady work through direct contracts. In the highly cost-sensitive world of logistics, shippers rarely pay premium rates just for peace of mind. However, they often reward trusted carriers in other ways, like assigning more favorable routes with better road conditions, less challenging terrain, or more desirable cargo. Like in the gig economy, truckers with high internal ratings have more perceived value to dispatchers and clients.

While building trust directly with shippers may not necessarily translate to higher rates, it gives you the power to choose more profitable and attractive jobs, ultimately improving your bottom line. This mirrors what we saw with Mazzi888 in the gig economy. Just as highly rated gig workers can choose to take on more work rather than raise prices, truckers with strong reputations can opt for more frequent or more lucrative jobs instead of increasing their rates.

Even though trucking might seem like a simple "move goods from A to B" business, having that hidden high score can make a real difference, providing a measure of security, stability, and flexibility in a highly commoditized industry. For truckers looking to do more than just get by, investing in these relationships is how you stay ahead in the game. By focusing on the key components of trust—credibility, reliability, and intimacy—you can set yourself apart in a competitive marketplace and gain access to better opportunities.

## The Uber Driver Who Drove Off the App

During a trip to Dallas, I caught an early-morning Uber to the airport with a driver named Jerry. As we set off, I noticed how well-kept the car was and how professionally he presented himself. With a warm smile and a confident air, Jerry greeted me and confirmed my destination before smoothly merging into the early-morning traffic.

I asked him about his favorite shifts, my go-to icebreaker with drivers. His reply caught me off guard. He mentioned that after dropping me off, he planned to go offline to pick up a private client. Curious, I asked him to elaborate. Jerry told me about a small group of clients who booked him directly without going through the Uber app. Most of these clients were business travelers who appreciated a clean car and a driver who was reliable and punctual. By working with him directly, they knew exactly what they were getting every time they needed a ride to or from the airport.

I was impressed and asked Jerry how he built his private client list. He explained that during his Uber rides, he would casually ask passengers about how often they traveled. If someone turned out to be a frequent flyer, he'd offer his personal contact details, inviting them to reach out to him directly the next time they needed a ride.

The reliability and credibility he established during that first ride were qualities that set him apart from other drivers in the competitive ride-sharing market. Jerry understood that many business travelers had experienced disappointing Uber rides and preferred a reliable driver they could trust over what amounts to a roll of the dice with traditional ride-share assignments. During his airport runs, he could sense which passengers appreciated good conversation and might value having a personal driver for their trips. The best part, he confided, was that even though the cost of the fare remained the same for the customer, he got to pocket a much larger share by eliminating Uber's fees from the equation.

Although Jerry's private client base was small and most of his earnings still came from Uber, the way he was acquiring new clients was organic and resourceful. Instead of investing in marketing, he tapped into his existing pool of Uber-sourced customers, identifying those who might benefit from his personalized service. By cutting out the middleman and managing his own repeat customer list, he was reducing his reliance on Uber and building his own microbusiness within the larger ecosystem of app-based ride-sharing apps.

Every small business should at least understand the value of a direct relationship with their customers. It's worth exploring ways to go off-platform with your best customers and building your own customer list. Direct relationships can offer a number of possible benefits:

- You can choose who you work with and focus on clients you enjoy serving.
- You keep a larger share of your earnings without platform fees.
- You reduce stress by working with familiar faces rather than a constant stream of strangers.
- You cut down on the unpredictability that often comes with platform-based work.

Moving off-platform can be tricky, though. Many platforms have strict rules against soliciting clients directly, and violating those rules can result in getting banned. While the bigger platforms use sophisticated software and have big marketing budgets to capture customers searching for your business online, there are software, services, and tools that can help you take ownership of your relationships, and legitimately too. Website builders like Squarespace and Shopify offer tools for creating your own online presence. Payment processors such as Square and Stripe help manage transactions, while email services like Mailchimp let you maintain customer relationships. The key is to establish these direct channels while respecting platform rules.

## Retention and Advocacy

In this chapter, we've seen how big businesses encourage repeat purchases through loyalty programs that track spending and offer rewards. These programs turn customer spending into points or miles that customers can exchange for real benefits. While these concepts can work at a smaller scale, incentives and rewards alone don't necessarily create genuine connections with customers. When it comes to keeping customers and turning them into advocates, trust matters more than points or rewards.

## Create Your Customer List

Your goal should be to find and nurture a base of customers who'll keep coming back, or if you're relying on partners to refer customers, focus on identifying and building relationships with those who align with your vision. Unlike airlines, which concentrate primarily on their most profitable travelers, small business owners aren't confined to the same model. Your market focus allows you to concentrate on customers who truly appreciate what makes your business special.

Quality matters more than quantity. Build relationships that will help your business grow sustainably. Focus on those who best understand and value your uniqueness. These are the connections worth nurturing.

The way you choose to run your business can draw in customers who share your values. For example, Toshi wants customers who are respectful, who love his food, and who don't question his rules. Mazzi888 identified clients who might need her services again, built trust with those she enjoyed working with, and reached out to them when moving off-platform. Jerry focused on passengers who valued his consistency and conversation, and also tipped well.

Once you've defined your ideal customers, be strategic about building trust with them. It's not about reaching everyone; it's about investing energy in the relationships that matter most.

Managing these relationships at scale often requires the right tools. While there are many options available for small businesses, sometimes specific industries develop their own solutions. Take Wridz, for example, an app-based carpooling platform that launched in Texas in 2022. It's perfect for the business that Jerry was building. Instead of taking a big cut of each fare like traditional platforms, Wridz charges drivers a small monthly subscription fee based on their region. Drivers can invite customers to add them directly, often after they've had a positive experience through a different platform. Customers benefit by curating their own list of trusted drivers, while drivers get to keep 100 percent of their fares and can choose the regions in which they want to work. It's a fresh approach to ride-sharing that allows drivers to earn more while still benefiting from the convenience of an app-based system.

Although Wridz wasn't around when I met Jerry, I hope he's using it now. Perhaps there's a similar tool in your industry that can help you take back ownership of your customer relationships.

## Deepen Your Customer Relationships

Now that you've identified your ideal customers, you can focus on meaningful ways to deepen these relationships that feel authentic to your business. Ask yourself: How can I better serve my customers at each stage of their journey with my business?

Some approaches that can work well for smaller operations might include:

- Exclusive access to special items or services not available to everyone
- Priority scheduling when your time or inventory is limited
- Added flexibility with appointments, orders, or services for your regular customers
- Personal acknowledgment of their continued support

Whether it's throwing in a free coffee, dessert, service upgrade, or offering special pricing, the key is to make your appreciation feel genuine. If you have a referral-based business, think about ways to encourage and reward the continued loyalty of your partners as well. Don't let concerns about profit margins hold you back; focus on retaining the customers and partners who matter most to your business.

## Create a Path to Direct Relationships

Whether you're a trucker, an Uber driver, a restaurant owner using delivery apps like DoorDash or Postmates, or any freelancer working through app-based platforms, relying too heavily on these intermediaries is risky. While they bring in customers, they also take a significant cut of your earnings and can leave you at the mercy of their rules and ratings systems.

Building a sustainable business on platforms like Fiverr and Upwork requires a careful balance between staying competitive and maintaining profitability. Many businesses get caught up in a pricing race to the bottom, feeling pressured to match competitors' rock-bottom prices just to stay busy. But this approach isn't sustainable. By constantly undercutting yourself, you'll end up with a lot of low-paying, one-time clients who don't value your work and are unlikely to become repeat customers.

I'm not suggesting you abandon app-based platforms entirely. They're great for reaching new customers and filling gaps in your schedule.

Instead, use them strategically as a springboard to build something that's truly yours. Be intentional about finding new customers and thoughtful about nurturing relationships with those who understand your value and are willing to pay a fair price for quality work.

Have a plan for bringing these potential long-term customers directly into your business. Whether it's including a feedback form that connects them directly to you or improving your search performance so that they find you before the platform that eats up your profits, make it easy for your loyal customers to work with you directly.

Here are some approaches to consider:

- Know your platform's rules. Many have provisions that let you promote specialized products or services that aren't available through their standard listings. This can create legitimate opportunities to connect directly with customers who want something unique that only you provide.

- Make it easy for customers to find you again by incorporating your contact information naturally into their experience, whether it's slipping a business card into packages, printing your phone number on napkins, or including branded magnets with your web address in shipments.

- Research alternative platforms that might better suit your business model. Some newer platforms (like Wridz for drivers or Shopify for retailers) offer better terms, more flexibility, and more control over your customer relationships.

- Build and maintain a strong web presence that highlights what makes you unique. Ensure your website clearly communicates what sets you apart and makes it easy for customers to book or buy directly from you.

- Take control of your online presence beyond the platforms. Claim and actively manage your profiles on Google, Yelp, and other industry-specific directories, including social media platforms like LinkedIn, Facebook, and Instagram. Regular updates and responses to reviews show potential customers you're engaged and professional.

Remember, even one-time customers can become loyal clients. With each transaction, look for opportunities to build lasting relationships. In a market that increasingly tries to commoditize your offering, the trust you build with clients becomes your unique advantage.

THOUGHT STARTERS

- Who are your ideal customers and key relationships, and how might you attract more of them?
- How are you showing these customers that you value them? What changes could you make to serve them better?
- What are you doing to encourage your customers to return to or advocate for your business?
- To build stronger client trust, which aspects of the trust equation need your attention: credibility, reliability, intimacy, or self-orientation?

## CHAPTER EIGHT
# WOULD YOU LIKE FRIES WITH THAT?

### Lessons in Culture

In January 2020, that last normal month before masks became everyone's new favorite accessory, I found myself hunched over, hands on my knees, sweat dripping onto the floor of a martial arts studio in Los Angeles. Next to me, my friend George was doing the same, both of us trying to catch our breath after a particularly demanding training session.

We were preparing for an upcoming Chinese New Year show, rehearsing a choreographed combat scene where I wielded a staff while George brandished a *dao*, a thin, flexible sword that, despite being a prop, was sharp enough to draw his blood once during practice. Our master, Hu Jianqiang, had performed alongside Jet Li in the 1980s film *Shaolin Temple*, the first martial arts movie ever filmed within the temple's ancient walls, and was now a legendary figure in the sport of wushu. He watched us with growing frustration.

"You guys look like old men up there," he called out. "You need to be more fierce and go a lot faster!"

George wiped his forehead with his sleeve and shot back, "But we ARE old men!" We both chuckled, though the truth stung a bit. Six years of training, and we were still moving like creaky garage doors.

We'd met at Master Hu's Shaolin Wushu Center years ago. We were two middle-aged dads whose kids were taking classes, and we decided maybe we should get some exercise too. Somehow, we'd earned our black belts along the way, and our wives had gotten used to their Tuesday and Thursday nights of peace and quiet.

In an attempt to change the subject from our less-than-impressive performance, I asked George if he was planning to join Master Hu's upcoming group trip to China. We'd traveled there together before, discovering both the roots of our practice and the strength of our studio community. I was particularly excited about this trip's itinerary. We'd be walking those same temple grounds where Master Hu had helped make history. For his students to explore this sacred place with him would be something special.

"Not this time," George said, straightening up and adjusting his grip on the *dao*. "Don't get me wrong, I'm sure the trip will be amazing for whoever goes, but lately, it feels like everything's becoming a sales pitch."

"What do you mean?" I asked.

"Well, this is a martial arts studio, right? I'm here to get a workout and learn this craft, but there's always something else to buy: trips to China, special workshops, branded gear . . ."

"But George, every 'extra' you've taken Master Hu up on has made you a better martial artist. Look what that workshop did for your technique last fall. His offerings have never felt like a hard sell to me. Everything he does comes from wanting to share wushu with his students as fully as possible," I said.

"I know he isn't just trying to make an extra buck," George sighed. "It's not even about Master Hu. I'm actually feeling the pressure to sell more in my own business. Every month, there's another sales rep at my door with some new dental product they want me to push on my patients. My colleagues are all adding spa services, cosmetic procedures, anything to boost their margins. Everyone keeps telling me I should do the same." He shook his head. "But that kind of aggressive sales mentality just isn't me."

"But don't you offer any additional services?" I asked. "Teeth whitening, at least?"

George cut me off with a wave of his hand. "I'm not running some McDonald's franchise trying to supersize your meal. Offering extra products and services might work for Master Hu's studio, but I'm not there to sell. My goal is to provide great care, not to squeeze every penny out of my patients."

George and Master Hu couldn't have been more different in their approach to business. Where George shunned any form of upselling in his dental practice, Master Hu embraced it. As a cultural icon and ambassador for the sport, everything he offered was carefully chosen to help his students develop a deeper connection to the ancient art of wushu.

The group trip to China he'd planned for the summer of 2020 had everything to do with sharing his life's passion, passing down centuries of tradition he'd lived and breathed since his early days in film. The trip cost about what you'd spend on a Disney vacation, putting it out of reach for some students, but it was just one of the ways Master Hu enriched our experience at the studio.

## UNCONVENTION

The studio offered a broad set of other services and products that went beyond his core offering. For his students, none of it ever felt like being sold to; everything Master Hu offered simply flowed from his role as a keeper of wushu tradition. Besides the regular branded gear that one would find at other martial arts schools, he used his connections in China to source traditional silk uniforms and premium wushu weapons, items you wouldn't find at online stores like Kung Fu Direct.

For students interested in the world of competitive wushu, he regularly brought in guest instructors, including China's reigning national wushu champion, Yu Te. I remember taking that class and watching Yu Te demonstrate a 720-degree tornado kick, a move I still can't come close to matching, but more importantly, I learned how to train like a national champion.

Throughout the year, the studio hosted events that would strengthen our connection with wushu culture. We had an annual tournament where students from across Southern California came to test their skills. The center also put on shows at the studio, at local schools, and at cultural festivals. And then there was our much-anticipated annual Chinese New Year celebration. It was for the 2020 celebration, a few short months before we left for China, that I was inspired to learn and perform my first choreographed form.

As we packed up our gear back in the training hall that day, I couldn't stop thinking about how triggered George was about selling anything beyond basic dental care in his practice. Here was my friend—my dentist and my sparring partner—taking such a principled stand against something I saw as a natural extension of any business. His McDonald's comment, however, got me thinking. Because the thing is, McDonald's knows exactly what it's doing when it offers you more than what you came for.

## Supersizing Your Business

Let's travel back to the summer of 1987. You're at McDonald's, ordering a Big Mac. "The combo meal, right?" the cashier asks. Before you can process the question, they add, "Would you like that supersized?" For just a dollar more, you could get a lot more fries and nearly double the drink size. What a fantastic deal, you think—a significantly larger portion for a relatively small price increase. Why not?

What started as a short-term summer promotion lasted over twenty-five years. The larger size was a hit, and while the price difference was small, it was almost pure profit. McDonald's finally discontinued supersizing in 2004, claiming customers had lost interest, but by then the term had become synonymous with upselling—offering an upgraded version of what you're already buying.

Then there's the other famous McDonald's question: "Would you like fries with that?" This is cross-selling—suggesting a complementary product to go with your burger. They're not asking you these questions because they think you look hungry; it's how they get you to spend more.

Think about the last time you dined at a sit-down restaurant. After taking your order, did the waiter ask if you'd like to start with drinks or appetizers? There's a good chance they did. And it's not because they were concerned that you might be dying of thirst; it's a script they've rehearsed with one goal in mind: to maximize the value of your visit.

To understand why this matters so much, let's break down the economics of a typical fast-food transaction. McDonald's, like many businesses, faces what economists call "sunk costs"—money they've already spent before a customer even places an order. These are a few of the expenses that need to be recouped:

- **Fixed costs:** These include expenses like rent, utilities, and equipment—costs that remain the same whether the restaurant is open or not and whether they serve one customer or a thousand.
- **Marketing costs:** This is what is spent on advertising, promotion, signage, and other campaigns to bring customers in. It's what we discussed in Chapter 6 as the customer acquisition cost (CAC).
- **Labor costs:** This covers the wages of employees opening the store, prepping the kitchen, taking orders, and handling transactions. All of these happen regardless of how much food they'll be preparing.

Let's say these costs add up to about five dollars per customer to bring them into the store and take their order. A six-dollar meal deal barely covers these expenses, let alone the cost of ingredients and labor. A restaurant relying only on small orders like this would struggle to make a profit. Given these sunk costs, it makes sense to maximize the value of each transaction. If you're going to spend time dealing with a customer, why not try to make that order as large as possible? Even if it means the line moves a bit slower, the increased order size can more than make up for it.

This is why you'll often see promotions like dollar menus or discounted items. These are called loss leaders—products sold at minimal profit, or sometimes at a loss, to attract customers. They might not make money on their own, but they bring customers through the door. It's the first step in a broader strategy: First attract customers with an appealing basic offering, then increase the value of their visit through upselling and cross-selling. That one-dollar soft serve can quickly turn into a five- or six-dollar transaction.

And while McDonald's might be the most familiar example, these strategies extend far beyond fast food. Let's look at how they work in a completely different industry.

## More Wallet in Wealth Management

While McDonald's asks, "Would you like fries with that?" wealth management companies have their own version of upselling. Instead of upgrading meal sizes, they're looking to expand their clients' portfolios.

Certified financial planners (CFPs) traditionally deal with stocks, bonds, and other publicly traded securities. Their goal is to grow their clients' net worth and prepare them for retirement. The economics are simple: The more assets they manage, the more they earn. It's a direct incentive to maximize the value of each client relationship.

I saw this strategy at work when consulting with Katherine's firm. She and her partners had left the wealth management division of a major bank to build their own practice. Katherine had strong opinions about everything, especially business growth.

"These days, our clients own more than just traditional investments like stocks and bonds," Katherine explained. "They've got Bitcoin, real estate, privately traded businesses—a whole range of assets," she continued. "But we're not interested in just managing what they already have. We're thinking bigger. We want to open doors for other clients to make similar investments."

"So what you're saying is that you want a bigger share of wallet from your clients?" I asked.

"Call it what you want," she said. "Does it matter what the asset is as long as we're managing it with our client's overall needs in mind? This is about expanding our service offering. It just so happens that it also means we're managing more of their wealth."

"We've found platforms that package alternative investments into smaller shares," Katherine explained. "It means we can take a major real estate project or a crypto fund and break it into pieces that our regular clients can afford."

She pulled up some numbers on her screen. "Look at what this means; it's not just about managing more assets. We would be bringing investment opportunities to people who couldn't access them before. Our clients who previously couldn't afford to invest in commercial real estate can now buy a small slice of a larger property. Instead of needing millions to invest in a building, they can participate with as little as five or ten thousand."

The projections confirmed what Katherine was saying: These fractional investments would transform their business. By diversifying their offerings and attracting a broader client base, they could significantly expand their assets under management. They'd move beyond just serving wealthy clients to making high-end investment opportunities accessible to a much wider market—their ultimate goal.

In the end, whether you're selling burgers or managing millions, the principle is the same. You've got the customer's attention, whether they're sitting across your desk or standing at a counter. Not all their money is coming to you as the service provider. So, just like McDonald's, these wealth managers are essentially asking their clients, "Would you like to add some alternative investments to your portfolio?" It's their version of "Would you like fries with that?"

While we've seen how this principle applies in industries as diverse as fast food and wealth management, the underlying concept is relevant to businesses of all types and sizes. Whether you're a solo entrepreneur, running a small business, or managing an online store, the question is the same: How can you increase the value of each customer interaction? You've already invested in getting a customer through the door (or onto your website), so you want to make the most of that opportunity.

## Derrick: The Business-Minded Dentist

Sometimes, life has a funny way of bringing people together. As it turns out, George wasn't the first dentist I'd found through martial arts. Years earlier, while living in the Bay Area, lightning had struck for the first time. Like George, Derrick and I met through our kids' martial arts classes. What started as a casual conversation between two dads watching their children train grew into a friendship. Over the years, I found myself not just in his dental chair but also engaged in conversations about his work and his passion for dentistry.

Having two friends who were both dentists and martial artists made for an interesting window into how differently they approach their practices. While George takes a principled stance away from anything that feels like selling, Derrick embraces a broader vision of what dentistry could be. For him, dentistry isn't just about healthcare; it's about building a business. For Derrick, every patient interaction is an opportunity to offer more services, and he's always on the lookout for the next big thing in dental care. From what I can see, his business-first approach is both fulfilling and profitable.

## The Treatment Plan

One thing Derrick is particularly good at is upselling. In the US, it's pretty standard to visit the dentist twice a year for a cleaning and checkup, especially if you have health insurance. Derrick sees these biannual visits as golden opportunities.

Here's how it works: You come in for your routine cleaning with one of Derrick's hygienists. Once they're done, Derrick makes an appearance. But he's not just there for a quick hello. He's got a whole list of extra services he can offer you, such as teeth whitening, corrective procedures, you name it. It's all part of what dentists call a "treatment plan."

Derrick doesn't just pull up these treatment plans at the end of an appointment like some dentists do. Instead, he spends time talking with his patients throughout their visit. "I want them to feel comfortable with me," he explained. "So I open up about myself, and I encourage them to talk about themselves too."

He'll chat with patients about their lives, their work, or their families while they're in the waiting room or as he's prepping for their procedure. It might sound like friendly conversation, but Derrick's being strategic. The more he knows about his patients, the better he can tailor his suggestions.

Then, he'll smoothly transition into mentioning additional services that might interest them based on what he's learned. "Would this be something you'd like?" he might ask, seamlessly weaving potential treatments into the conversation. It's a subtle way of personalizing his upselling approach, making it feel natural and considerate rather than pushy.

## Pushing Boundaries

Lately, dentists have started branching out into more interesting areas. Traditionally, dentists have used Botox for specific dental procedures, like managing teeth grinding, because it helps relax the jaw muscles. Now, some are considering offering it purely for cosmetic treatments. Derrick had been mulling over this trend.

"I could do more to promote Botox," he told me one day. "Imagine the conversation with patients: 'Those new veneers look great! You know, a fuller upper lip would really complement them.'"

"Wow," I said. "That's quite a leap from dentistry!"

"There are legitimate dental uses for Botox, like treating a gummy smile," Derrick said. "It's just about starting those conversations. Whether it's Botox or any other service, I'm not pushing anything. Patients make their own decisions. You want them to know what's available. If they're interested, great. If not, there's no pressure. After all, being at the dentist is uncomfortable enough without feeling pushed into a sale," he added with a wink.

Derrick also shared an interesting insight about the economics of these additional services. Many of these treatments, like cosmetic procedures, aren't covered by insurance. This means patients pay full price, which can be more profitable for the practice than routine cleanings. On the flip side, there are important treatments that insurance does cover generously, which patients are often eager to pursue once they know about them.

This approach benefits both Derrick and his patients. By providing just two or three of these services each week, he sees a meaningful increase in his personal income without necessarily increasing his workload. At the same time, patients get access to a wider range of dental and cosmetic services.

## The Natural Promoter

Derrick's influence extends beyond his own practice. He is an active leader in local and state dentistry associations, which puts him at the forefront of the dental community. He's particularly passionate about continuing education, a requirement for all dentists to maintain their licenses.

"We need to get twenty hours of medical education every year," Derrick explained to me. "And you know what? Some of those hours can be spent learning how to sell more services."

This intersection of medical education and business strategy has turned Derrick into something of an evangelist. He regularly shares his business insights with other dentists, whether through casual conversations or formal classes.

"I've developed a cheat sheet," he told me with a grin. "It's got scripted questions to help dentists bring up additional services, even Botox."

Derrick walked me through his teaching approach, showing how he trains other dentists to upsell. "I tell them to start with simple questions about how happy patients are with their smiles," he explained. "Then it's all about listening for the right cues to suggest treatments."

He gave me an example: "If someone mentions their teeth looking a bit yellow, that's your chance to talk about whitening. If they're worried about crooked teeth, it's time to bring up Invisalign."

Derrick's big on reading patients' reactions. "It's not about pushing treatments. It's about spotting needs they might not have mentioned and offering solutions."

Derrick isn't just practicing dentistry, he's building something bigger. Through upselling, Derrick found a way to grow his practice while expanding what dentistry could offer his patients. He's always looking for smart, ethical ways to do this while helping other dentists do the same. He's mastered the art of asking, "Would you like fries with that?" and showing others how it's done.

## Land and Expand

When you've got a customer in front of you, you've already done the hard part. They're there, giving you their time and attention. The question is: What else can you offer them?

Take a hair salon, for example. You've got a captive audience sitting in your chair for an hour or more. Why not offer them professional hair products, accessories, or styling tools? It's surprising how many salons miss this opportunity. After all, you're not just selling a haircut; you're selling a complete hair care experience.

The same principle works for nail salons. Once a customer is in your chair for a manicure, why not introduce them to nail care products, hand creams, or even jewelry? They're already investing in their appearance; they might appreciate knowing about products that extend and enhance their salon experience.

This approach isn't just for service businesses. Whether you're running a bookstore, a pet shop, a café, or an online craft business—or any small business for that matter—every customer interaction is an opportunity to provide more value. The key is offering products or services that naturally complement what your customers already want.

Business strategists call this systematic approach "land and expand." First, land the customer with your core offering, then expand the relationship through upselling and cross-selling. For small business owners, every customer interaction presents an opportunity to build a stronger relationship. Like Derrick in his dental practice, successful business owners understand that getting a customer through the door—landing their business—is just the beginning. The real opportunity lies in growing that relationship over time.

But how do you approach this systematically? How do you build these opportunities into your business in a way that feels natural and serves your customers better?

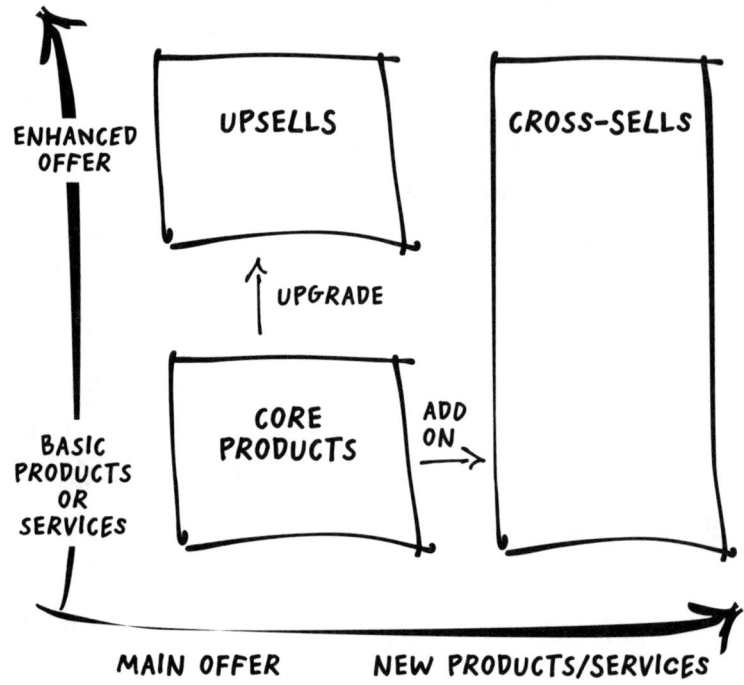

A land-and-expand strategy typically focuses on three key areas:

### CORE SERVICES OR PRODUCTS

This is why customers come to you initially. For Derrick, it's routine dental care. For a hair salon, it's haircuts. For a tax preparer, it's the annual tax return. This is your "land" opportunity—your core business and the main way you show customers the quality you deliver.

### RELATED SERVICES OR PRODUCTS (CROSS-SELLS)

These are natural extensions of your core offering. It's like Derrick suggesting cosmetic dental work during checkups or the tax preparer offering tax planning sessions. These offers might be closely related to your main offering, or they could stretch a bit further, like a dentist offering Botox or the tax preparer offering referrals for financial advisory or estate planning services. Either way, these cross-selling opportunities let you expand into areas that complement your core business.

### PREMIUM OPTIONS (UPSELLS)

These are ways to enhance the basic experience. When a hair salon offers a deep conditioning treatment with a cut, or when a café suggests upgrading to premium beans, they're upselling by adding value to the core service. This is another "expand" strategy—offering customers a way to get more value from their visit.

Earlier, we saw how Master Hu ran his studio. His approach tells us something important about small businesses: They can grow beyond their core offering without it feeling forced, especially when that growth serves a deeper purpose. Master Hu's students embraced his expanded offerings because they felt like natural steps in their journey, not sales tactics. This is what sets small businesses apart. When you're driven by more than profit, expanding your offering becomes a natural extension of your purpose.

## George: The Patient-Focused Dentist

The choreographed fight went well enough that George and I mostly got applause and compliments at the Chinese New Year show at Master Hu's Shaolin Wushu Center. Our celebration and festivities afterward turned out to be one of our last gatherings before the world changed. Within days, China closed its borders, and our trip to visit the Shaolin Temple in Zhengzhou was canceled.

As the pandemic set in and businesses everywhere scrambled to adapt, I wondered how George was handling the financial pressures in his dental practice, especially given how adamant he was about not offering his patients additional services. Months later, when the chaos of lockdowns and mask policies started to subside, Crystal and I invited George, his wife, Shirley, and their kids over for dinner.

"How's business?" I asked, knowing full well that, like many businesses across the country, his practice had taken a beating.

"I'm seeing patients again, and business has picked up nicely," George said. "Although, we're nowhere near our usual numbers. And I'm still waiting for that PPP money to come through."

I shared my take on the PPP and how it was failing businesses like his. I assured him the funding would come through if his paperwork was in order. George just shrugged it off, saying he'd believe it when he saw it. Right now, his focus was simply on keeping his practice running, with or without government help.

Never shying away from controversial topics, I brought up what was really on my mind: the idea of driving more revenue per customer. "Wouldn't offering other services to your patients while you've got them in your chair help you through this period?" I asked.

George put down his chopsticks and gave me that familiar look—the same one he'd given Master Hu when told to speed up our routine months earlier.

"That's not what my patients come to me for," he said. "If someone needs something, I'll tell them. If they want something extra, they can ask."

"But George, if you're not offering additional services, how do you plan to grow your bottom line?"

"Growing my business isn't just about making more money," he replied. "It's about building a stable practice with loyal patients."

He explained that his practice was built on routine care and preventative maintenance. "I make most of my money from cleanings," he said. "It's not the most profitable service, but it's what people need. Shirley likes to call it the low-margin stuff," he said as his wife smiled at him from across the table. "But when patients keep up with their cleanings, they don't need as much extensive work down the line. It's better for them in the long run."

I could see this wasn't just about business strategy anymore; George was getting fired up about something deeper.

"Do you know what people in healthcare management say about preventative care?" he continued. "They say it doesn't make money, that the best margins come from emergencies." George shook his head. "Am I supposed to just let people have dental emergencies so that I make a lot more money? That's not why I became a dentist. I want to prevent those emergencies from happening in the first place. Besides, I've got patients who pay on time, trust me, and recommend me to their friends. That's organic growth right there."

He went on to explain how passionate he was about the quality of his work and that he genuinely empathized with patients who had tight budgets.

"I understand not everyone can afford extensive dental work," George explained. "My job is to provide the best care possible within their means."

He told me about how important it is for him to connect with each of his patients on a personal level. Unlike Derrick, when George talks to his clients, there's no rehearsed script or strategic conversation. He sees those interactions as personal rather than business-oriented.

"How do you think the Niners will do this season?" he might ask a patient. Or, "How's your son adjusting to college life? Is he remembering to brush his teeth?" His approach spoke for itself. His patients loved him, and his practice was always busy, even if it meant working harder for a lower financial reward.

"You know what my best marketing tool is?" George added. "Yelp. We've got tons of positive reviews. I don't even have to ask my satisfied patients to share their experiences online; they just do it."

## Playing the Long Game

I sat back in my chair, took a long swig of my wine, and smiled. I'd been barking up the wrong tree trying to convince George to expand his services. He had a clear vision for how he wanted to run his practice, and he wasn't going to change it for industry trends, or my advice.

"The smartest move I made last year was bringing on a dental hygienist," George said, interrupting my thoughts. "I'd considered partnering with another dentist, but since most of my work is focused on preventative care, a hygienist made more sense. They cost less than another dentist would, and they've allowed me to see more patients."

The decision had paid off exactly as George had hoped. "It was a game changer," he said. "With the hygienist, I could take on more first-time patients without getting overwhelmed. Sure, I might not make as much per patient this way, but I get to do what's important to me—providing good care and regular cleanings."

Initially, George's stubborn refusal to offer more elective procedures didn't add up for me, especially in the face of a monumental business challenge like COVID. But watching him now, seeing his unwavering commitment to his broader purpose, even under all that pressure, I finally understood what made his practice work. He wasn't trying to build the kind of business that gets written about in management books. For George, being a great dentist meant putting patient care above profits. His success came from that commitment, not in spite of it. George's version of success had nothing to do with upselling services, proving that success in business can be measured in more than just dollars and cents.

## Two Paths, One Profession

While George and Derrick couldn't be more different in how they run their practices, they do have one thing in common: They both care about their patients and their work. They've just chosen different ways of going about it. Each has found a way to practice dentistry that aligns with their own broader purpose.

Derrick's not just pulling teeth and filling cavities. He sees himself as a one-stop shop for all things dental, from cleanings to cosmetic work. To him, offering extra services is like doing his patients a favor. He's quite comfortable asking them, "Would you like fries with that?" George, on the other hand, isn't out there trying to make money outside of what he sees as necessary dental care. He's selective about what he recommends, focusing instead on building long-term patient relationships. For him, it comes down to necessity—repairs, crowns, anything directly related to dental health. These aren't optional extras in his mind; they're important for his patients' well-being.

George's commitment to dental health has earned him a loyal customer base that comes in regularly for checkups and cleanings. Thanks to his focus on prevention, his patients' teeth are typically in good health, making those routine visits quick and easy. But this focus on preventive care means sacrificing the higher margins that come with a broader range of services. There are times when George is at the office six days a week, and he's keenly aware that when he's not there, the practice isn't generating income. A family emergency or illness could seriously impact his earnings. Maybe he could work one less day and make the same money by offering more elective procedures, but that's not the kind of dentistry he wants to practice.

Derrick's range of expanded offerings, on the other hand, gives him more flexibility. He can take weekends off and step away when needed. His business continues even when the chairs aren't filled all day long. George's principled approach doesn't offer that kind of security.

I had to admit, I'd been quick to side with Derrick's approach. After all, wasn't his way of doing things exactly what I'd been advocating? But that was the beauty of it; both approaches worked, just differently. What I'd initially dismissed as George's stubbornness was actually something I'd observed in many of the most resilient small businesses I'd studied—a deep connection to purpose. George had unknowingly positioned himself as the "no-frills" dentist, serving a market segment that other dentists weren't actively pursuing—patients who primarily needed regular cleanings and preventative care. He wasn't trying to be everything to everyone. Instead, he'd positioned his practice precisely where he felt he could make the most difference, even adjusting his business model to better serve these patients. Derrick, on the other hand, had taken a different path, but his choices were equally rooted in purpose. He saw dentistry as an opportunity to offer his patients comprehensive care that went beyond basic dental health.

George's decision to restructure his practice around a hygienist rather than another dentist, and Derrick's decision to expand into complementary services, were deliberate changes that allowed each of them to practice dentistry their own way, without compromising their principles. Their stories added another layer to what I was learning about small business success. There's no one-size-fits-all approach to running a successful business, and, as a small business owner, you have the freedom to play by your own rules, not those of big corporations driven by shareholder objectives. In the end, it's about building your business around what matters most to you.

## Expanding Your Offer, Your Way

The choices George and Derrick make about upselling reflect a broader challenge that every business owner faces: How much should you expand beyond your core service? Let's look at another example: your typical annual GP visit. These days, it's not just about checking your blood pressure and your heart rate. Doctors are now asking about hair loss, addictions, and sexual health. It's not the doctor's idea; it's the practice or the hospital system pushing these questions. Why? Because treatments for these issues are profitable. They're not forcing anything on you. But by asking the question, they're opening the door. And let's face it, if someone's worried about hair loss or erectile dysfunction, they might appreciate the opportunity to discuss it, even if they wouldn't have brought it up themselves.

If you're not at least thinking about additional services or products you could offer, you might be leaving money on the table. So, how much upselling and cross-selling should you do? There's no one-size-fits-all answer, but your strategy should be rooted in the three advantages you have as a small business: your positioning, your proximity, and your purpose.

## Finding Complementary Products and Services

Growing your customer relationships not only helps you increase revenue, it also helps you serve your customers better. Think back to Suzy Takacs, whose story I shared in the opening chapter. She combined her passion for wine and books to open The Book Cellar. Her unique offering didn't need to appeal to everyone, it just had to create value for the right customers.

Of course, not every business can build both related products and premium options around their core offering, and that's okay. What matters is that you're bringing genuine value to your customers. When an optician suggests anti-glare coating based on your screen time, or when Derrick recommends a specific toothbrush to a patient with sensitivity issues, they're solving real problems—ones they've identified while working directly with their customers.

As a small business owner, your proximity to your customers can help you quickly discover your own authentic version of "Would you like fries with that?" Here are some questions to guide your thinking:

### What Else Do Your Customers Need?

- What else are your customers trying to accomplish when they visit you?
- What products or services naturally complement your current offerings?
- What related needs might your customers have that you could address?

### What More Could You Offer That Aligns with Your Broader Goals?
- Where are your customers currently going for related products or services?
- How receptive might they be to getting these from you instead?
- What opportunities are you missing by not asking?

### What Are Others Offering?
- What additional products or services are your competitors providing?
- Which of these offerings appeal to your customers?
- How could you offer something similar but better?

## Introducing Your Expanded Offer

Once you've landed your customer and proven your value, growing the relationship becomes easier. Whether through related products or premium services—or both—you need to know when and how to introduce these opportunities. For Derrick, it's during treatment plan discussions. For Katherine and her partners, it's using quarterly reviews to discuss alternative investments.

This is what it looks like in practice:

**Time Your Suggestions:** Choose moments when your customers are most receptive to upsell or cross-sell. For instance, Derrick waits until after a successful cleaning to discuss additional treatments, recommending specific dental products before mentioning optional cosmetic services. A bookstore might suggest a bookmark or a reading light at purchase, then later introduce their premium first editions collection to regular customers who show interest in collecting. A café might pair pastries with coffee orders, saving their premium bean selection for customers who express interest in different flavors. When you time your suggestions strategically but thoughtfully, customers are more likely to be receptive to what you offer.

**Be Authentic:** For your expanded offer to be truly authentic, it must align with your purpose. When these offerings complement your main business goals, you can confidently recommend them to customers. Take Derrick's dental practice: He's seen how cosmetic procedures boost a patient's self-esteem, so he feels confident suggesting dental products and cosmetic work during routine cleanings. When your expanded offerings align with your purpose, the right customers will see their value.

**Build on Your Wins:** Broaden slowly and learn from your customers. Each interaction will reveal what else they might need. Start with natural extensions of your business, like related accessories or premium versions of what you already provide. Master Hu's martial arts studio evolved gradually from cultural events to local tournaments, and, finally, to cultural exchange trips as student interest grew. When customers are happy with your core service, they become more open to new offerings. Each successful addition strengthens the relationship, allowing for new opportunities.

## Tending to Your Business

Whether you choose to expand through upselling or cross-selling, or you decide to stay focused on your core offering, you need to shape your business around the customers you want to serve.

While George's practice is attracting enough patients, he can't afford to be complacent. Just look at what's happening in the dental industry today. Big dental chains like Western Dental are buying up small practices and turning independent dentists into employees. They're handing out scripts: "Ask about teeth whitening. Suggest Invisalign. Mention Botox injections."

These big players have deep pockets. They can pour money into advertising, drawing in patients that independent dentists have worked hard to win over. And they're recouping their marketing costs by promoting the extra services George won't offer. But George has found his niche—patients who don't want to be sold on extras and may even be turned off by them. To better serve these customers, he's adapted his practice by extending his hours and bringing on a hygienist.

To stay competitive, you don't need to copy what everyone else is doing, but you do need to remain alert to changes in your industry while staying true to your broader purpose. Be aware of what your competitors are offering your customers, but focus on the products or services that align with your values and your broader vision for your business. Maybe that means adding new offerings, or maybe it means doubling down on what you do best.

Before making any changes, think about what this means for your business: How will expanding your offering affect your daily operations and profitability? What changes in staffing or scheduling might you need? How will it impact your work-life balance?

## Thought Starters

- As your industry evolves, will your current approach remain competitive?
- What other products or services might your customers be looking for?
- Would changing your range of offerings—either expanding or reducing—create more value for both you and your customers?
- How could you create more value using what you already have?
- How might you expand your offering while staying true to your purpose?

CHAPTER NINE
# NO DAYS OFF

## Nanoscale Challenges, Massive Stakes: Optimizing the Semiconductor Industry

In the early 2000s, when I was consulting for the semiconductor industry, I found myself spending a lot of time in fabrication plants, or fabs as we called them. These are massive factories where microchips are made, and they cost a fortune to build—about $5 billion each. That was fifteen years ago. Today, that figure's closer to $50 billion.

Working in a fab was unlike anything I'd ever experienced. Before we could step onto the fab floor, we had to suit up in what we called a bunny suit—a head-to-toe white coverall that made you look like an oversized Easter Bunny. The process started in the "clean room." They weren't exaggerating about the clean part; they didn't want so much as a stray eyelash floating around those precious semiconductors. Hairnet on, beard covered if you had one, hands gloved up. Then came the bunny suit, made with a special fabric designed to keep fibers from floating around.

I'd spend my entire day in my bunny suit, only taking it off during my lunch break. It wasn't the most comfortable situation. Most of my time was spent scribbling notes on special fiber-free paper and making observations, constantly aware that one wayward sneeze could cost the company millions. All the while, I'd be sweating buckets inside this suit, my breath fogging up the visor. Sometimes, I'd wonder if I was breathing too hard or if I was going to pass out from the heat. But discomfort aside, it was fascinating to see firsthand how these tiny, powerful chips were made.

The semiconductor industry, I learned, is all about volume. When you're running a fab that costs billions to build, you need it to run at full capacity all the time. The goal is simple: get as much volume out as possible. You've already invested the money in the asset, so now it's all about maximizing output. This is where I came in.

## Efficiency and Bottlenecks

In the semiconductor manufacturing world, efficiency is everything. In an efficiency project, the first step was always to find the bottlenecks—the places where things got stuck or slowed down. We'd spend hours watching machines, taking notes, and asking questions about why things were done a certain way.

Making a microchip is a complex process with multiple stages, each requiring specialized equipment. Imagine an assembly line, but instead of putting together a car, you're crafting microscopic circuits on a slice of silicon. One machine in this high-tech assembly line plays a starring role: the lithography machine.

The lithography machine is like a super-precise, incredibly expensive printer. It doesn't create the whole chip at once. Instead, it applies the blueprint for each layer of the chip onto a silicon wafer. Think of it as a map that guides the rest of the manufacturing process. After the lithography machine does its job, the wafer moves on to other machines that etch away parts of the silicon, deposit new materials, and slowly build up the intricate layers that make up a microchip.

Back then, a lithography machine would set you back about $50 million. Today, they're probably closer to half a billion. With that kind of price tag, you'd expect these machines to be running nonstop, churning out chips like there's no tomorrow. But more often than not, this was exactly where I'd find the bottleneck. My job was to figure out how to squeeze every bit of productivity out of these costly giants.

One of my first assignments took me to an analog semiconductor manufacturer's fab. I spent hours watching these machines at work, scribbling notes about every step of the process. Why does the wafer turn three times before it goes in? How long does it take to swap one wafer for another? One thing caught my eye: Before each wafer went into the main part of the machine to get printed, it stopped in a separate chamber to get positioned correctly. This positioning step was happening while the main part of the machine sat idle. It got me thinking—couldn't we do both at the same time?

When I brought this up with the engineers, they explained that getting the positioning exactly right was crucial for quality. If it was off even by a hair, you could end up with a batch of useless chips. They had designed the process for perfection, not speed. That's the thing about manufacturing: What works perfectly in a lab doesn't always make sense on a factory floor. In the lab, they're focused on getting it right. In the factory, it's about getting it right and doing it fast.

After some back-and-forth and a bit of tinkering, they managed to get the positioning to happen at the same time as the printing. It wasn't easy; there were plenty of kinks to work out. But in the end, it increased the machine's throughput by more than a percent. This was a big win on the semiconductor scale, but it was just one piece of the puzzle. After visits to other machines, those wafers come back to the lithography machine multiple times for every layer, with a total of twenty-five or more visits before becoming a finished chip.

## Managing Demand

Another problem that some fabs faced was fluctuating demand. I remember working with older fabs where demand for a particular chip would drop but not disappear entirely. It's like being stuck in limbo. You can't justify a full production run, but you can't stop making them, either. Instead of churning out hundreds of thousands of chips, you're down to making just a handful. Suddenly, this high-tech factory, designed for mass production, was juggling small batches of different chips. One wafer of this, three wafers of that, fifteen of another.

When demand for certain chips dropped, it threw a wrench into the whole operation. The fab isn't just one machine but a carefully choreographed dance of multiple processes. If one type of chip wasn't in demand, it would leave expensive equipment idle at various stages of production, including the lithography machine.

In one particular fab I worked with, they specialized in manufacturing high-end, expensive chips. These were their biggest moneymakers, with each chip needing sixty passes through the lithography machine during production. The problem was that demand for these chips fluctuated, and production targets kept shifting. In periods where demand slowed, the lithography machine—remember, that $50 million piece of equipment—would sit idle.

We had to get creative. One solution was to take a hard look at what we were asking that bottleneck machine to do. Did it really need to handle every step of the process? Could we offload some tasks, like positioning the wafers, to other machines? Another approach was to rethink our production schedule. We even ended up talking to the sales team, asking if we could produce some lower-end chips to keep the machines busy. It wasn't ideal—you don't want to make stuff you can't sell—but in manufacturing, an idle machine (especially a multimillion-dollar one) is like burning money.

This experience taught me that maximizing efficiency in a fab isn't just about speeding up processes. Sometimes, it's about being flexible and adaptable. Can the production line be reconfigured to handle varying demands? Are there ways to keep expensive equipment running even when the main products aren't in high demand?

This kind of thinking isn't unique to the semiconductor industry. You see it in other sectors where expensive assets are central to the business model. Take cruise lines, for example. They start by selling seats at standard price. As the embarkation date gets closer, they might drop the price to fill empty seats, or take the price up if demand is high. It's all about maximizing the use of that expensive asset, in their case, the cruise ship.

In the end, it's all about utilization. Whether you're running a semiconductor fab or an cruise line, the principle is the same: Your expensive assets need to be working as much as possible. Because in business, nothing costs more than idle capacity.

## Adapting to Survive

Remember that stat about 30 percent of small businesses failing in three years? I thought about it often while researching how some small businesses managed to survive COVID. That's how I came across Nick's story. His martial arts studio should have become another casualty; he'd opened his doors just a year before the lockdowns began. His spacious studio, once his prized asset, had transformed into his biggest liability during the pandemic.

When I visited Nick to understand how he'd adapted to keep his business running, I discovered an entrepreneur who'd found new ways to make every square foot count.

"People were still nervous about physical contact after restrictions lifted," Nick explained, showing me around his five-thousand-square-foot studio. "I knew it would take time before students came back. Meanwhile, this space was eating me alive with rent payments. I had to figure something out."

Listening to Nick, I thought about those semiconductor fabs; instead of an idle lithography machine, it was the fixed cost of all that unused space that threatened to sink his business.

He walked me through his studio, past the main practice room, and into a smaller office space. "This room was just sitting here, gathering dust," he said. "Then, one day I thought, why not find another business to share the space? Someone who could use it and help cover the rent?"

"The solution came from just watching what was happening in the space," Nick explained. "Parents would rush in from work, drop their kids off, then rush off to another activity. These kids would just hang around before and after class with nothing to do. And then the idea hit me. Why not give them something productive to do with that time?"

"I knew some Chinese tutors, so I called them up and suggested they set up shop here. 'You'll get a ready-made customer base, and I'll get help with the rent,' I told them. The tutors gained a whole new customer base, and the parents loved it. They had one drop-off for martial arts and Chinese lessons. It was a win-win for everyone."

"Then I started thinking bigger," he added. "I noticed my weekend adult students were really into health and fitness, so I turned this space into a pop-up shop. Health products one week, beauty items the next. It kept things interesting for my regulars and brought in curious newcomers."

The Chinese tutoring proved the most sustainable, at least for a while. But as his martial arts students got older, their interest in language lessons naturally declined.

"These were kids who wanted to kick and punch, not conjugate verbs," Nick said with a laugh. "But by then, my student base had grown enough that I needed that extra room for more classes."

Looking back, Nick's journey showed how necessity drives innovation. What began as a desperate move to cover rent had evolved into a lesson in utilization. As a small business owner, he found creative ways to make his unused space serve both his business and his customers. This is a perfect example of positioning in action. By finding ways to squeeze more value from every corner, he was able to weather the storm while the world, and his martial arts studio, got back on track.

Seeing your resources with fresh eyes and finding new ways to create value from what you already have is an idea fast-food joints caught on to too. Take Taco Bell in the US. Up until 2014, they had these fully equipped kitchens—expensive grills, fryers, and prep stations—all sitting idle during breakfast hours. Meanwhile, the fixed asset meter kept ticking, whether they were serving customers or not. So what did they do? They started serving breakfast.

At first, people scratched their heads. Tacos for breakfast? But now it's as normal as bacon and eggs. You can grab a cheesy toasted breakfast burrito on your way to work, jazzed up with bacon, sausage, jalapeños, or guacamole. Just like that, a space that used to sit empty all morning is now buzzing with hungry customers.

Other restaurants have long used similar tactics, just at different times of day. Take the classic happy hour. It's a time-tested way of dealing with the lull between lunch and dinner. They're not giving drinks away—they're just offering lower prices to draw people in when the place would typically be empty. It's all about maximizing utilization. These restaurant owners look at their quiet hours and ask themselves: How can we keep our expensive equipment and space working, even when our usual customers aren't around?

These stories show how business owners can transform their most challenging resources into opportunities. But finding and fixing these bottlenecks in your own business requires a systematic approach.

## Attack the Bottleneck

In the semiconductor industry, it's a $50 million lithography machine that often becomes the bottleneck that holds back an entire production line. For most small businesses, that bottleneck might just be you, the owner. Just like that expensive piece of equipment, your time and energy are valuable resources that need careful management.

That $50 million lithography machine taught me something important about business constraints. The entire factory was organized around keeping that critical piece of equipment running at peak efficiency because its capacity determined the entire factory's output. Manufacturing experts call this the theory of constraints. This is the idea that in any system, one constraint determines how much that system can accomplish.

While this theory was developed for large manufacturing operations, its fundamental approach—finding and addressing whatever holds back your entire system—can help any small business owner make better use of their most valuable resource: themself.

These four steps, adapted from manufacturing principles, can help you identify and overcome the constraints holding back your business:

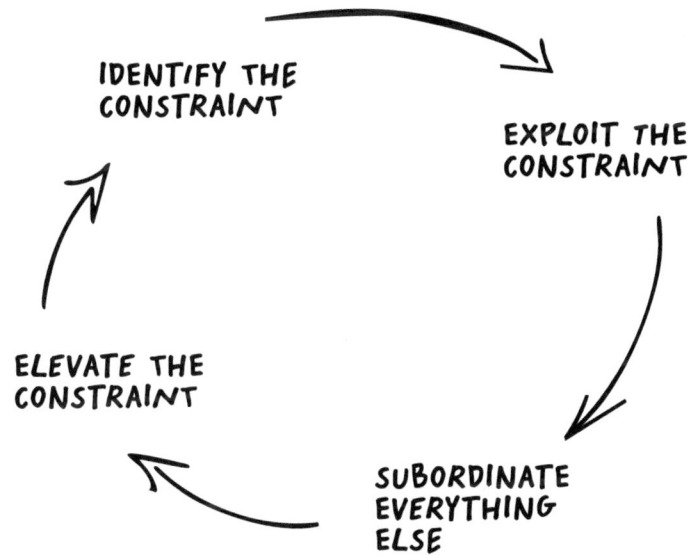

## IDENTIFY THE CONSTRAINT

The first step is recognizing where your business gets stuck. In a small business, the constraint is often the owner's time and energy, but it could be another resource, like your workspace or a specific piece of equipment, that's holding things back. You, or this constrained resource, might be the only one who can handle certain tasks or deliver specialized services. Finding your bottleneck means taking an honest look at your daily operations. Where do things slow down or stop completely without your direct involvement? Which tasks can only you handle? What work consistently piles up waiting for your attention?

Like that lithography machine in the fab, your constraint determines your entire operation's output. These bottlenecks do more than frustrate. They set the limit on what your business can achieve.

## EXPLOIT THE CONSTRAINT

Once you've identified your constraint, focus on making the absolute most of this limited resource. Remember how we reworked the wafer positioning process to keep the lithography machine running continuously? Apply that same thinking to your constraint. If you're the bottleneck, this means reducing interruptions, delegating tasks that others can handle, and focusing your time on activities that truly need your expertise.

Every minute of constraint capacity wasted, whether it's an idle machine or your scattered attention, means lost potential. Look for better scheduling systems or improved processes to optimize how you use your most precious resources. Just like we kept that expensive equipment running efficiently, make sure your constraint is always focused on its most valuable work.

## SUBORDINATE EVERYTHING ELSE

This step means organizing your entire business around making the most of your limited resource. Just as semiconductor fabs arrange their entire production schedule around keeping expensive equipment running, structure your business operations to support peak performance at your constraint.

Think about a lawn care business limited by its number of trucks. The solution isn't immediately buying more trucks—it's finding ways to accomplish more with each one, like planning routes with less driving time or using equipment that speeds up work at each home. The same principle applies to your constraint. This might mean training staff to handle more tasks independently, investing in technology to automate routine tasks, or restructuring your service delivery to reduce pressure on your constrained resource.

## ELEVATE THE CONSTRAINT, REPEAT THE PROCESS

The final step is finding ways to expand your constraint's capacity. In manufacturing, this might mean investing in new equipment. In your business, it might mean hiring key staff, developing systems that reduce your personal involvement, or finding creative ways to serve more customers without working longer hours. Sometimes, like those semiconductor fabs facing varying demand, you might discover opportunities to generate additional revenue from underutilized resources.

This cycle never really ends. As your business evolves, new constraints will emerge. The key is to keep identifying and addressing these bottlenecks, always looking for ways to make better use of your limited resources. Whether you're running a restaurant, a professional service, or a retail shop, understanding and managing your constraints is essential for sustainable growth.

The semiconductor industry taught me something valuable: Managing constraints isn't about pushing resources to their limits, it's about focusing your limited resources where they create the most value. Think of your time and energy as if it were an expensive piece of equipment—valuable, limited, and worthy of careful management. Building a sustainable business means creating systems and building teams that extend what you can do on your own while giving you room to breathe. The goal isn't working yourself to exhaustion; it's about making the most of your resources while still leaving room for the life you want to live.

## Hooked on Efficiency

A few years back, while attending a conference on Florida's east coast, Crystal and I were treated to a deep-sea fishing excursion, courtesy of the organizers. It wasn't cheap. I'd heard that these trips could run up to $1,500 or more. But this was covered for us, so we happily joined in with seven others, eager for a taste of the high seas.

As we boarded, I noticed three crew members for our group of nine. Quick math told me we were in for some first-class service. The open ocean stretched out before us, promising a day of relaxation. Not a bad way to start a Monday.

Deep-sea fishing, I discovered, is a far cry from the lake fishing I did as a kid in Michigan. Here, you don't even need to hold the pole. You just kick back, sip a beer, and let the crew do all the work. They bait the hooks, cast the lines, and set everything up while you soak in the sun.

On our way out to sea, I struck up a conversation with the captain, who introduced himself as Hamish. He mentioned it was a better day than yesterday because the sea had been choppy then. Since the previous day was a Sunday, I asked him if he ever took a day off.

"I work every day," he casually replied. Then he started talking about the boat in an oddly personal way. "We've got to be on the water," he said, and I realized the "we" meant him and the boat. "She's pretty hungry. I've got to feed her."

Curious, I asked if he enjoyed being on the boat. Hamish's eyes lit up. "It's my favorite thing in life," he said. Then, with a wry smile, he launched into the story of his former life, a world away from the open seas, where he spent his days surrounded by sawdust and kitchen cabinets.

"Back then, I was running on fumes," he admitted. "The business was just a means to an end, you know? Keeping food on the table and a roof over our heads."

Then came the divorce, and his ex-wife wanted half his company.

"She didn't realize the business was worth nothing without me," he chuckled. "When we split, I saw my chance to start over. She got half a worthless company, and I bought this boat and became a fishing captain. Best decision I ever made."

He told me that he spent more time on the water than anywhere else and that he'd never been happier.

"What's the minimum you need to bring in per day to cover your costs?" I asked.

"Fifteen hundred dollars," he said. "The boat's financed, and paying off that loan is my biggest cost." He chuckled, adding, "I used to work for my wife. Now I work for my boat."

I laughed. "At least you don't argue with the boat, right?"

"Oh, she has her moods. But I've learned not to rock the boat," Hamish said.

"And what do you do during the off-season?" I asked, knowing that in Florida, the quieter months run from May to October.

Hamish grinned. "Oh, I keep busy. You've got to be creative in this business. Can't let the boat sit idle just because the tourists aren't biting."

He went on to explain his year-round strategy. When the fishing crowds thinned out, he'd shuttle people up and down the coast. Sometimes, he'd do private charters for wealthy folks who wanted the boat to themselves.

"I'll even sail people all the way to the Bahamas," he added. "Once we're there, I'll anchor offshore and catch some shut-eye on the boat. There's no need to pay for a hotel. We'll stay for a day or two, and I charge the passengers for all three days. It's a win-win: They get an island getaway, and I keep the boat earning."

Listening to Hamish talk about his schedule, one thing became clear: This was a "no days off" business. He hadn't taken a real break since buying the boat. Every day was about keeping that expensive asset working, earning enough to cover the payments, and hopefully turning a profit. He'd escaped his cabinet-making business only to find himself tethered to something even more demanding: a boat that needed constant feeding.

## An Asset or a Liability?

Hamish's story got me thinking about all the small business owners I've met over the years. What looks like freedom from the outside often turns into a different kind of trap. These entrepreneurs might have escaped their 9-to-5 jobs, but many end up slaves to their debt or the very asset they've bet their lives on.

Take my dentist friend George. He's always going on about "empty chairs." The first time he mentioned it, I thought he was talking about some new minimalist decorating trend. But it wasn't that at all. In George's world, an empty chair is money down the drain.

Now, you might think, *Hey, isn't it nice to have a breather between patients? A chance to rest your arms or grab a coffee?* But for George, every empty chair is a missed opportunity. It's not just about having his hands in someone's mouth for eight hours straight. It's about keeping the lights on, paying his staff, and feeding his family.

It's the same story with Hamish and his boat. Like George managing his dental chairs, Hamish has to keep his boat earning. During peak season, he prioritizes private charters because they bring in the highest margins, with wealthy clients wanting the boat to themselves. He fills the rest of his schedule with tourist fishing trips, and during slower periods, he keeps the boat earning by offering shuttle services up and down the coast.

But even with all this careful planning, a single breakdown could derail everything. I asked him if he'd ever had to take the boat offline. He nodded grimly.

"I once had the engine fail on me," he said. "The part alone was going set me back five grand, plus a couple thousand for installation."

The supplier told Hamish it would take three weeks to get the part shipped. But for another $5,000, they could airfreight it in a couple of days.

"I absolutely had to do it," Hamish explained. "I don't have any choice because I've got to keep this thing sailing. I'm still paying for the boat, even if it's broken." He did the math faster than I could blink. "Twenty-one days times $1,500 a day? That's way more than five grand. I paid for the express shipping without breaking a sweat."

This is the kind of decision-making that separates small business owners from everyone else. Anyone not in tune with the no-days-off concept would probably opt to save the cash and take a forced vacation. But not Hamish. For him, it wasn't just about fixing the boat, it was about keeping his business afloat, quite literally. Every day of downtime meant lost revenue, and in his world, that could quickly spiral into a make-or-break situation.

## The Subordinate

When I asked if he ever took a break, Hamish shrugged. "I don't really need time off, but it'd be nice to feel solid ground under my feet once in a while. That's why I'm bringing my son into the business," he said, nodding toward one of the crew members.

"He's my exit strategy," he continued. "Right now, he's not ready to handle a full boat of tourists, but I'm teaching him the basics like how to steer and the important safety stuff. He can already handle private charters and ferry runs. The economics of each trip is different, but they all have one thing in common—they've got to pay for the boat's upkeep. And the key is, whether it's me or my son at the helm, somebody's always keeping this ship busy. That's how we stay afloat in this business."

As Hamish spoke, it hit me—this guy really understood utilization. Whether it was tourist season or not, he was always finding ways to keep his biggest asset, the boat, working and bringing in money. It was the same principle I'd seen in the big semiconductor fabs, just on a smaller, saltier scale. Like those factory owners, he lived with the constant pressure of keeping an expensive asset profitable, a pressure that shaped everything from his daily schedule to his plans for succession. *Running your own business might mean freedom from a boss*, I thought to myself, *but that freedom comes with a weight that never really lifts.*

As we talked, a few fish nibbled at the lines. Some of the other guests reeled them in. Then something big hit. Crystal got excited and handed me the rod. I fought with that fish for what felt like ages, my arms burning, following the crew's instructions. "Pull! Now let it slack!"

Finally, we saw it—a barracuda, all teeth and attitude. But just as we were about to bring it in, something massive erupted from the water and snatched our catch. Maybe it was a shark, maybe not, but it scared the living daylights out of everyone on board.

As we headed back to shore later that afternoon, I realized I'd gotten more than just a deep-sea fishing trip. I'd seen a master class in small business asset utilization, all while working on my tan and nearly catching the ugliest fish I'd ever seen. Not a bad way to spend a Monday, and a poignant reminder that whether you're running a massive semiconductor fab or a charter fishing boat, the principle's the same: keep your assets working, or watch your profits swim away.

## Coloring Outside the Lines

Elena's salon was one of the businesses that we helped through the PPP application process in the summer of 2020. The expanded capacity she'd invested in just months earlier was beginning to pay off when the pandemic lockdowns brought everything to a halt. The PPP money, along with her commitment to her customers and stylists, helped the business survive.

Years later, with the business back on solid ground, I visited to hear her story. She had presented a compelling case when she first approached ForwardLine for financing. She had so much demand that she was turning customers away and needed capital to purchase more chairs.

"How long did it take to get back on your feet?" I asked, looking around at her now-packed salon.

"The demand returned pretty quickly," she smiled, gesturing around her bustling space. "But even after the lockdown ended, we faced strict limits on how many people could be in the salon at once. Social distancing meant we could use less than half our chairs. Here I was with this beautiful expanded salon, and we couldn't use all of it."

"How did you manage with those restrictions?" I asked.

"We had to get creative," she said. "First, we extended our hours. We started opening earlier and closing later, creating shifts so more of our stylists could still work, just not all at the same time." She paused to check on a client, then continued. "But the real challenge was balancing everyone's needs. I knew if our junior stylists didn't get enough chair time, their skills wouldn't develop. So we created a rotation system that gave everyone, including our newer team members, a fair share of the available hours."

"Many salons only kept their most experienced stylists during that period," she explained. "But I took a different approach. I believed in investing in our whole team, even if it meant taking a hit in revenue in the short term."

She gestured toward a junior stylist, confidently working with a client. "Teaching and mentoring young stylists is fundamental to how I run this business," she said. "When you invest in teaching these young professionals, you're not just helping them develop technical skills. You're showing them how to build a sustainable career. Every stylist here knows that their growth and earning potential matter as much to me as the salon's bottom line."

Elena's commitment to her team paid unexpected dividends. While other salons struggled to retain staff after pandemic restrictions were lifted, she had maintained a full roster of skilled stylists. But this created a new challenge. "We were turning away clients," she explained. "And other salons were trying to poach our best stylists with promises of higher earnings."

That's when Elena spotted an opportunity. Her experienced stylists could handle certain services more quickly than others. "A regular client coming in for a trim might only need forty minutes with a senior stylist," she said, "not the full hour we'd always blocked out."

She turned to technology for help. New scheduling software allowed her to customize appointment lengths based on both the type of service and the stylist's experience level. An experienced stylist could complete a trim in forty minutes instead of the standard hour block. "Simply tightening the schedule helped my stylists earn 25 to 50 percent more per day," she explained. "Now, we can serve more clients while still maintaining the high standards our customers expect."

Like Taco Bell adding breakfast service to their offering and Nick reimagining his martial arts studio's space, Elena had found ways to create more value from her constrained resources. Just as my semiconductor clients had discovered, there was a way to get more done without adding more resources. But she also showed me that managing one's constraints isn't just about maximizing revenue; it's about aligning your decisions with your business philosophy. For Elena, carving out the time and capacity to develop her younger stylists was what set her business up for long-term success, and that's what she optimized for.

## Maximizing Utilization: Putting Your Capacity to Best Use

In any business, making the most of your available resources is key. We've seen how Hamish keeps his fishing boat busy and how semiconductor fabs push their machines to the limit. Just as businesses must maximize the use of their physical assets to stay profitable, small business owners must also consider how they manage their most important resource: themselves.

In small businesses, bottlenecks often come down to one thing: you. Just like that lithography machine in the semiconductor fab slowed down the entire production process, you might be the constraint on your business's growth. Maybe you're a graphic designer who insists on handling every project personally, or a baker who feels only you can create the perfect pastry. Your skills are in demand, but there are only so many hours in a day. When you're the bottleneck, your business can only grow as far as your personal capacity allows.

Making the most of your time and energy doesn't mean working longer hours, it means being strategic about what you take on. Instead of trying to serve everyone, use your freedom to focus on the customers and services that matter most to you and your chosen market. This might mean turning down projects that don't align with your vision, automating routine tasks, or training others to handle work that doesn't require your expertise. Ask yourself each day: Am I spending my time on the things that only I can do? Or am I getting bogged down in tasks that someone else could handle?

## Tighten the Schedule

Once you've identified where you can delegate work, the next step is making the most of your newfound time. By letting others handle routine tasks, you can focus your energy on the work that truly needs your expertise.

Take a fresh look at your schedule. Are there gaps that could be closed or transitions that could run more smoothly? Maybe you're a hairstylist who realizes some cuts take less time than others. Or a mechanic who could squeeze in more oil changes between bigger jobs. Even small changes to how you organize your day can make a big difference to your productivity without affecting the quality of your work.

Remember, maximizing your schedule doesn't mean pushing for 100 percent utilization every day—that's a recipe for burnout. Unlike big corporations, you can structure your time around what matters most to your business, just as Elena did when she prioritized developing her junior stylists. Your drive for efficiency should support, not compromise, your approach to running your business. The goal is to find that balance where your business runs smoothly and everyone, including you, still enjoys the work.

## Maximize What Matters

Making conscious decisions about where you spend your time can increase the volume of business that you can handle, but decisions on what matters most will transform your business. When you focus your energy on high-value work, you'll achieve more without burning out. Take Toshi, the yakitori chef. While his restaurant could probably make more money and serve customers faster if he hired extra staff and focused solely on cooking, he deliberately chooses to cook the food and serve his customers himself. Making that personal connection is his choice, and that's what makes his restaurant special.

Remember, there's no one-size-fits-all answer. Hamish found freedom by training his son. Toshi found satisfaction in maintaining a hands-on approach. Your solution will be unique to you and your business.

Your role in day-to-day operations should reflect what matters most to your business. Whether you delegate decisions or maintain hands-on involvement, the right balance will keep your business running smoothly, your customers happy, and your work fulfilling.

## Find Creative Solutions for Underutilized Assets

Running a small business means juggling a lot of numbers, but two big ones are always staring you in the face: your operating costs and your fixed costs. These are the bills you've got to pay whether you have one customer or a hundred. Maybe it's rent for your space, equipment you've leased, or staff you've hired. Like that lithography machine in the semiconductor fab, they're costing you money whether you're using them or not.

So what do you do? You might think the answer is simple: just keep busy. Fill every hour, take every job, and keep those assets working nonstop. But as we saw with managing your own time, pushing resources to their limits isn't sustainable or fulfilling.

Unlike big corporations, you have a deep understanding of your customers and the flexibility to be creative with your resources. Your skilled staff, unused space, equipment, and even quiet periods all hold potential for creating additional value—potential that might be hiding in plain sight. The key is finding ways to leverage these assets that align with your broader business objectives while meeting your customers' needs. Nick discovered this when he turned his martial arts studio's spare office into a tutoring space. Taco Bell found it in their quiet morning hours. Elena uncovered it in her salon's scheduling. The challenge is to look at your business with fresh eyes and ask: What else could I be doing with what I've already got?

- When your business is operating at capacity, are you the bottleneck? If not, what constraints are limiting your potential?
- How could you use your time and resources differently to focus on what matters most?
- Could adjusting your services or schedule help you serve different types of customers better?
- During slower periods, how do you decide which tasks deserve your immediate attention versus which can wait?

CHAPTER TEN

# ARE WE WINNING YET?

## Defining Success

My journey to understand what makes small businesses successful began with a simple question: How do some businesses thrive in the face of bigger, better-funded competitors? What I discovered at ForwardLine, studying thousands of business cases, wasn't what I expected. The most resilient small businesses—the true underdogs—weren't trying to beat the giants at their own game. They succeeded by embracing what made them different. They knew exactly who they wanted to serve, they built real connections with their customers, and they stayed true to their purpose. In this final chapter, we'll explore how losing sight of these strengths, particularly your core purpose, can shake even the most stable business, and how rediscovering them can set you back on course.

## Greed Is Good

Big businesses often get a bad rap for being cold, impersonal profit machines. But there's a reason these companies operate the way they do. In large corporations, everyone typically rallies around a single, clear goal. Usually, it's to maximize profits or drive up the stock price. It's easily understood, easy to measure, and it gets everyone pulling in the same direction. Business experts call this an "objective function." It's the one thing a company chooses to improve above all else. In the corporate world, this laser focus can be incredibly effective. When everyone agrees on the objective function, it becomes a lot simpler to get things done.

The problem is, most business advice assumes profit and growth are everyone's primary objectives. Flip through a business book or attend a seminar, and you'll probably hear the same old advice: grow faster, maximize profits, scale up! It's as if every business owner secretly dreams of becoming a tycoon.

For many small business owners, though, this is simply not the case. Your reasons for starting a business might have nothing to do with becoming a corporate giant. In fact, many people leave the corporate world precisely to escape its relentless focus on growth and profit, which often comes at the expense of personal fulfillment.

That's not to say making money isn't important—of course it is. But it doesn't have to be your only measure of success. As a small business owner, you have the freedom to define success on your own terms. Your main objective could be achieving a better work-life balance, making a difference in your community, finding personal fulfillment, or any combination of factors that matter to you.

Small businesses don't have to follow the big-business playbook. When you own a small business, your objectives aren't dictated by a board of directors or shareholders; they're personal and can evolve over time. Unlike big corporations, where the objective of returning money to shareholders remains largely unchanged, your goals as a small business owner will likely shift. What seemed important when you first started might not be your focus now.

Remember, your business should fit into your life, not the other way around. You might start out chasing rapid growth, only to realize later that having time for your family is more important. Or perhaps you'll find that contributing to your community brings you more satisfaction than maximizing profits. It's perfectly normal for your goals to evolve.

One of the advantages of running a smaller business is the freedom to define success on your own terms. Unlike large corporations that are locked into the same performance measures year after year, you can change direction when you need to. Take a moment to step back every now and then and ask yourself, "Is this business still giving me what I want?" If not, you have the power to adjust your course.

But how does this play out in real life? Allow me to introduce you to my friend Darren. He's a lawyer who stepped off the corporate treadmill to redefine success on his own terms.

## Breaking Free from the Corporate Grind

I first met Darren at an event hosted by our kids' elementary school. Calling this event a "production" would be far too generous. It wasn't a talent show either. The school had thrown together a mishmash of class performances, and every child in every grade got their moment in the spotlight.

From past experience, I knew the show would resemble something of a dog's breakfast. One class would stumble through a scene vaguely resembling a play, while another would belt out songs with more enthusiasm than skill. Uncoordinated dance moves, forgotten lines, and the occasional wandering child would be par for the course. Yet there I was, among a sea of parents elbowing each other to snap photos like our kids were headed for Broadway.

Our kids would each have no more than three minutes on stage, but as devoted parents, we were committed to sitting through all three hours of the show. Both of my kids were done with their parts within ten minutes of the first act, leaving me little to do but fiddle with my phone or scan the room from my uncomfortable folding chair in the stuffy auditorium. I couldn't help but notice Darren a few seats down. Like me, he had already seen his child perform and was now visibly restless, enduring the ongoing cacophony of children's music.

During intermission, we both made a beeline for the refreshment table, desperate for some caffeine to power through the second act.

"Well, that was . . . something," I said, trying to keep a straight face.

"Indeed," Darren grimaced. "Our kids were great, though."

"Of course," I agreed quickly. "Absolutely brilliant."

We both chuckled, the shared understanding of parental pride hanging between us.

"So, two more acts to go," I said. "Plus the dreaded PTA meeting at the end."

"Please don't remind me," Darren groaned. "I love my daughter. She was fantastic, but this PTA thing is torture."

"Tell me about it," I commiserated.

"All those helicopter parents who think their constant involvement is somehow helping the teachers," Darren scowled, coming in hot. "They're the ones interrupting family dinners to discuss why their precious angel's every misstep is the school's fault. And don't get me started on how entitled they act, insisting that kids should only be taught the same way they were taught decades ago!"

Right there, I knew I liked Darren. I'd never met someone who could so candidly express their disdain for a social gathering while literally standing in the midst of it.

Just then, a harried-looking mom rushed past us, arms full of hastily made props. "Excuse me! Coming through! Act two, scene three!"

Darren's eyes followed her. "Unbelievable," he muttered. "Why can't people get organized?"

I raised an eyebrow. "Rough day?"

"It's been a rough week," he sighed.

"So, what do you do when you're not enduring school performances and PTA meetings?" I asked, thinking a change of subject might improve his mood.

"I'm a lawyer," he replied.

"Oh? What firm?"

"Actually, I have my own practice," Darren said.

"Really? I'd love to hear how that came about," I said.

Before Darren could answer, a frantic teacher burst into the hallway. "Has anyone seen the Dawn of Civilization kids? They're on in five minutes!"

"Listen, why don't we step outside for a bit and get some air?" I suggested.

Darren nodded gratefully, and we made our way to the exit, dodging excited kids and frazzled parents.

Once outside, Darren seemed more relaxed. "So, what made you decide to start your own firm?" I asked.

Darren took a sip of his coffee. "Let's just say it was survival instinct."

As we stood there, Darren shared his journey from being a lawyer at a small firm to running his own practice. His story was eye-opening, filled with the kinds of details you'd never expect to hear at a school event.

Darren's blunt honesty was a breath of fresh air. Plus it turned out that the PTA meeting gave our wives a chance to meet and hit it off, so much so that our families soon became regulars at each other's New Year's parties and summer vacations. From Yosemite camping trips to late-night discussions about the ups and downs of entrepreneurship, that conversation outside the school auditorium was the beginning of a long friendship and a front-row seat to Darren's ongoing journey —one of stepping out on his own, facing down new challenges, and finding himself.

## The Door to Independence

Darren spent many years climbing the corporate ladder at various law firms before deciding to strike out on his own. A commercial real estate lawyer specializing in complex contracts for big deals, Darren was intelligent and introspective, but he had always been his own toughest critic, constantly questioning the quality of his work. This self-imposed pressure followed him from high school through law school, into his career at major firms, and even into his personal life.

"Am I as good as I can be?" The question plagued him, driving him to push harder, work longer, and chase perfection in every aspect of his life.

Darren's disillusionment with the world of big law firms began early in his career. As a young associate, he understood the importance of client development, even though it wasn't something he particularly enjoyed. One day, at a country club event, he found himself mingling with potential clients, business cards in hand.

"I met this wealthy guy," Darren recalled, thinking back to his early career. "We talked about what I do, and he seemed really interested. He asked for my card, and I was thrilled. 'Look at me,' I thought. 'Developing clients!'"

Eager to share his success, Darren approached the senior partner whose name graced the firm's letterhead. "I told him that I met this guy, and I thought there was a lot of potential work there." Darren said. "I was sort of expecting some praise for that," he added.

But instead of patting Darren on the back, the partner's response was cold and dismissive. "He's a golf buddy of mine," he said. "I know him well."

"He was marking his territory, you know," Darren added. "Like a dog pissing on a tree."

The interaction left Darren deflated. His efforts to contribute to the firm's growth had been brushed aside, leaving him questioning the value of his work. This incident, while disappointing, was just the beginning of Darren's growing disillusionment with the corporate law world.

As Darren's career progressed, he found himself at a different firm, on the cusp of becoming a junior partner. During this time, Darren had a mentor he respected and considered a good person. Client development still formed a large part of his responsibilities, and he threw himself into the work, believing it to be essential for his success and the firm's growth.

One day, after a successful early-morning meeting out in California's Inland Empire region, where he'd landed a new client over breakfast, Darren joined his team's weekly update meeting, led by his mentor. When it came time to update the firm's partners on client development, Darren was enthusiastically sharing his client development efforts when his mentor cut him off with a mocking comment: "Thanks for the Darren show."

The remark stung, leaving Darren feeling disrespected. As he reflected on the incident later, it dawned on him that his boss, the very person he looked up to, felt threatened by his success and that even their relationship wasn't immune to the pressures and politics of the law firm.

Similar experiences with other lawyers had already painted a bleak landscape where everyone was out for themselves. Darren started to see beyond the glossy exterior of prestigious firms and high-profile cases, noticing the toll it took on the partners around him.

That day, walking through the office, he looked at his colleagues with new eyes. There was the overweight partner, burning the midnight oil in his office. Another partner, now juggling his third marriage, was grinding away just to keep up with his alimony payments. Everywhere Darren looked, he saw partners working themselves to the bone, but none of them were fulfilled, and all of them looked unhealthy.

What Darren saw that day shook him to his core. *If I stay here,* he thought, *I'm going to work myself into an early grave with nothing to show for it.*

That day in the office was the final straw for Darren; he had seen enough. He felt a desperate need to break free, to do the work he loved, and to make money on his own terms. He was done with the corporate grind, the office politics, and the constant pressure. Most importantly, he was determined not to end up like the other partners—slaves to their jobs and miserable despite their success, with no life outside work. He wanted to be his own master.

Darren had a clear vision of what independence could offer him: a chance at a better work-life balance. Confident in his ability to bring in clients and handle the work, he looked forward to being able to control his own schedule, attend his kids' school events, or take a day off without having to justify it to anyone.

He had always been good at building relationships, a skill he modestly referred to as "selling." But it was more than that. Darren had a knack for connecting with people, for making them feel heard and understood. He could build trust quickly, balancing a bit of humor with the seriousness of legal matters.

"I figured, if I'm good at what I do and I can sell my services, why shouldn't I be able to have both a successful career and a fulfilling personal life?" Darren told me. "This was my chance to focus on the parts of being a lawyer that I enjoyed the most."

So he quit. He walked away from the firm and set out to start his own private practice. Now, as his own boss, Darren was free to utilize his relationship-building skills—talents he hadn't been able to fully express in the rigid structure of a large firm—and grow his practice in a way that felt true to himself.

## The Art of the French Press

Our first trip to Yosemite with Darren's family found us at Housekeeping Camp, a halfway point between roughing it and glamping. With its canvas-covered structures and electricity, it gave us the illusion of camping without completely abandoning creature comforts. It also revealed more about Darren's journey, and exposed my utter incompetence with a French press.

While preparing for the trip, I'd gone out and bought this fancy camping French press. Everyone else seemed to view it as an essential piece of gear, a gateway to morning accomplishment, but for me, it was just another way to mess up perfectly good coffee.

That first morning, as I fumbled with the contraption, Darren watched without attempting to hide his amusement. "You're supposed to let it sit for a bit before pressing," he offered unhelpfully.

"Right," I muttered, staring at the murky liquid. "And how long is 'a bit'?"

"Long enough," Darren replied mockingly. "But not too long."

I had ground my coffee before the trip, feeling smugly prepared. Little did I know I'd pulverized it into dust. The result was a bitter, silty mess that could probably strip paint.

As I grimaced through my first sip, Darren chuckled. "Maybe you should stick to giving coffee shops business advice and leave the actual coffee making to them?"

I rolled my eyes but couldn't help laughing. Here we were, surrounded by Yosemite's majesty, and I was being defeated by ground beans and hot water.

On our second morning in Yosemite, I was eyeing my French press with dread when I spotted Darren, backpack in hand, heading for his bike at the ungodly hour of 6:30 a.m.

"Where are you off to?" I called out, desperate for any excuse to avoid my homemade brew.

"Curry Village," he replied, checking his watch. "Need to get some work done before everyone else is up."

I had to chuckle. Here was Darren, who'd left the corporate world to be his own boss, still chained to his work even in the heart of Yosemite. And my wife thought I was the workaholic.

"Mind if I tag along?" I asked. "Curry Village has real coffee. Four bucks a cup, but worth every penny to avoid my sludge."

## ARE WE WINNING YET?

As we grabbed our bikes and prepared to leave the campsite, I couldn't help but ask, "So, Darren, what's so urgent that you're racing to Curry Village at this hour?"

He hesitated for a moment, then sighed. "There's no internet here. I need to send some important documents and do a little bit of research. There's good connectivity in Curry Village."

"Research?" I asked. "On vacation?"

Darren let out an exasperated sigh. "Yeah, well, it's complicated."

Sensing there was more to the story, I decided to probe gently. "Sounds like running your own practice isn't quite the freedom you imagined?"

That seemed to open the floodgates. As we pedaled out of our campsite and toward Curry Village, Darren began to share the realities of his journey into entrepreneurship.

"You know," he said between breaths, "it's not just about freedom. Having your own practice means you're always on, either doing the work or being ready for it. I am good at winning work. I have the freedom to do things my way. But big firm or not, in this business, clients expect you to always be available."

I nodded, encouraging him to continue while switching gears to keep up with him. It had been a while since I'd been on a bike, and the mechanics of it all seemed to have escaped me.

Darren's rant grew louder as he pulled ahead. "It's not just that I have to be a good lawyer. Early on, I learned that I'm also the bookkeeper, the marketer, and the office manager!"

"It's nonstop!" he shouted as we rounded a bend in the road. "If I'm not working, I'm not earning. It's that simple. And with a family to support, the stakes have never felt higher. I'm constantly juggling priorities like financial security and independence and keeping myself intellectually stimulated with sexier deals and sophisticated clients. The problem is, they rarely align."

Darren pedaled furiously as he vented, while I struggled to keep pace. "I'm constantly spinning plates and waiting for it all to come crashing down," he said. "I'm always worrying about what I need to work on the next day and who I need to call to bring home the bacon. The idea of taking a vacation or dealing with an unexpected illness seems like a luxury I can't afford."

"It sounds like you've been dealing with the same trade-offs I've seen other business owners struggle with," I ventured, awkwardly shifting to a lower gear.

Darren nodded, his wheels turning both literally and figuratively. "Exactly. Everything I spend time on is either delivering work I've promised or winning more work. Sometimes I wonder if I'm really my own boss or if I've just traded the pressure of dealing with selfish partners for a different kind of pressure. Am I any freer if my family's financial security is still driving the outcomes and goals of my professional life?"

I raised an eyebrow, narrowly avoiding a low-hanging branch in the process. A bead of sweat, from exertion or the near-miss, I wasn't sure, trickled down my temple. The frustration in his question was clear, delivered in that familiar aggrieved tone of his. Darren wasn't always this heated, but it wasn't uncommon to hear him express himself honestly and openly.

"You know, I do what I have to do for my family, and I'll sign up for that over and over again," he said, his voice softening.

## Catching the Big Fish

As we rolled into Curry Village, Darren made a beeline for an empty table and quickly set up his laptop. I decided to take a leisurely cycle around the site before joining the queue for coffee. By the time I returned, steaming cup in hand, Darren had been online for a good half an hour and was in a noticeably better headspace.

Settling into the chair opposite him, I took a grateful sip of my hard-earned caffeine fix. "So," I asked. "What's so urgent that it couldn't wait until after vacation?"

Darren glanced up from his screen. "Remember how I was telling you about trying to land bigger clients? Well, I started working with this guy, Jacob, about eight months ago. He's a huge real estate mogul in LA."

My eyes widened. "Sounds like a big deal."

"You have no idea," Darren said, his fingers pausing on the keyboard. "Jacob's probably the biggest player in the city, maybe even nationally. For someone in my field, landing him as a client is like striking gold."

"Is that why you're working on vacation?" I asked.

"Yeah. Even though he knows I'm away, he asked for something urgently. I can't risk dropping the ball this early in the relationship."

"So, how did you land him as a client?" I asked.

"It's been a long game," Darren explained. "I've spent months, maybe even the last few years, talking to various real estate management companies. These firms usually have their own in-house lawyers, but they often need someone on the other side of deals."

"And that's where you come in?"

"Exactly. I've been putting myself out there, exploring every opportunity. With Jacob, I started with some small projects. I knew I had to knock them out of the park to show him I was worth the investment."

"And it worked?" I asked.

Darren nodded. "It did. He's started giving me more and more project-based work, and I think it could eventually make up 60 percent of my practice."

"That's a huge chunk of your business," I said.

"It is," he replied. "It'll pack my schedule and give me more than enough billable hours. For the first time since going out on my own, I won't constantly be worrying about where the next job will come from."

As we continued to chat, I noticed a change in Darren. He seemed relaxed, the uncertainty that had been hanging over him for years now lifted. He had a big client on the hook, a vision of steady work, and the security he'd been chasing.

"Just give me a few minutes to add some finishing touches to this document," Darren said, turning back to his laptop.

I nodded, sipping my coffee and enjoying the morning air. After a short while, Darren closed his laptop with a satisfied sigh.

"Research complete. Documents are on their way," he announced. "But knowing Jacob, this might not be the last time he texts me this trip."

We cycled back to Housekeeping Camp, the morning sun now warm on our backs. As we approached our campsite, I spotted Crystal sitting outside our tent with a steaming mug in her hands.

"How was your ride?" she called out.

"Enlightening," I replied, eyeing her mug suspiciously. "Is that actual coffee?"

Crystal's smile widened. "French press. Turns out, it's not rocket science after all."

I groaned good-naturedly as Darren chuckled beside me. "You too?" I muttered, realizing I was now the only one in our group incapable of producing a decent cup of camp coffee.

## The Blowup

Years had passed since our first Yosemite trip, and once again, we found ourselves in the shadow of Half Dome. This time, we booked ourselves a spot in Curry Village. I was preparing for an afternoon at the Yosemite Village pool with my kids when I spotted Darren. His face was a storm cloud of frustration.

"Damn Curry Village Wi-Fi," he muttered, furiously tapping at his phone. "Can't even make a call."

I raised an eyebrow. "Everything okay?"

"Jacob's been blowing up my phone. I need to talk to him, but the reception here is terrible."

"I might have a solution," I said. "There's a tiny library near Yosemite Village. Great Wi-Fi, and hardly anyone knows about it."

Relief washed over Darren's face. "Lead the way."

The library was a hidden gem—a single-room cabin that felt more like a time capsule than a county facility. As Darren set up for his call, I found myself surrounded by what seemed like a shrine to John Muir. The Dewey decimal number 508.7 dominated nearly every spine, each book a window into the life of Yosemite's patron saint.

While Darren talked in hushed tones, I flipped through the pages of Muir's adventures. The man had lived alone in the wilderness for months, exploring and documenting his surroundings with an almost obsessive dedication.

When Darren finally emerged from his call, he was as white as a sheet.

"Everything alright?" I asked cautiously.

Darren shook his head. "That call with Jacob? It was worse than I thought. We had a disagreement. A contract clause that I wrote came back to bite him—we're talking millions."

I winced. "Ouch."

"Yeah," Darren sighed. "He's furious. Kept yelling, 'You didn't write that clause the way I wanted. It should have protected us!' But I know we discussed the risks. Now, I'm not sure he'll ever work with me again."

"What now?" I asked. "Doesn't he make up a big chunk of your business?"

Darren nodded grimly. "If I lose Jacob . . ." he trailed off, but I could fill in the blanks.

As we walked back to the campsite, Darren's frustration seemed to deepen with each step. He kicked a pebble along the path.

"You know what makes this whole situation even worse?" he said. "We're in the middle of converting our garage into an in-law suite."

He let out a bitter laugh. "Turns out, even a small construction project has to have a nightmare of expenses and bureaucratic red tape. The backyard is a construction zone, and the kids are in the house all summer, so I've got no peace and quiet in the home office. And now my biggest client might walk."

The next morning, I found Darren outside, phone in hand, pacing back and forth between the tents.

"You okay?" I asked.

He shook his head. "More bad news," he said. "The building inspector says we need a separate connection to the power grid. Adding another electric meter is going to cost a small fortune, and we need city approval first. Construction will be delayed by another month."

He ran a hand through his hair, looking more stressed than I'd ever seen him. "The timing couldn't be worse. We've spent so much on the project, banking on my practice to cover the costs. But after this thing with Jacob, what if all the work disappears? I'll be back to square one, scrambling to fill my pipeline."

As I listened to Darren, I realized how precarious his situation had become. Nobody wants their boss—or, in Darren's case, their main client—to think they're inadequate or incapable. That's a one-way ticket to sleepless nights and constant anxiety.

For years, Darren had been riding high on his relationship with Jacob. The steady stream of work had given him newfound confidence in his practice, allowing him to handle a large volume of Jacob's work while maintaining a few other clients on the side.

Darren had left his firm years ago to be captain of his own ship, to do things without people getting in his way. But, by relying so heavily on Jacob, he'd simply traded one boss for another. Now, he was paying the price.

"You know, John Muir once wrote, 'The mountains are calling, and I must go.' Maybe what you're going through is just another mountain to climb," I said, trying to lighten the mood.

Darren managed a small smile. "Let's hope it's not as steep as Half Dome."

## The Rebuild

The collapse of his relationship with Jacob took a big chunk of Darren's business away, plunging him into the work habits of the partners he'd been trying to escape when he left the firm all those years before. For months on end, Darren found himself working late nights and weekends, spreading himself thin in an effort to win over new clients that would keep his practice afloat. He was unaware that he had fallen into the "I'm-going-to-work-myself-to-death" mindset that had driven him to independence in the first place. The fear of failure loomed large, and he wasn't sure he could pull himself out of this tailspin.

Watching my friend struggle, it dawned on me how easily the very thing that often drives people to start their own businesses—their deeper purpose—can get lost in the daily grind of keeping that business alive. Here was Darren, who'd left corporate law specifically to avoid working himself into an early grave, doing exactly that in his own practice. The pressure of losing Jacob had pushed him right back into the life he'd tried to escape. I'd seen this pattern before in other business owners, but never quite so clearly as I did with Darren.

But Darren wasn't one to stay down for long. As he pushed through the stress, he forced himself to take a step back and reevaluate. Why had he started this journey in the first place? What were his strengths? He'd always been good at winning people over, selling his services, and closing deals. It was a skill he'd let slide during the comfortable years with Jacob, but it wasn't gone—just underutilized.

Darren realized he didn't need to stress over losing a client because he had the skills to win new ones. He hadn't gone out on his own for an easy life; he'd done it to avoid dying from overwork, confident in the strengths he could count on. It was time to put that talent back to work.

"I've got to focus on winning just one or two," he told himself. "I don't need to replace Jacob. I just need more balance, more flexibility. If one client is unhappy, I'll have others to fall back on."

So Darren focused his client development around relationship-building, something he'd always been good at. But this time, he approached it differently, leveraging the reputation he'd built over the years. He still worked hard to find clients that he could connect with, but he was smarter about it. He reshaped his practice, focusing on the aspects of his work that truly fulfilled him.

He started writing articles about complex real estate law issues and sharing them online. At first, it felt like shouting into the void, but, gradually, it led to new connections and opportunities. He even began interviewing past clients about their experiences, sharing these stories online to give potential clients a real sense of the work he did and the value he provided.

Within a year or two, Darren had rebuilt his business. He developed strong relationships with a broad range of clients, confidently managing their varied demands. He even rekindled his relationship with Jacob, but this time on his own terms.

As the work poured in, Darren recognized that he no longer needed to spread himself so thin. This realization led him to a deeper epiphany about his entire approach to his practice. With more work than he could handle, Darren became selective, taking on only the deals that really interested him, turning away the less-sophisticated clients he'd once thought he needed. He noticed that some of his smaller clients were taking three times the effort for the same billable hours.

*What if, instead of chasing every potential client, I charged more for my specialized knowledge and aimed for quality over quantity?* he wondered. The idea was terrifying but exhilarating. It would mean fewer hours chained to his desk and more time to actually run his business—and maybe even have a life outside of work.

Darren took the plunge. He raised his rates and focused on the clients he genuinely enjoyed working with. It was nerve-racking at first, watching some clients walk away. But he soon found that the clients who stayed valued his expertise more. The higher rates meant he could work fewer hours, yet his income held steady.

For the first time since striking out on his own, Darren had breathing room. He no longer felt the need to constantly chase new clients. He had enough volume spread across his client base that if one or two clients left, he could easily step up his work with others to fill the gap. This diversity gave him better control over his work, allowing him to take care of his family without spending every waking moment worrying about billable hours.

But while he'd finally reached a place where he felt truly in control, Darren was about to discover that true success meant more than just financial stability; it was about having that work-life balance he'd seen so sorely lacking in his corporate law days, where his colleagues seemed to have one foot in the grave and the other chained to their desks.

## The Payoff

It was our last joint family camping trip to Yosemite. Our kids were graduating high school, and for the first time in years, Darren wasn't sneaking off to find internet connectivity or obsessively checking his phone for client emails. As we sat by the campfire under a canopy of stars, our teenagers off exploring the moonlit grounds, I noticed a calmness in him that I hadn't seen before. It was a far cry from the anxiety-filled and expressive Darren I'd known for years—the one who could never truly disconnect from work, even in the midst of Yosemite's natural splendor.

"You seem different," I said, poking at the fire. "More relaxed than I've seen you in years."

"I finally have something I almost forgot existed," he smiled. "Free time!"

"Free time?" I laughed. "You? What's brought this on?"

"I've reset my expectations of what being my own boss really means," he said. "It wasn't just about financial independence anymore. I realized I wanted to invest in myself and live a life beyond my law practice."

"That's a big shift," I said. "What made you come to that realization?"

"Losing a chunk of Jacob's business was a wake-up call," Darren admitted. "It forced me to look at how I was living. I started taking care of myself by seeing a therapist, exercising regularly, even trying some of those LA health trends I used to mock."

I chuckled. "Don't tell me you're into organic foods and that Goop that Gwyneth Paltrow's selling these days."

He laughed. "Believe it or not, I am. Who knew I'd be swapping burgers for kale smoothies?"

We both laughed.

"But the biggest change was rediscovering my passion for comedy. When I'm not drafting contracts or meeting clients, I'm writing material and performing at local comedy clubs," he continued.

"Seriously?" I asked. "Stand-up comedy?"

"Yep," he nodded. "I forgot how much I love making people laugh."

"That's amazing," I said. "How did you get back into it?"

"I needed an outlet," he said. "I took a class on writing jokes, and now I'm going to open mic nights. I'll never be as good as Dave Chappelle, but I've figured out a persona that really works for me."

"Oh?" I asked. "What's your angle?"

Darren grinned. "I'm going up on stage as the Angry Asian Man."

I burst out laughing. "Darren, it took you fifty-five years to figure that out? You've been an angry Asian man ever since I met you!"

He chuckled, shaking his head. "Well, now I can finally be myself and people will appreciate me for it."

"But seriously," he continued, "it fits me. So why not lean into who I am? I can't be that guy as a lawyer, but I can as a comedian. It works."

"Sounds like you're finally finding balance," I smiled.

"Yeah, I think I am. Looking back, it's ironic. I left the firm to avoid ending up like those partners working themselves to death, but I almost did the same in my own practice. Losing Jacob's business shook me out of that cycle."

"Sometimes it takes a setback to make us reevaluate things," I said.

He nodded. "I quit because I wanted to control my destiny, but somewhere along the way, I lost sight of that. I got so caught up in running the business that I became trapped by it. I was right back where I started, letting something else control my life."

"And now?" I asked.

"Now, anytime there's uncertainty in my workload, I lean on the confidence I have in landing clients," he said. "I went off on my own because I wanted to have a sustainable business that supports the life I want to live. I'm still dedicated to my clients, but I'm also making time for my passions and well-being."

"That's a valuable lesson indeed," I said.

"Who knows?" Darren said with a chuckle. "Maybe my next act will be as a world-famous comedian and author. Book deal, comedy tour—anything's possible!"

As we sat there, the crackling of the fire the only sound between us, I thought about how far Darren had come. From a stressed-out lawyer to the Angry Asian Man on stage, he'd found a way to be true to himself while building the life he wanted.

I thought about another friend, Satish, who took a different path but learned a similar lesson about forging your own way. Back when I was running my startup, Talytica, Satish and I were part of the same entrepreneurial circle, sharing ideas and supporting each other's ventures. Little did I know how his story would unfold.

## Redefining Success in the Startup World

I remember when Satish first shared his idea during one of our startup group meetings. We were all gathered in the conference room of the startup lab, a diverse group of founders eager to bounce ideas off one another. Satish stood at the whiteboard, clearly excited as he described his vision for a food delivery app called Clorder—a mashup of "cloud" and "order."

"We're going to focus on smaller, local establishments," Satish explained, marker in hand. "The big players are overlooking this market, but I think there's real potential here."

Richard, a software developer who was trying to disrupt the flower delivery business, raised his hand. "That's an interesting niche, Satish. How do you plan to compete with the big players' tech infrastructure?"

"And what about customer acquisition?" Jennifer added. She was working on a baby seat installation service. "The giants have huge marketing budgets."

Satish nodded, clearly energized by the questions. "Good points. We're building a lean, flexible platform that can adapt quickly to smaller restaurants' needs. As for marketing, we're betting on word-of-mouth and targeted local campaigns. It's not about outspending the big guys; it's about being smarter and more focused."

In the crowded market of food delivery apps, Satish and his cofounder had spotted an opportunity that others had missed, and the room was abuzz with interest.

I was impressed by how committed Satish was to bootstrapping his startup. He wasn't looking for quick money from investors; he was in it for the long haul. Satish intended to run Clorder like a business that was going to go public someday, reinvesting every penny they earned back into the business. The family he needed to support was on board too. In his mind, all this sacrifice would pay off when their equity became massively valuable in the future.

As the months passed, Satish and his team built the code, cold-called restaurants, and slowly but surely, started signing them up. I remember meeting with Satish for coffee one morning. He was excited. "We're making money on every transaction," he said. "Sure, it's a small amount, but we're growing."

Years passed, and while Clorder had managed to onboard hundreds of restaurants, they were nowhere near the exponential growth they'd envisioned. Without venture capital (VC) funding, they couldn't match the aggressive customer acquisition strategies of competitors like Grubhub and Uber Eats. These giants were burning through venture capital on massive marketing campaigns, sacrificing profitability for market share. Meanwhile, Satish and his team had to be more conservative. They were making money, but at a much slower pace than their VC-backed rivals.

## The Backyard Breakthrough

In the summer of 2021, with the world slowly emerging from COVID, Satish reached out to meet. "Let's catch up, but maybe in your backyard? I'm still not ready to brave the great indoors," he said. I chuckled, thinking how even a simple meetup had become an exercise in pandemic protocol.

When he arrived, we sat down outside, and I handed him an ice-cold beer. I asked how Clorder was doing, and his face dropped. As he spoke, he sounded utterly deflated. All the enthusiasm he'd once exuded was gone.

"We're not growing fast enough," he sighed, absently peeling the label off his beer bottle. "No one's interested in buying us out. The big players are leaving us in the dust."

As I probed into the business, I realized something didn't add up. "Satish," I said, "you've hit all the little goals you set out to achieve. That's a fantastic success, at least in my opinion. I don't get why you're struggling."

It turned out he was feeling pressure from his family because he wasn't bringing home the proverbial bacon. The dream of hitting it big, selling the company, or going public was long gone. He was grinding away on a very low salary, building business value but not taking any of it home. In fact, he and his cofounder were scraping by on $80,000 a year each, and in Los Angeles, that's barely enough to get by. Here they were, running a profitable company, and yet they were living like struggling entrepreneurs.

Satish was feeling the destructive consequences of losing sight of his purpose. It was a sobering realization for me: The goals we set for our businesses—whether it's going public or staying private, growing exponentially or sustainably—directly impact our day-to-day happiness and well-being as business owners.

"Wait a minute," I said, eyeing the beer label he'd been peeling away. For a split second, I considered scribbling some numbers on it, but thought better of it. "Let me grab something to write on. This calls for proper paper."

I dashed inside, returning with a notepad and pen. "Okay, so you're not happy because this business doesn't pay you enough?"

"Well, no," he replied. "It's because it's not going to sell and be an IPO."

"But if it's not going to sell and be an IPO, then why aren't you paying yourself?"

Satish looked at me as if I'd just punched him in the nose.

"Why don't you run me through your numbers," I said.

We spent the next hour filling the notepad with calculations.

"So, instead of spending all this money on marketing, if you paid yourself more, what would happen to the business?" I asked.

Satish thought for a moment. "We'd lose a little bit of growth, but we'd still be profitable, and we'd still keep growing. We'd still be able to run the business."

"Then why don't you do that instead of giving up on it?"

Satish agreed, albeit skeptically. "Let me go talk to my cofounder, let me talk to my family, and let me figure this out."

After that conversation, I didn't hear from Satish for another few years. When we finally reconnected, I was greeted by a changed man. Gone was the stressed-out, frustrated entrepreneur I'd last seen. In his place stood a confident, energized business owner.

"How's Clorder doing?" I asked.

"It's doing great," Satish beamed.

It turned out that Satish and his cofounder had indeed raised their salaries. Once Satish started paying himself properly, his passion for the business returned. The drag of having to explain why he was sacrificing so much time and energy disappeared. He was making money, putting more energy into the business, and loving it again.

"Can you believe that was the problem?" Satish laughed. "All I had to do was pay myself more."

"You know," he continued, "when I started out, I loved this business. But somewhere along the way, I started hating it because it wasn't giving me what I wanted. The funny thing is, I didn't even know what I wanted anymore."

Satish explained how he'd been so caught up in following the startup playbook—reinvesting every penny and chasing exponential growth—that he'd lost sight of why he started the business in the first place. He realized he didn't need to create a billion-dollar unicorn. He just needed to build a sustainable business that allowed him to do work he loved while providing for his family.

He was following a different formula now—one that wasn't written in the startup playbooks. Unlike other startups running at a loss forever in hopes of a big payday, Satish had found a path that worked for him. He could get something out of the business and still keep growing it, but on his own terms. And most importantly, he was happy again.

## Rewriting Your Business Playbook

Darren and Satish both started their businesses with one vision, only to find themselves chasing objectives that had changed over time. Their stories remind us that running a business isn't about following a straight line. It's more like navigating a winding road, with unexpected turns and the occasional need to pull over and check your map.

Remember how we started this chapter? Big businesses have their objective functions—those clear-cut goals that keep everyone marching in the same direction. But for small business owners like you, Darren, and Satish, the objectives are personal, and they can shift over time. Unlike large corporations, you have the flexibility to set goals that align with your values and aspirations, and adjust them as your life and priorities change.

Darren set out to escape the corporate grind, determined not to work himself into an early grave like his former colleagues. He wanted control, freedom, and a chance at a better work-life balance. But somewhere along the way, he found himself right back where he started—chained to his desk, constantly chasing billable hours. It wasn't until he reassessed his situation, remembering why he'd started his own practice and the relationship-building skills that had served him so well since his firm days, that things began to change. By reconnecting with his talent for building relationships and trust, Darren was able to diversify his client base and raise his rates. This not only improved his financial security but also allowed him to build a sustainable practice that gave him life beyond the office. He rediscovered his passion for comedy and finally achieved the work-life balance he'd been seeking all along. Darren had come full circle, leveraging his strengths to create the life he'd originally envisioned when he stepped away from corporate law.

Satish, on the other hand, dove headfirst into the startup world, convinced he needed to build the next tech unicorn. He followed the Silicon Valley playbook to the letter, reinvesting every penny and working himself to the bone in pursuit of exponential growth. But in doing so, he lost sight of why he started Clorder in the first place. When he finally took a step back and adjusted his objectives, focusing on building a sustainable business that provided for his family rather than a billion-dollar unicorn, he rediscovered his passion. By paying himself properly and reframing what success meant to him, Satish found not just balance but a renewed love for his work.

Their stories teach us a valuable lesson: Your business should fit into your life, not dominate it. It's easy to get caught up in conventional ideas of success, like having more clients, higher profits, and rapid growth. But the real power lies in stepping back periodically to ask yourself, "Is this still what I want?"

Think of your business as a custom-built home. When you first designed it, you might have thought you needed a formal dining room. But as the years went by, you realized what you really wanted was a cozy home office. There's no shame in renovating to fit your changing needs.

Throughout this book, we've met business owners driven by purposes as unique as their stories. For Darren, it was about having control over his life rather than letting work control him. For Satish, his purpose was to build something sustainable that could support his family. For Hamish, the fishing boat captain, it was about preserving his independence. And for Toshi, the yakitori chef, his purpose was to serve food that he loves, in a restaurant run his way, to customers who appreciate what he offers. What matters isn't whether your purpose fits someone else's definition of success—what matters is that it's meaningful to you.

As you move forward, keep checking in with yourself. Are you still excited to start work each morning? Does your business give you the lifestyle you want? If not, what small changes could you make to bring things back into alignment? Remember why you started your business in the first place and the skills you leveraged to get it off the ground. These can be powerful tools when facing challenges.

There's no universal blueprint for success. What works for one person might be completely wrong for another. Don't be afraid to reassess, realign, and reimagine what success looks like for you—right now, in this phase of your life—and then reshape your business to support that vision, whatever it may be. By regularly checking in with your goals and leaning on your strengths, you can build a business that not only thrives, but also brings you personal fulfillment.

After all, it's your business, your rules.